M Hettich
6/87

One More Time

One More Time

A Memoir by

Carol Burnett

Random House New York

Grateful acknowledgment is made to the following for permission to reprint previously published material:

Warner Bros. Inc.: Excerpt from "Carolina in the Morning," words and music by Gus Kahn and Walter Donaldson. Copyright 1922 by Warner Bros. Inc. Copyright renewed and assigned to Gilbert Keys Music Co. & Donaldson Publishing Co. All rights reserved. Used by permission.

Famous Music Corporation: Excerpt from "My Ideal," words and music by Leo Robin, Richard A. Whiting and Newell Chase. Copyright 1930 by Famous Music Corporation. Copyright renewed 1957 by Famous Music Corporation. Excerpt from "True Blue Lou," words and music by Leo Robin, Sam Coslow and Richard A. Whiting. Copyright 1929 by Famous Music Corporation. Copyright renewed 1956 and assigned to Famous Music Corporation.

Kenneth H. Welch: Excerpt from "I Made a Fool of Myself Over John Foster Dulles," words and music by Kenneth H. Welch. Copyright © 1957 by Ben Bloom Music. Copyright renewed 1985 by Kenneth H. Welch. Published by Little Jug Music, Inc.

Manufactured in the United States of America

For my daughters
and
for Peter, who said
I should, and could

One More Time

1

Dear Carrie, Jody, and Erin,

When you were all little girls, I'm *sure* you recall my telling you count-less stories about what it was like when I was little:

"I remember it as if it were yesterday. . . . It was my ninth birthday, and I woke up with the chicken pox. . . ."

And the three of you would roll your eyes to heaven because you had heard it a million times. I don't blame you. It had to drive you nuts.

But now that you're older and I'm older, I felt that it was important to go through it all one more time. Actually I'm hoping you might recog-nize parts of yourselves in me, when I was growing up—recognitions that have nothing to do with "the times" ("the covered wagon days," as you always put it) when I grew up but have everything to do with the same feelings that I think we all have in this world, no matter when we were born . . . feelings we should share as much as possible. . . .

So here it all is, in a letter.

And you can read it whenever you want to.

I started scribbling it on Wyndham Hotel stationery in New York about two years ago. After a few weeks I graduated to a rented type-writer. I amazed myself. I taught myself to type all over again—and on an electric one, not an Underwood. I wound up buying tons of Liquid Paper and Avery self-adhesive correction tape. When I realized that what I was writing was turning into a *book*, I got one of those little one-page-at-a-time copiers. This was getting serious.

I wrote as much as I could whenever I could, and it took a lot longer than I expected. Not because I couldn't remember but because I remem-bered so much more . . .

It was like a limb when you stretch it. My memory was stretching. I began to dream of moments—long-buried moments that I thought I had forgotten almost as soon as they had happened. I'd wake up in the middle of the night, turn on the light, and scratch out a key word on a notepad I kept on the nightstand, making sure I'd have the information in the A.M.

when I woke up. Then I'd lie there with my eyes wide open the rest of the night.

I started putting my tape recorder by the bed, so that if I woke up wanting to remember something, I could mumble it into the machine—at least I wouldn't have to turn on the light. That worked a little better. I was able to go back to sleep . . . most of the time.

Three months ago I got a word processor! I know. None of *you* could believe it either. I'm proud of myself for doing it, although I almost returned it when the instructor turned out to be twelve. I'm glad I didn't, or I probably never would have finished.

And I *had* to finish.

Why? I don't know . . . yes, I do.

I wanted to go through it all, one more time, to let you in on my growing pains, dreams, goofs and what-have-yous, so that maybe you could figure out, in case you'd ever want to, just how your mom turned out to be the kind of hairpin she is. . . . Lord knows, I can't. But I guess people never can when it comes to themselves.

And more than anything, I wanted you to get to know Nanny and Mama and Daddy, since there's no other way now.

I wrote it for you, but it turned out that I wrote it for me, too.

I hope you'll do the same thing someday for yours . . . and for you.

So, here goes. . . .

My earliest memories are of being bathed in the kitchen sink in the old house. I couldn't have been much over two, because I fit in it. Mama kept the door on the stove open, and I'd stare at the waves in the air the heat made. I remember her drying me, holding me, kissing me, and putting me to bed. It felt good. Sometimes she'd wake me up after I'd fallen asleep, when she'd pull my thumb out of my mouth. It made me mad. She left for somewhere after that.

The sidewalk was all cracked and wavy, like little hills, and the weeds pushed their way up through the cement. I had to roller-skate there anyway, because they wouldn't let me out of their sight, and they could watch me from the swing on the front porch of the old house. It was hard to skate there, and I kept falling down and getting sores on my knees. I screamed so loud when I'd see the iodine coming that they finally decided to let me skate on the wood floor in the slanted hallway. I'd stand at the high end of the room, put my hands out in front of me, and roll to the other wall, stopping myself with my palms. Then I'd hang on to furniture and half walk and half skate back up to the starting point and begin all over again. They didn't seem to care that my skates scratched the floor and made deep marks in the wood. "They" were Nanny and Goggy, my grandmother and great-grandmother.

Forty years later I was invited back to my hometown, San Antonio, by the Board of Education. It was a very special day. I was driven through town in an open convertible, and everybody was smiling and waving. After all the festivities were over, as a surprise, I was driven to the old house on West Commerce Street. The car pulled up to exactly where the cracked cement had been. There was the big old house with the porch that wound around from the front to the side. The paint was chipped, and it looked pretty much the same, except for some new cement steps leading up to the entrance.

I climbed the steps with one of the city officials and knocked on the screen door. An elderly Mexican man answered. He was wearing an undershirt and a pair of work pants held up by suspenders. He was alone in the house, he explained in Spanish. His wife was at the store. He was blind. He talked with the city official and said he'd let me, and only me, come into the house. He unhooked the screen door, and I walked in. Everybody else waited out in the hot Texas sun. It took a few seconds for my eyes to get adjusted to the dark interior. It was just the two of us, alone in the old hallway. I looked down at the wooden floor.

The skate marks were still there.

If I really begged her, Nanny would take her teeth out and smile at me. I never saw anything so funny in my life. She kept them in a glass by the bed. She didn't wear them all the time because they were kind of loose and clicked around in her mouth. She'd run her tongue over the uppers to put them back in place. She said they made her gums sore, and she was mad at the store where she had bought them because they wouldn't give her her money back. I was glad she had to take them out a lot because the sight of her shiny gums grinning at me got me hysterical. One time I hid her teeth from her, and she really got mad and said she'd never smile for me again if I didn't give them back right away.

I was around three and didn't have to go to school yet, so Nanny took me everywhere she went. I was crazy about her. I was worried, though, because she wasn't well. She felt her wrists all the time and talked about "skipping beats." At night, when she was asleep, I'd sometimes grab her wrists and try to feel something. I never could, but as long as her chest was moving up and down, everything was okay.

We went to the Christian Science church. Nanny would be in the grown-up section, and I'd go to the Sunday school. I hated being separated from her, and I'd make such a fuss in front of the other kids that the teacher would give up and kick me out of the room early. Then I'd hightail it over to where the grown-ups were, peek through the main door, and try to find her in that sea of heads and hats. I wouldn't relax until I could spot her, and then I'd stand there and wait, keeping my eye on her, until church was over.

Afterward we'd go home and have hotcakes with Goggy. If Nanny had ever known I'd been bad, she never told me about it.

I was her little shadow, and that was just the way I wanted it.

Goggy was two hundred years old and would let me chase her all around the big old house and tickle her. When I caught her, I didn't tickle her

too hard because she could've broken. We laughed a whole lot. She liked
to play games. We'd sit on the porch and play checkers for hours, and
sometimes I almost won. But on Sunday she wouldn't do a thing but read
the Bible. She wouldn't even talk. Not a sound.

I was always glad when Monday rolled around.

We had an old upright in the living room. I'd roller-skate while Nanny
would play "Maple Leaf Rag" and "Old Rugged Cross" and tell me all
about how talented the Jones family was. She'd talk about how she was
the middle of six—four brothers and one sister—and how her daddy,
F. C. Jones, had been a wealthy and powerful man in Arkansas. Nanny
had been known as the Belle of Belleville, until her daddy had lost everything (she never told me where) and died a "broke and broken man."

Nanny's real name was Mabel Eudora, but she liked people to call her
Mae. Boys had come from miles around to court her, but she gave her
heart to big Irish handsome Bill Creighton, a railroad man. They got
married, and Nanny had two daughters, Eudora (1907) and Ina Louise
(1911). Louise, as she was later called, was my mama. Something happened, and Nanny "divorced" Papa Bill way back when, and he died
when Mama and my aunt Dodo were still little bitty things.

Herman Melton was Nanny's second husband, and for a while Nanny
changed Mama's name to Louise Melton. But Mama named me after
Papa Bill—my middle name, anyway: Creighton. The Carol was for Carole Lombard, Mama's favorite actress, Nanny said. Something went
wrong with Mr. Melton, and Nanny up and left him, too.

The grandfather I knew was Papa John: John White. Nanny was Mae
E. White. He lived with us in the old house for a little while, and then he
went to Kerrville, Texas, and died there. He was the first dead person I'd
ever seen. We all had to kiss him in his coffin so he wouldn't come back
and haunt us. I was real little, so they had to lift me up.

We were on something called the WPA. It meant that we were poor and
that every once in a while I'd get some clothes that had been worn by
other little girls, and they'd be in a grocery bag. It also meant we'd get a
chicken to fry at Christmas.

I liked it better when we'd get a dead chicken we didn't know because
one time I saw Nanny wring one's neck in the backyard and I didn't
want to eat it.

* * *

Nanny never missed a night looking under the bed before she got in it. She said she wanted to make sure there wasn't a man under there. I always thought if there was, she'd scare him more than he'd scare her because she wore long underwear with a drop seat that sagged and her teeth were out.

Mama and Daddy weren't around anywhere.

They were in a place called Santa Monica, California. I went out there to be with them. I think I was around four. I don't remember the trip. I just remember being with them for a while. They were still living together then.

Daddy had a job. He'd go to people's houses and knock on their doors and try to get the people to buy some pink coupons he was selling for a local photo store. The coupons cost a quarter, and the customers would get a discount if they wanted to get their picture portraits taken, and Daddy would get a "commission." He could choose his hours that way. Everybody knew Daddy had a problem. Mama would break the bottles she found, and he'd just stand there and say, "I'm sorry, Lou."

One time she dug her nails into both sides of his face and scratched him from his temples to his chin. He didn't even budge, and it took the longest time for the blood to pop out. It came in tiny red dots at first, and then it looked like four satin ribbons on each cheek. He never moved.

I couldn't understand that. I would've run like hell. It never occurred to me that he probably didn't feel it. I remember it took forever for the scabs to fall off.

Everybody liked Jody, my daddy. I did, too. He was sweet and tall and lanky, and his smile made me feel warm. He liked to tell me about when he and Mama had been sweethearts in school. "Your mama and I were crazy about each other from the very first."

We lived in a little place on Montana Avenue, and I'd play with my dolls in the front yard every day and look for him to come home from his job. I'd see him round the corner, and if his legs were wobbly, I knew Mama would be mad, and he'd catch it. I'd run to him and he'd sweep me up and kiss me and ask how his "punkin" was.

It wasn't long after that that I was shipped back from Santa Monica to San Antonio and Nanny and Goggy. I guess that was when Mama and Daddy stopped living together.

* * *

I'm lying on the grass, looking at the sky and making up pictures with the clouds. It's hot, and I have on shorts and a sun top. I'm four. It's very still, and the clouds have stopped moving.

I don't know how long it was—it dawned on me only after it was all over—but for a time there, I was everything and everything was me. I've never felt that way since.

But it's possible.

I didn't want to go to school, and that was that. Ever since I got back from staying with Mama and Daddy in California, I hadn't been away from the old house, or Goggy and our games, or Nanny. Especially Nanny. I was her little shadow, more than ever. Uncle Parker would crack, "It's like they're joined at the hip." I was scared she might die on me.

Sometimes she'd wake up in the middle of the night and start pacing up and down the room, poking her fingers against her chest and feeling her pulse. "I'm having a hissy fit . . . I'm having a hissy fit . . . help me, God, help me." Then she'd lie down and put a cold rag on her forehead and clutch the Bible and *Science and Health* to her breast, moaning, "There is no death, God is all in all. . . ." I'd start to panic when she'd jump up again, swallow some medicine, then give up and say, "Watch me . . . I'm going. Know the truth for me!" One time I banged my head against the wall and begged God to take me first. She made me go to school anyway because she said she didn't want to get arrested.

I was thrilled when my first day of school was over. I figured it was done with, for good. Then the teacher said she'd see us all again . . . tomorrow. I ran as fast as I could . . . away . . . away from Crockett Grammar School. I didn't have to go back for a whole month. I had willed myself the measles.

This was the first time I ever remember being really sick. Nanny took care of me. A big sign with red letters on it was nailed right up on the screen door: QUARANTINE. I didn't understand the word at first.

After a while I knew it meant I wasn't going anywhere, and nobody wanted to be around me. When I felt like it, Nanny would let me get out of bed and I'd sit in a chair with a blanket around me and look out the window. But I had to wear dark glasses because the measles could make you go blind if you weren't careful, they said. My eyes got so used to the dark that I could see the lizards skitter across the walls and into the cracks where they lived in the bedroom.

Before I got sick, I used to catch fireflies in the front yard and put them in a preserves jar. Then Goggy and I would take them into the living room at night and turn out all the lights and watch the jar glow. I would've liked having my firefly jar when I had the measles because the glow wouldn't have been too bright for my eyes, but the fireflies weren't around that time of year.

"You should've seen me when I was young," Nanny said. "My daddy had to beat the boys off with a stick." I asked her how come her teeth were all gone, and she told me that rotten teeth could kill you every time, and except for big brother Edgar, who had every tooth in (and not a gray hair on) his head, just about everybody in the world who was her age wore false teeth. "Just you wait, it's a fact of life." Nanny wouldn't ever tell me what that age was, no matter how many times I pestered her. I decided to ask Goggy sometime, when Nanny wasn't around, how old Nanny was. I figured she'd know since Nanny was her daughter.

Goggy took her own sweet time answering my question. She leaned way back in her rocker on the porch, took off her glasses, and closed her eyes and thought. "Well, now, let me see . . . your grandmother is the middle one. Edgar was my firstborn, then Fred . . . Lester . . . Mae (Nanny) . . . Ina . . . and the baby, Hubert." She kind of choked a little when she said "Hubert." I had been told the story about how Hubert had dropped dead on the spot when a baseball had hit him smack-dab in the chest during a game. He was fourteen. F. C. Jones had been in the stands and had run out on the field and picked Hubert up in his arms and screamed, over and over, that he'd give away every cent of his fortune to anybody who could bring Hubert back to life. They said Mr. Jones never was "the same" after that. He had worshiped Hubert. Nanny always said *she* had been her daddy's favorite.

Goggy's eyes were still shut. She had been thinking for a real long time. I heard the crickets start up. I was beginning to wonder if she was ever going to tell me how many years I had left before I would have to buy *my* teeth in a store. She finally opened her eyes and looked at me. "Now promise me you won't tell her I told you how old she is." I swore I wouldn't. She whispered in my ear. I breathed a sigh of relief. It would be a hundred years before I was ever fifty-one.

* * *

Nanny and I would go downtown to the main street where all the stores were and window-shop. She'd hold on to my hand real tight so she wouldn't lose me. She walked pretty fast, and when she'd spot a bargain, she'd get so excited and so scared that somebody might beat her to it I thought she was going to jerk my arm clear off my body and leave the rest of me there without ever turning around. I was pretty little, so I had to run a lot to keep up with her.

I liked the times we went downtown because it meant she wasn't sick that day. She'd get dressed up and put on stockings and everything— even lipstick. Sometimes she'd stop at a window and pretend to be look- ing at the things that were on sale, but I could tell she was really looking at herself. All decked out, and with her teeth in, I knew nobody in the world would've dreamed she was so old.

Before they left me with Nanny and went away to California, there was a little while when Daddy was the manager of a neighborhood movie house in San Antonio. Sometimes Mama would take me there and leave me with him. I'd take a nap in his tiny office. I'd try my best not to get sleepy because I wanted to watch the picture shows. I loved it when he'd let me sit in the dark theater by myself. I watched the movies and cartoons over and over. I remember Betty Boop and something with Joel McCrea and Bonita Granville. Mama said I was almost born in a movie house. She was watching a reissue of *Rasputin and the Empress* and never made it to the end.

I had a Snow White doll, but *Pinocchio* was my favorite movie, until I saw Linda Darnell kiss Tyrone Power in *Blood and Sand*.

When we were downtown, I'd hold on to Nanny for dear life whenever we got anywhere near the Buckhorn Saloon. There was a giant ape in the window. King Kong. They said it was just some old ape that was stuffed, but I knew better. It was King Kong. He was alive, and he was after me. I knew it, and he knew I knew it, because I could see him move when nobody else was looking. Nanny didn't believe me at first, but I screamed so loud one day that we started walking on the other side of the street after that.

The first food I remember is enchiladas.

Mama told me the first food I really ate was Cream of Wheat. She said it was Cream of Wheat that saved my life. I'd been born with a "wall" across the inside of my stomach, and the milk wouldn't stay down. Mama was scared I was a dead duck. I just kept spitting and throwing it back up. Then the doctor told Mama to feed me Cream of Wheat every two hours for a few days. He was hoping it would form a little hard ball and push through the wall. Mama said each feeding took a whole hour and I screamed constantly and she was on the "verge of a nervous breakdown from worry and sheer exhaustion." But it worked, and the doctor didn't have to cut me open. I always liked that story.

When I started Crockett, I bragged about my stomach to the other kids in the first grade. I was known as "the kid with the brick wall in her gut," and I was quite popular for a while there.

The first time I ever remember having my picture taken was by Mama when I was with her and Daddy that time in Santa Monica. I had on my old wrinkled dress that was the color of medicine pink, and I hated it. I hated my haircut. It was a Buster Brown, and everybody in the world thought it was cute. They were nuts. I was playing with my dolls on the grass, waiting for Daddy to come home, when Mama pointed that thing at me, told me to quit playing and stand up and smile. I didn't want to. She wouldn't let up, so I threw my dolls down and made a face. I heard a click. I could've killed her.

The next time I had a picture taken, I was back in San Antonio with Nanny. We were in front of Joske's department store, and there was a sidewalk photographer with a camera that looked just like an accordion. I posed, he clicked, and Nanny took the ticket stub. She got the snapshot a few days later. I looked pretty relaxed.

When Nanny didn't talk about how sick she was, she talked about money. She said it was a crime Mama hadn't married James Trail, whose daddy owned a bank, because we'd all be sitting pretty now and wouldn't have to depend on the WPA for everything. "But noooo, your mother had to go for that *love* bunk, and look where it got her."

The three of us, Nanny, Goggy, and I, would sit on the porch, and I'd listen to them talk about the family. Nanny did most of the talking.

"Louise thought Jody was *cute* when he drank." She'd switch back and forth from me to Goggy. "I told her it wouldn't be so cute when he couldn't come up with the grocery money."

I liked it when we sat on the porch. It was usually sundown, my favorite time. They'd be sitting there with cooking pots in their laps, peeling and shelling. Every once in a while Nanny would wind down and it would get real quiet and I could hear Goggy humming very softly under her breath. It was usually "Old Rugged Cross." Sometimes I'd shell the peas. I liked the sound they made when I snapped them open and they landed in the metal pot. It made me feel kind of grown-up. But it was about as grown-up as I wanted to get. I wasn't in any particular hurry. Everybody looked so serious all the time. Sometimes I'd pretend to be an adult when I played with my dolls. It was easy. I just didn't smile much.

Nanny would pick up a carrot to scrape and start in again. "She's as bad off now as she was when she was living with Jody. Not a red cent to her name . . . staying out there in *Hollywood*! Thinks she's a hot patootie . . . thinks she can be a big-shot writer. . . . Well, nobody's knocking her door down as far as I can see. She just up and leaves Carol here with me, like she's not even her mother. But Louise never did think of anybody else but herself."

She'd pick up another carrot to attack and get on the subject of my great-grandfather. Goggy still called her husband "Mr. Jones." He'd been gone a long, long time, but Nanny still missed her daddy. Nanny said he was the only man she had ever known who wasn't worthless. He was the finest man who had ever lived, the only man she had ever really loved, and it was a crying shame that there never was, and never would be, another man like her father.

Goggy would just sit and rock and not say anything.

Nanny would hang the ICE sign on a nail outside the old house. The ice truck would pull up, and the iceman would get out and walk around to the back of his truck, carrying those big metal things that looked like claws. He'd stick the claws into a big square piece of ice and grunt and lift it up to his shoulder, lug it up the porch steps, and Nanny would hold the torn screen door open for him. He'd cart the load into the house and head for the kitchen. The ice block would go in the icebox, and things would get cold again. By the time he came out of the house, I'd be sitting on the back of the truck, chipping small pieces of ice off one of the blocks with a pick and sucking on them. He'd let me stay there while he made his rounds.

Sometimes I'd ride two whole blocks before I'd jump off and run all the way back home.

* * *

God made grown-ups sad. You couldn't laugh in church. I never got it when they said, "I really enjoyed this morning's lecture." It sure didn't look like it.

I got a laugh in church once. As usual, I'd been let go early from Sunday school, and I was waiting for Nanny to get sprung from the main room. I was wearing my Sunday suit Nanny had made for me and a blue felt hat with a red feather that stuck way up in the air. I peeked through the crack in the big double doors, but I couldn't find Nanny anywhere. I could usually spot her pretty fast because she was the one who fidgeted the most. I started to feel scared, and then panicky. I didn't see her . . . anywhere.

She was gone. Maybe dead.

I slipped into the room and hugged the back wall. I stood on my tiptoes, but all I could see were the backs of the heads of the people sitting in the last row. The lecturer was talking all about how God is Love, and I figured God wouldn't be too mad at me if I tried to find Nanny in the quietest way possible. I dropped to all fours and began to crawl down one of the aisles, scanning the pews on either side. That way I could see her if she had keeled over on the floor during one of her spells. If she *had* keeled over, nobody would know it in church because you weren't supposed to get sick if you were a good Christian Scientist.

They'd just think she was taking a nap.

So it was up to me.

I started inching my way down the aisle, on the verge of a hissy fit.

I don't know how long it had been quiet, but I do know I was about to scream for her when somebody said, "Why, look at the little Indian." They all started to laugh. Even the man up on the stage.

I stood up and started to cry. I felt a familiar hand grab my elbow and usher me out of there. I just hadn't seen her, that was all. I threw my arms around her and started to scream louder.

"*Now* what's the matter?"

"Everybody was laughing at me!" I was mortified.

Nanny said, "They weren't laughing at you; they were laughing at the feather on your hat."

There was one dumb old lion.

Some of his teeth were out, and some of his hair was, too. I couldn't understand why that man in the tight pants had a whip with him. The dumb old lion sure couldn't have done anything.

We were at the circus, my first one. I remember the big top and the sawdust on the floor. There were the three rings. The lion, the man with the whip, and a lady in sparkly shorts all were in the middle one. They were the stars. The lady had holes in her stockings, and the man's belly hung out over his tight pants.

I was disappointed as hell. Even the cotton candy was fake. It went away in your mouth as soon as you tried to bite it. I wanted to go home. The circus was supposed to be exciting and scary.

They finished their acts and the lights went out and some horns went "TA-DA."

Then the clowns came on.

They wore wild outfits, and they were all in Technicolor—purple and orange and yellow and red and green and blue. Their painted-on grins were a mile wide, and they were all teeth and flashing crossed eyes.

They were mean.

They slapped each other, and it hurt. They squirted fire hoses and slammed each other in the face with pies and hit each other over the head with rolling pins . . . hard . . . and everybody was screaming with laughter.

Then one of them came toward me with a gun in his hands and aimed it right at my face. I screamed. He shot me, and a parasol came out. People were falling down laughing.

I wanted to kill him.

He scared me to death, and I hated him.

I hated all of them.

They weren't funny. They were scary. There was something wrong with them, and I was the only kid in the world who was on to them.

Mama and Daddy weren't living together anymore, and Nanny talked a lot about how we were going to go out to Hollywood and live with Mama real soon. It didn't make much difference to me one way or the other as long as I'd be with Nanny.

I sort of remembered the time I'd been in California with Mama and Daddy, the time she scratched his face so bad, and the time she took my picture when I didn't want her to.

We got separate letters from them all the time. I was around six or seven and couldn't read very well, but Nanny would read them to me and kind of snort when she was finished, as if she didn't like what was in them.

I'd draw them pictures, and she'd put the pictures in with the letters she wrote back.

I didn't think about my parents a whole lot. I could hardly remember them.

Mrs. Carol Burnett
3301 West Commerce St
San Antonio, Texas.

Friday P.M

Dear Mrs. White –
    I received yours
and my baby's letters
this afternoon and I
can't tell you how
happy they made me.
Yes, I am definitely
off hooch of any
kind – Tomorrow will
be the first month-
I'm feeling so much
better and gaining
good honest weight-
I'm sending Carol
$2.00 and I'm sure
she can use it –
I'll send more as
fast as I can make
it, but you know

the old coupon
racket — you never
know how much, if
any, you will make —
I can go to work
at one of, the air-
craft Co. assoon
as I can pass a
physical exam —
I drank for so long
that it will take
time to get back
on my feet —
Kiss the punkin'
for me and I'll
write again next
week —
Love to all,

Daddy

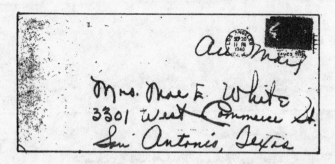

Monday Eve.

Darlings:— Got your special Saturday—and it certainly "got me down"— I hope and pray you're feeling better—and that some one is looking after poor little Carole.

I've had quite a bit of a "break" from "Pic"—and can't even concentrate long enough to do my work. Frank gave me another assignment to do a story on Cary Grant. But I'm re-writing the Zon Grey story today—as it wasn't exactly what I wanted—So, after it's through—I'll contact Cary & start on that—then, practically have one lined up on Ceasor Romero— But it

It seems I just can't keep my mind on things - and don't sleep at all -

I hope my registering for you will cheer you up some. Haven't talked to Eudora yet today - guess she'll call me after the afternoon mail - I sent your special to her. Don't get to see very much of her either as don't have the car here - and have to try to concentrate on my work. Had lunch at Universal Friday - with the heads of publicity dept. and met Gloria Jim, Nancy Kelly - etc - Had a ~~fun~~ nice day - considering. Also, went out to Nan Grey's

& again - She's so sweet -

It'll really be something to get a story on Cary Grant. I'm really very thrilled over it. Hope I do all right.

Aunt Ina hasn't come out yet - and I doubt if she does. I don't think Eudora will be here very much longer either.

This land lady job here is the bunk - They want me to take over & do all the cleaning, answering phones etc - for just half off the rent - and it darn'd sure isn't worth it - So as soon as I get all my stories off my mind - I'll look for that part time job - Then we'll make some kind of

4. arrangements to get you and
Carole here. She simply has to
be in school — I'll bet the
poor doll is worried sick
over you —

Well, dear — have to get
back to my story — will add a
line — after afternoon mail —

Later — nothing from you —
Talked to Eudora and she hasn't
heard from Parker in over a week.
She's getting plenty disgusted too —
So wouldn't be surprised if she
doesn't head that way very soon —

Called R.K.O. and Cary Grant
won't be back for 10 days — So will
work on something else 'til he
does — Please feel better —
      Kiss thy baby —
       Love, Dad

AFTER FIVE DAYS RETURN TO
Jody Burnett
915 Wilshire Blvd.
SANTA MONICA, CALIF.

VIA AIRMAIL

Miss Carol Burnett
3301 West Commerce St.
San Antonio, Texas

Wednesday

Dearest Punkin' Kid,
          I received yours
and Nanny's letter last
week and I'm sorry
I haven't answered
sooner, but have
been pretty busy try-
ing to get a job
and haven't had
much time – I may
be able to get on
at one of the smaller
aircraft parts co's,
soon – I sure hope
so –
          How are you
getting along in
school? I'll bet
the other kids are

awfully jealous
of you for being
able to draw so
well - your draw-
ing was sure swell
I didn't know you
could write so well
Gee! you can write
better. than I can
Daddy is sending
you $5.00 for your
lunches & anything
else it will buy -
I'll send you
more as soon as
I can make it -
Went to Bob
Hope's broadcast
with Mother - Last
night, she is well
and we both love

you very much —
You be the sweet
girl I know you
are and daddy
will try and find
a way to send
for you & mommy
soon — Daddy
hasnt taken a
drink yet and I
never will as long
as you pray for
me —
        I love you —
                Daddy —
P.S. Hello mrs. White
we are all still up
& kicking & I hope
you are all well. my
best to all — Love, Jody

Sunday afternoon

Dear:— Got your spec'l - but
haven't had a chance to answer
~~sooner~~ - and besides, can't get hold
of a spec'l - air-mail stamp - So,
I hope you're not mad -

I hardly know how to
answer your letter anyway - as
- I've ~~so often~~ said - I don't see
how we can manage to keep you
even 30 days - and I have no
assurance of a job. even part
time. If only you could wait
just a little while - as I am
so thoroughly unprepared -
I don't think you'll like
this room here any way - as it's
too noisy - and I don't think you'll

care for these vibrations -

I've talked with Eudora
everyday - and I'm glad you
wrote her - as I knew
Parker was making most of
that stuff up..

She'll get Jan's other
audition this week - and
then she'll know just what
she's going to do -

I saw Frank, "Pic" editor,
yesterday and he wrote one
the swellest letter to the
Hays office so I can get my
card - I'm going to the Hays
office tomorrow and see about
the card - I'm sure with
this letter. That's all I'll

3 need. and it will surely
mean a lot to me — I'll be
in a position to really get
around with that. I've been
wanting one for 7 years — and
guess I've got it at last.

Bobby & Maryeon came over
and took me home with them
for supper last night. Thursday
Bobby & Rosamae come over
for the afternoon — first I've
seen of them in months —

Must get this off —
Please let's wait & see what
Eudora is going to do — and
give me a chance to locate
a better place — or at least
an apartment here — There may
be a vacancy (apt.) here soon —

4- I'll get you here soon-
but I do want it to be
half way right-
I'll let you know about
the card tomorrow.
Kiss my baby-
Lots of Love,
Lou

Tuesday A.M.

Dearest little Punkin' Kid—
        Just got Nanny's card
saying you are sick—Daddy
is so sorry—I know that
old cold and rainy weather
makes it easy for anyone
to get sick—I hope you
are all right when you
receive this letter—It
makes me hurt all over
to know you aren't well
and that I am way
out here in California
and can't see you—
        You hurry up and get
well and Daddy is trying
awfully hard to get a
job so you and Nanny
can come out here

and get away from
that old cold weather
back there — I know
Nanny is taking good
care of you and will
have you well in no
time —

Daddy still is
~~not~~ ~~drinking~~ anything
and is ~~trying~~ ~~to find~~
a way to get you here —

So you be a sweet
girl and write me as
soon as you feel like
it — I love you, love
you, love ~~you~~,

Daddy.

P. S. Dear Mrs. White —
I'm so sorry Carol is
sick — If you need them

please call either
Dr. Sharp or Dr.
Kalisky and have
them send bill to
me here — I'm en-
closing a # all I
have, I'll send more
as soon as I can —
Coupon business slow
as you probably can
guess — I hope you
are feeling better by
now — Worry as little
as you can and
maybe things will
break for the better
soon —

Love to all

Jody

Wednesday Eve

Dears:— Got your air-mail
yesterday — and have tried all
night and day to figure out a
sensible answer — and I'm
stumped —

All I can say is — I'm flat
broke — and am hardly in a position
to offer a sensible suggestion
under this awful strain —

Eudora has two auditions
for Janice tomorrow — one at
R.K.O at 2:30 — then one at
M.G.M at 2:30 — It's a funny
coincidence they had to happen
on the same day — but that's
the way things seem to work
out. I'm going with her — and
I surely hope some thing good

'works out for her. At least she'll know "the score" all at once — and won't have to wait around wondering. So, she'll be making up her mind one way or the other very soon —

I'm so worried over you, too dear — Oh, God I wish I knew what to tell you to do — but I won't know anything 'til after my story. Now Grey haven't come back yet — but they're expecting her any day — and I have to sit around and wait for the phone to ring — It's hell.

Rook, the editor, called

yesterday - and gave me a new scoop to cover for "Pic" — they assigned me to ~~table~~ entertainment dept. In other words, writing about unusual & different hobbies of the stars. So I have a better chance to get more stories in now.

Why don't you wait until we find out what Eudora is going to do? Maybe, we can work out something then — but I just have to have a few days to "think" —

I hope Carole is all right at least — seems everything else is all 'll screwed up –

     I go around so dizzy
all day – can hardly hold
my head up –

     Well, darling – Eudora
or I will write you after
the auditions tomorrow –

     Please try to cheer up –
and we'll work out
something very ~~soon~~.

      Kiss my hoky –

       Love,
        Lou

Louise Barnett
2500 Mr. Pasadena
Hollywood, California

Mrs. Mae ..... Nr.
5 East Commerce Stree
San Antonio, Texas

Thursday Eve.

Darlings:-

Just got your airmail xxxxxxx about all the sweet things
Parker said to you. Why, the son of a b----. I didNt say
any such thing and you hurt me because you believe it. All
I've said, and still say, is that I wish it were possible for
you to wait until I had a little money of some kind, and that
that was driving me crazy, but I've written that to you time
again. It also drive me crazy that I haven't been able to help
you and Carole, I worry all the time about it. But I did NOT
say that about you, as I'm too well acquainted wibt all the hell
you're go ng through there. PLEASE, darling, don't let that
thing get you down, 'cause thats probably just what he wants to
do, and you're playing right in his hands. I don't believe
Eudora said those things either, and I'm going to let her read
the letter xxx as I think she should...I don't see why he should
get by with all that crap and her not know it.

I spent the night in Culver xxx with them last night and
Janice had to postpone one of the auditions, at RKO because she
had been sick. However she was going to MGM and then to RKO
next week, they gave her another appointment for the first of
x the week. I surely hope she makes it OK.

I can hardly sit up myself, but wanted to write you, so
you wouldn't believe all that hooey. I've got the darndest
cough and cold. Guess its the flu, there seems to be an ep-
edemic going around here, and I have a date with Tony tomorrow
too, don't know whether I'll be able to keep it or not, guess
that would break my heart if I couldn't.... I'm going to bed as
soon as I finish this, and try to 'get well'...

Carole that was a darling picture you drew for mother, and
believe me, darling, mother wants to see you too. And we xxxxxx
will before very long. I know you weren't a bad girl.. you're
too good to Nanny, you couldn't be bad. Always be good to her
dear, and mother will never let anyone separate you...when I
get married next time, they're going to have to take Nanny too!

I had a letter from the editor of Look magazine and he wants
me to write for them too, so I'm working on some ideas for them,
and mebbe one of them will xxxxx click too. It won't be so hard
now, that I've had something in print... So I have a feww good
prospects in view anyway..

Dears, I've just gotta' lie down...please cheer up, and
write me anything you want to...I can take it...

                    I love you gals,

3

The next thing I remember is sitting up on the train with Nanny. The chairs looked as if they might have been a very dark blue a long time ago. The color had worn away where the people had sat on them and leaned their heads back to try to sleep.

Nanny kept saying, "We're headed west! We're going to Hollywood!" She also kept saying, "Three days and three nights . . . Dear God, let me make it." She'd feel her pulse. Over and over. I prayed to Dear God to let her make it, too. It was taking forever. The train sounded like Nanny: It belched. We ate the sandwiches we brought with us: ham on white with mustard. And we drank water out of little paper envelopes while we jerked along down the tracks.

I missed the old house, and I missed Goggy.

When we finally pulled into the depot in Los Angeles, after the three days and three nights, we were full of soot and my eyes were full of sleep. A man called the porter lifted me down off the train because the stairs were too steep and he was afraid I'd fall down and hurt myself. The station was noisy, and it smelled. I saw this lady waving at us. She looked familiar. She ran to us and grabbed me up and kissed me. Then she kissed Nanny, who told her how long it took us to get here and how she'd been afraid she wasn't going to live to make it. She helped us carry our stuff up some stairs.

Mama. It's Mama. Oh, that's who it is.

We took a bus and a red trolley . . . to Hollywood.

The sky was real blue, and there were mountains that looked as if you could touch them if you stretched your fingers out extra-hard.

There was a different smell: orange. It felt different: dry. San Antonio was wet and smelled like chili. I missed it.

One of the mountains had big letters on it that spelled out where we were. HOLLYWOODLAND. That's what it said then.

Mama took us to a building that had a lot of rooms in it. It was an apartment building, and she lived in one of the rooms. She got another key from a lady at the desk in the lobby. Nanny asked what apartment was going to be hers and mine, and Mama pointed to a door right behind us. It faced the lobby, and it was number 102. She put the key in the lock. We went in. It was a room. Just a room. There was a little kitchen and a little bathroom. I couldn't see the bed anywhere. My eyes had crust in them. Mama reached up into the wall and grabbed a handle from out of nowhere. She yanked at it, and a bed came right out of the wall. She called it Murphy. It was the Murphy bed.

Nanny snorted a little and felt her pulse. I crawled up on Murphy and fell asleep.

Mama was really pretty. I hadn't remembered her being that pretty or young.

I didn't know where Daddy was. He just wasn't around. Mama lived alone in her room down the hall.

People said she looked a lot like Joan Crawford, and Nanny said Mama did everything she could to live up to the comparison. Her eyes were big, and she had long eyelashes that she loaded down with mascara. She'd put on her fire engine red lipstick over her lipline and blot her mouth with some toilet paper. Then she'd smile at herself. She used to let me watch her get dressed. I loved looking at her. She wasn't tall, and she was round everywhere. Her breasts were big, but they didn't sag the way Nanny's did. Her legs were slim, with little ankles. I liked it when she carefully pulled her stockings up her legs and rolled them over the little elastic garters. She'd put on her high heels and back away from the mirror and look this way and that and pose a lot.

She got a kick out of looking at herself.

I wished she loved me as much as Nanny did.

I met Joan Crawford years later, and I said, "You look just like my mother did." Boy, Mama would've loved that.

Cuz and I were around seven, and she had a pair of little Texas cowboy boots with pointy toes she wore all the time, even when it was boiling hot. We fought a lot. I'd chase her around the house, looking to kill her, screaming, "Light somewhere, damn you! Light! You son of a bitch!"

I cussed a lot when I was little. I was famous in the family for it. Nanny said she didn't know where I got it from, and everybody else said I sure knew how to use it.

When Cuz would finally light, it was usually on the bed or the couch.

She'd fling herself down on her back and kick her feet wildly in the air, as if she was having a hissy fit. The pointy toes on her boots would land smack-dab on their target: my shins. My legs would be black and blue and red and yellow for weeks. The thing was, I never physically fought back. I'd just stand there, at the end of the bed, and let her kick the bejesus out of me with those goddamn boots, and I'd spew out every bad word I had ever heard.

Uncle Parker would scream with laughter and say, "Boy howdy, JoJo (his nickname for me) cusses like a sailor, doesn't she?"

Aunt Dodo would go "Tsk, tsk," and Mama would say I must've got one in the head, " 'cause only a dumb jackass would just stand there and take it like that."

Janice and I are first cousins. Mama and Aunt Dodo (Eudora) were sisters. Janice was Aunt Dodo's daughter. We called each other Cuz. She was nine months older than I was, and beautiful and blond and talented. She could act and sing and tap-dance. Aunt Dodo had brought her to Hollywood to get her into the movies because "all the studios were looking for another Shirley Temple."

But Cuz never seemed too interested, even though we played "movie stars" in her backyard. We'd be Nelson and Jeanette. I was Nelson. We'd be Tarzan and Jane. I taught myself the Tarzan yell.

I thought they were rich because they had a house, and Uncle Parker had a job, and Cuz got shoes that fit her, so that she didn't have to wait to grow into them. I envied her because she was as pretty as a birthday package and had a closet. I liked her when she wasn't kicking me in the shins. We giggled a lot, especially in church, and when we did, Aunt Dodo would reach across me and pinch the daylights out of Cuz, making us laugh even harder. Once we poked the glass eyes out of a fox-head fur some lady was wearing in the pew in front of us while we were singing a hymn. We were trying to stifle our laughter so hard we started to pee in our pants at exactly the same time. We looked down at the two little puddles on the floor, and the dam broke, and all hell broke loose. I thought I was going to die. I had no idea I had that much water in me. I also thought Dodo was going to murder us right there in the Christian Science church on Hollywood Boulevard, in front of God and the practitioners. She could look mean as hell. It only made Cuz laugh harder.

Except for Mama, we all went to that church. Nanny still kept trying to "know the truth," but she still kept stocking the medicine cabinet with aspirin, milk of magnesia, and phenobarbitals. It made perfect sense to me to have a backup system.

For her own reasons, Mama liked the Catholic Church. I think it was because she said her daddy, Papa Bill Creighton, had been a Catholic.

Nanny couldn't understand it because Mama wasn't ever one to take orders of any kind.

"You make my ass want to chew tobacco."

That's what she said.

I was scared to go to school.

Not because of what would happen there, but because of what would happen at home if I wasn't there. If I left home to go to school, Nanny could up and die on me because I wouldn't be around.

It really made Mama mad.

It was a major event every day to get me to go to school, and Mama was disgusted with me.

When I got there, I'd sit at my desk and pray-to-God-please-let-Nanny-live-one-more-day-until-school-was-over-and-I-could-get-back-home-to-her.

This one morning I was fidgeting in my seat, and I knew I couldn't last till three. I raised my hand, and the teacher gave me permission to go to the toilet. I headed for the girls' room and passed it, making a beeline for the front entrance and freedom.

I ran all the way home, down the side streets so the policeman wouldn't catch me.

I threw open the door.

Nanny wasn't anywhere to be seen. She's dead. I knew it. I'm too late. Mama was there. She stared at me . . . hard.

"Why aren't you in school?"

"My hip hurts."

She had that disgusted look. "You're lying." I tore past her to look in the kitchen. No Nanny. I had to pass her again to look in the bathroom. It was empty. Mama just stood there.

I started to cry. "Where is she? Oh, *God,* where's Nanny?" Mama didn't say anything for the longest time . . . she seemed to be searching for the right words.

Finally she spoke. "You make my ass want to chew tobacco."

Thank God, I thought. Nanny was still alive.

* * *

When Mama pulled the Murphy bed out of the wall the day Nanny and I moved into 102, it was down for good. It was never lifted up and swiveled back into the closet again. Nanny kept it down for her heart attacks. I slept on the couch.

After a while Murphy couldn't have gone back in its slot in the closet even if Nanny had felt better because there wasn't any room left anymore.

The whole closet, including the space meant for the bed, was loaded with old newspapers, rags, magazines and clothes. Nanny never threw anything away.

Since she never felt too good, she didn't clean because it wore her out.

The rest of the apartment looked pretty much like the closet. There were old scarves and handkerchiefs and dishtowels hanging on the lampshades. More newspapers and magazines were thrown in the corners, on top of the brown grocery bags from the store. Old sweaters and underwear and dresses hung from the backs of the chairs and sat in piles on top of the radio and the end tables and the couch. When I went to sleep at night, I shoved the stuff to the bottom of the couch with my feet.

Save everything. You'll need it someday.

The kitchen looked as if it had blown up and everything had stayed where it had landed. Old cracked dishes and knives and forks grew up out of the sink and took root on top of the counter, the stove, and the dingy red and white checked oilcloth that covered the little card table. Inside the cupboard were empty peanut butter and jelly jars (for water glasses), the Crisco can filled with bacon grease (for cooking), and more newspapers and magazines.

Nanny was going to cut out the recipes, as soon as she could get to feeling better. All my clothes hung on the shower curtain rod in the bathroom. I only took baths because I didn't want to keep taking my clothes down and putting them back. We didn't have a shower curtain anyhow. The bathroom looked as if there were more stuff in it than the rest of the apartment—probably because it was the smallest room.

The bathroom was always damp and smelled moldy because Nanny was scared of catching pneumonia, so she never opened the air shaft window, which led up to the roof. It was shut tight as a drum, so I never went to school in the morning wearing anything completely dry. I couldn't understand why Nanny was scared of pneumonia because she hardly ever took a bath. She hated water. She liked to tell the one about falling through the ice when she was four and how she'd been terrified of drowning ever since. She said that's why she took only "whore baths." She said her beautiful complexion came from not going overboard in the water department.

The bathroom looked like an old used drugstore. There were medicine bottles, full and empty, in the cabinet and all around the sink. Something would usually fall over when you reached for the faucet. The cabinet was so full you couldn't fit a toothpick in it. Nanny kept her Big Ben clock in there, too, because its tick was so loud it made her nervous. If you wanted to know what time it was, you had to go into the bathroom and open up the medicine cabinet. And then all the bottles would crash into the sink.

Except for my best friend, Ilomay, I played with most of my friends outside or in the lobby. I wouldn't let them set foot in 102 because I didn't want to get teased about the mess. If they wanted to use the toilet, I told them ours was out of order and sent them to the Shell station across the street.

There were a lot of kids in the neighborhood, and Ilomay Sills and I hit it off right away. She was kind of plump and very friendly. We were the same age, and she lived with her grandmother and had a pretty mother, too.

Her grandmother would cook stuff I'd never heard of. I'd go to their apartment in the building next door, and she'd make me eat things like borscht with sour cream. I didn't like it at first because we never ate much of anything that wasn't fried. Nanny made a face when I told her about some of the funny food I was eating over at Ilomay's, so I didn't say much about it after that. But I got to like the borscht, and it wasn't long before I was opening my mouth to every spoonful of anything Ilomay's grandma wanted me to taste.

I was starting to like Hollywood better. It was kind of spread out and green, and the sidewalks were a little smoother than the one in front of the old house in Texas, and Ilomay and I could skate clear around the block without hitting too many cracks or bumps. We'd fall down anyway and limp home with a bloody knee once or twice a week, blaming it on the pepper tree roots that shot up straight through the cement. Skating was our passion for a while. So was playing jacks on the tile floor in her bathroom. Sometimes we'd go up to the roof of my building and scream at the top of our lungs down the three-story bathroom shafts and marvel at the wonderful sound of our own voices bouncing off the little square cubicles and coming back up to us. When the tenants screamed back at us to cut it out, we'd run out onto the creaky fire escapes and hide, pretending we were spies.

I took her home to meet Nanny and Mama. I didn't know what a Jew was until then.

After Ilomay left to go home, Mama said something kind of mean about her. I don't remember what it was, but I know she meant it to be funny, and I know she meant it to make me not want to play with Ilomay so much anymore.

It didn't work.

I loved to listen to the radio. And I loved to hear the big bands, like Harry James.

But sometimes Nanny just couldn't take it, and she'd make me shut that darn thing off. It gave her a headache. She'd lie down on Murphy and ask me to pull the shades down and please give her a wet rag for her head and a little peace and quiet for a *few* minutes. I'd sit in the chair in the dark room and watch her very closely. If her breathing was smooth, it wouldn't be too long before she'd start to snore, and then I could relax and know she was okay.

Then I'd tiptoe out of the room and go down the hall to Mama's. She was only a couple of doors away, and I knew she'd have the radio on. She loved music more than anything, and I could count on her singing with Harry's trumpet when I walked into her apartment. She sang great. Like Alice Faye.

One time I got up the nerve to join in. And when I did, she stopped singing and looked at me kind of funny. It was as if she were pleasantly surprised and a little sad at the same time. I stopped singing, too, and for the longest time we sat there staring at each other, with Harry's horn wailing in the background.

Her eyes got wet, and she finally spoke. "I miss you, baby."

I didn't get it. I was right there in front of her.

Mama had a boyfriend . . . Bill Burgess.

He wasn't really her boyfriend, but I could tell he sure wished he was.

The first time I saw him, he was at Mama's door with a bunch of flowers in his hands. He was nice. His hair was a light curly brown, and he was pudgy. He wore glasses.

Nanny was crazy about him, and she told Mama she'd better hook him while she had the chance.

Mama liked him okay, but she sure didn't want to hook him.

He kept coming back anyhow, bringing Mama flowers and us groceries.

Ilomay and I had just walked home from school one day, and I opened the door to 102, and Daddy was there.

He was sitting on the couch, talking to Mama. Nanny was at the store.

He hugged me, and he had a little bit of that smell on his breath. I was scared Mama might scratch him again, but they seemed to be getting along okay. I figured it was because he was still living in Santa Monica and she wasn't.

He started showing up every once in a while. I liked it when he did. He was handsome, and he smiled. I could tell he didn't feel like smiling sometimes, but he did anyway.

When he'd had a good week selling those discount coupons, he'd give Mama a dollar for me, and Nanny would snatch it up, as if she didn't trust Mama with it.

I was eight, and it was Mama's birthday. I asked her how old she was. When she told me, she was crying. "Kiddo, your Old Lady is an old lady. I'm thirty—I'm *thirty*! Oh, God . . ." She was really crying.

The mascara was running down her cheeks.

I figured her days were numbered.

Nanny said, "Don't be a fool, Louise. You shouldn't ever tell anyone how old you are."

I guessed Nanny meant that I was "anyone."

Things weren't too good between Nanny and Mama. They fought just about all the time. About money. And our not having any.

Nanny would say it was awful the way Mama had brought us clear out here and stashed us in that stinky little one-room dump . . . we were better off in San Antonio. That would really get Mama to screaming back.

"Who *asked* you? I *told* you, I *wrote* you! *I wrote you I was broke! You knew it!* You *knew* I didn't have a job yet! You *knew* I couldn't take care of you and Carol yet. I *begged* you to wait until I could get on my feet! But no! *You* were the one who wanted to come to Hollywood. It was *you*!

Don't you blame me. You got just what you asked for, god*dam*mit! Why can't you ever let up?"

Then Nanny would say, "Why can't you get a job or a man?"

Mama would shriek, "Because I'm not like *you*! I'd never marry a man because he's a meal ticket."

Then Nanny would say, "Well, see then . . . I'm right! You *don't* love Carol."

We lived on the first floor in the three-story building on the corner of Yucca and Wilcox, one block north of Hollywood Boulevard.

Warner Brothers Theater, where I got my first full-time job, as an usherette, a few years later, was on Hollywood and Wilcox.

Room 102 faced the lobby, and our windows butted up against the Mayfair apartment building, just around the corner. I used to sit on the couch and listen to all the voices and noises coming out of the different apartment windows of both buildings. There would be radios blasting away, record players spinning big band music, and lots of people fighting —seemed like the whole world fought about liquor and money. When Nanny was down the hall at Mama's or at the store (by now I was around eight, and I didn't have to be with her every minute, as long as I *knew* every minute where she was), I would try to fool the neighbors by doing a "radio show" through my window. I'd lower my voice and pretend to be the announcer: "Welcome once again, ladies and gentlemen, to our show, featuring the brightest new talent to appear on the Hollywood scene in a L-O-N-G time!"

Then I would introduce my "Discovery of the Week," me, and proceed to interview myself. I would ask myself to "render us a little ditty, without benefit of musical accompaniment," and then I'd belt away at the top of my lungs.

I was thrilled once when a man next door at the Mayfair opened his window, stuck his head out, and screamed, *"Turn that goddamn thing off!"*

There were about a hundred thousand movie houses on Hollywood Boulevard, from LaBrea to Gower.

I could see a double feature, cartoons, news, and coming attractions for eleven cents. I averaged three trips a week to the movies. Sometimes I saw as many as eight second runs in five days if Nanny and I hit the boulevard on keno night at the Admiral. We'd get in before one or six, so we could "beat the prices." Ilomay and I would go together on Saturdays and then come home and play the movies we'd just seen. Lots of jungle stuff—Nyoka, queen of the jungle, and Sheena (another queen of the jungle)—lots of pirate stuff—Tyrone Power—and *lots* of Betty Grable. I had the upper hand in our relationship because Ilomay always played the second leads.

Nanny liked Ilomay. She made us capes out of pillowcases, and we dyed them black and tied the strings she sewed on the edges around our necks. We'd put on the black Lone Ranger masks we'd bought at the dime store and run like the wind down Cahuenga Boulevard, with our capes flapping behind us. We'd come to a screeching halt when we got to the Bank of America, where we'd flatten ourselves up against the building and hang around most of the afternoon, on the lookout for robbers.

I was enrolled in Selma Avenue Grammar School, and the first year I was absent more than I was present. I was still scared to leave Nanny at home. I would pretend to be sick so I could get out of going to school. She needed me to keep an eye on her.

It was okay with her. In fact, she wrote some pretty good excuses.

To Whom It May Concern:
 Please excuse Carol's absence from school the past two days. She was suffering from a severe stomachache and a temperature of 102 degrees. I felt it was best to keep her home, for her own benefit and for the well-being of those who would be exposed to her.

Sincerely,
Mrs. Mae E. White (Grandmother)

Sometimes it would be bronchitis and a sore toe. I'd stay home, and we'd play cards (high, low, jack, and the game) or sneak out to a movie.

Once in a while Ilomay would pull the same thing, and I'd visit her and we'd go in the bathroom for a few rounds of jacks.

Mama had given up on me.

102 remained a mystery to most of my playmates, except for Ilomay.

Whenever one of them would knock on the door, wanting me to come out and play, I'd open it just wide enough for me to slip out into the lobby without giving the person a shot at the view inside.

But there was nothing I could do about the whiff they'd get of Nanny: Ben-Gay, Vicks, and gas.

Nanny would lie down on Murphy and say, "This is the worst day yet," and if I would "know the truth" for her, she might pull through.

I learned about "knowing the truth" in Sunday school, so it was up to me.

I could, and did, keep her away from "death's door" many times.

I would pace up and down the room for hours, reciting Mary Baker Eddy's "Scientific Statement of Being." I didn't really know what a lot of the words meant, but Nanny liked to hear me recite it over and over: "Therefore, man is not material, he is spiritual . . ." and she'd lie there with a cold rag on her forehead and let out these big, long belches.

Then I'd start the whole thing all over again. Once in a while I'd slip in my "Please, God, take me first," and she'd be gulping down a phenobarbital.

I believed in God, or something.

It wasn't the God *they* all talked about. I didn't seem to know or trust that God, maybe because it didn't look to me as if they did either.

It's just that whenever I shut up long enough and listened, something would talk to me.

It still does.

If I just shut up and listen.

There was a tiny "dressing room" leading into the bathroom that had a cracked full-length mirror on the door. I would shut myself in there and look in the mirror and pose and sing—mostly Betty Grable stuff. But I seldom got to finish a whole routine because Nanny was always running to the medicine cabinet.

If I got into the theater before the prices changed at 1:00 P.M., on Saturdays and Sundays, I'd sit through Betty, or Mickey and Judy, or Fred and Ginger, or Cary and Irene, or James Stewart, twice or maybe three times, just as long as I got home before dark. The only sour note was leaving and walking out into the glaring sunshine.

They said Hollywood Boulevard was glamorous, but it sure wasn't in the daytime.

* * *

Mama wanted to interview movie stars and write about them for magazines. She wanted to do that more than anything. She was always hoping for, and trying to get, a regular job on a magazine staff.

Nanny said she should forget all that bull hockey and come down to earth and look for a real job.

But Mama wouldn't give up on it. She said Nanny was forever sticking pins in her dreams, and Nanny said it didn't make any difference anyhow because they were "pipe dreams," and somebody around here had to have her feet on the ground and her head out of the clouds. Mama would say that her head was *not* in the clouds and that she would make it big someday, and "Thanks a lot for all your faith in me."

Mama did get a chance to write about some stars on a "free-lance basis." She hustled up a few, on her own, and sold stories to *Pic* and *Collier's* for a few dollars. I was very impressed. She brought home autographed pictures of the people she had interviewed. There was Rita Hayworth, and George Montgomery, and Nan Grey, and Bob Hope, all hanging on her wall in a row and all signed, "To Lou." She loved to tell the one about how Rita Hayworth borrowed a nickel from her because she didn't have change for a phone call. She got a big kick out of saying, "How about that, Rita Hayworth owes *me* a nickel!" The neighbors would "Ooh and ahhh," and Nanny would sniff and say, "Too bad we don't have it now."

Mama went out a few times with a famous comedian. He called her on the phone a lot. I answered it once, and I recognized his voice right away when he asked for "Lou."

Years later I met him for the first time when we were on a TV show together. I asked him if he remembered her. He said no.

I think he did.

Nanny would tie a string around her waist and stick a rolled-up *Christian Science Monitor* under it, so it pressed hard against her stomach. She did it so her "insides wouldn't fall out."

She could belch louder than any boy in the whole school.

Ilomay and I would get hysterical.

She'd fart, too. I'd get awfully embarrassed because she did it in front of Ilomay, and she'd excuse herself and shrug it off with "More room *out* than *in.*" When the Relief Lady would show up, Nanny would lie on the bed, feel her pulse, point to me, raise her eyes to heaven, and let 'er rip.

The Relief Lady would hightail it out of there as fast as she could, and the welfare check would come another month.

I'd hear the trap snap in my sleep.

It used to wake me up when it first started happening.

Then, after a while, I got used to it. It became part of the night.

At first I'd pull the covers up over my head and bury my face in the pillow on the couch.

Nanny would be snoring. Finally I'd get up the nerve to go into the bathroom and check on what time it was. I'd open the medicine cabinet and look at Big Ben. It was always after midnight. It made me nervous to have my feet touching the floor because even in the bathroom I could hear the mouse in the kitchen dragging the trap around by its neck, back and forth across the linoleum, and bumping into the walls.

I'd run real fast and dive headlong back into my safe nest in the couch and wait for the noise to stop. If the mouse was little, it wouldn't take long. But sometimes it seemed to go on for hours. That's when I knew we'd caught a big one.

Nanny would always throw it out in the morning.

Lord, I hated the bus. It was the fumes. It still is.

Even now I get nauseated when I see a bus. About once a week Nanny and I would take two or three buses, transferring from one to the other, to visit Aunt Dodo and Cuz and Mary Lou, Cuz's older sister, and Uncle Parker. The Vances lived in a house off Pico and La Cienega. I liked playing with Cuz, but the trip was just plain awful.

It would be nighttime when we would leave to go back home. We'd sit on the bench, waiting for the bus, and I'd start yawning. My feet would dangle, not quite touching the sidewalk. I'd be just about asleep when I smelled it. It would lurch up and stop, and Nanny and I would drag up the steps through the folding doors. The bus would pull away from the curb, and we'd try to keep our balance and make it to the first empty seats we could find. If there weren't any, Nanny would announce to everybody on the bus that she had a bad heart, and somebody would always get up and give her a seat. I'd shield my eyes from the glaring neon overhead lights and pray I'd keep my dinner down, while we bounced all the way back to Hollywood Boulevard.

* * *

A few years ago, I was driving my car along Fairfax Avenue after rehearsing at CBS one night, and I saw an old woman and a little girl sitting on a corner bench, waiting for the Fairfax bus. I stopped for the light and stared at them for a few seconds. I checked my wallet, rolled down my window, and called to the woman. She looked up, and I reached across the seat of my car and handed her a fifty-dollar bill through the window. I think I told her to take a cab, or some such thing, before I drove off.

It was Sunday, and Ilomay and I were playing hopscotch on the sidewalk in front of the building. My best lagger was two bobby pins hooked together. They were the perfect weight for tossing. I had a pretty good eye, and I'd just successfully tossed and landed in the chalked-off number six square without even touching a line. I was in the middle of hopping on my left foot to pick it up when Old Mrs. Wolff, who lived on the second floor, appeared on the fire escape and began to scream, *"We've been bombed!"*

I tore into the lobby and burst into 102. Nanny and Mama were sitting there, staring at the radio . . . and we all listened to some radio announcer talk about a place called Pearl Harbor. Then the next day President Roosevelt talked about "infamy."

Nanny had pretty legs and ankles. So did Mama. They compared them. Nanny said her own were prettier, and Mama said hers were.

Now that the war was on, Mama started wearing leg makeup. Everybody was supposed to do his or her part for the "war effort." I couldn't understand why the soldiers wanted her silk stockings. Nanny darned and redarned her own stockings on a dead light bulb.

Once, when I was playing with Cuz at her house, we invited some neighborhood boys in to judge a leg contest. Cuz and I made ourselves the contestants, and we had the boys rate us from the toes up. She won "overall prettiest," and I won "longest." We were eight.

One thing I hated about visiting Cuz's was that Dodo would make her take naps. Nanny never made me take a nap. We weren't on any kind of schedule. We'd stay up till all hours of the night and go to bed when we felt like it. Naps were stupid and for babies. Cuz and I would be having a great time playing, and then Dodo would bust it up with her nap bit.

We'd drag our feet into Cuz's room and lie down on her twin beds, and I'd be out like a light.

Nanny had a habit of watching me leave for school when I was little until the very last possible moment. We had a routine. I'd kiss her good-bye in 102, and then I'd open the door and leave. When I had crossed the lobby and opened that door, I'd turn around, and there she'd be, waving, about seven feet away. I'd wave back, blow her a kiss, and go through the lobby door. I'd look back, and she'd blow one back at me. Then, when I got outside to the sidewalk, I'd look back again, and there she was, at the lobby door: kiss, kiss; blow, blow; wave, wave. Halfway down Wilcox, on the way to Hollywood Boulevard, I'd turn around again, and I'd see her little head and her hand held up, around the corner of the building . . . as if I were going off to the war. We kept it up until we couldn't see each other anymore.

The next morning it would start all over again.

Whenever I asked Nanny what time it was, she'd pause and say, "Time all fools are dead. Ain't you sick yet?" And then she'd howl with laughter. It was a family saying. Another one was: "Happy as a dead pig in the sunshine." I'd wonder how they'd been passed down, and why. I liked Mama's "sayings" better: "Most comedy is tragedy plus time," and "Jesus *had* to have had a sense of humor; otherwise so many people wouldn't have paid attention to Him."

Mama started drinking. Not much at first.

I went to bed the night before my ninth birthday, real excited about the party the next day.

Mama and Bill Burgess had had a couple of shots in the kitchen, and Bill had hinted that he'd got me a swell present, but I'd just have to wait until the next day. I woke up around two in the morning, feeling sick. My stomach itched, and my head was hot. Nanny looked at the bumps on my stomach and said it was the chicken pox.

Then she went down the hall and woke Mama. Mama came in the room, and she didn't look much better than I felt. She had thrown on her old chenille robe to wear down the hall, and her hair was stringy, and her eyes were kind of red. I was scared she'd be mad at me. And then she did a wonderful thing. She made me a chocolate cream pie. Right then and there.

And when it was done, Mama and Nanny and I ate the whole thing and watched the sun come up.

Every so often Daddy would show up and pay us a visit, but only when he could give us a dollar or two. Otherwise, Nanny wouldn't let him in. He was usually a little drunk. He and Mama would sit on the couch and talk.

They were divorced now.

Sometimes he'd come over when Mama wasn't home. He'd knock at the door, Nanny would open it, and he'd reach in his pocket, hand her a dollar, and wobble into the room. He was always real sweet and polite.

The only time I can remember his being upset was when he came by to wish me a belated happy ninth birthday. Nanny asked him to baby-sit me while she went to J. C. Penney's to buy me some pajamas. He said he'd be more than happy to.

I didn't want her to leave me. Ordinarily I would've gone with her, but this time I wasn't faking it. I was really sick, with a full-blown case of the chicken pox and a 102 temperature. I didn't want her out of my sight because she could have a heart attack or get hit by a car, and I wouldn't be with her to "know the truth." But off she went, saying she would be back in a few minutes, and "Don't be so silly."

I looked at him, and he looked back at me. His eyes were a little bloodshot, and he smiled at me and said, "Now, Punkin, don't you worry, your Nanny'll be back before you can say 'Jack Robinson,' an' in the meantime, you're in safe hands with your ol' daddy here."

I started to scream.

I was yelling at the top of my lungs for God to spare Nanny and bring her back to me . . . *now!* He tried to calm me down, but I wasn't having any of it. "Jack Robinson! Jack Robinson!" I grabbed the Bible and begged *it* to make her appear. "Matthew! Mark! Luke and John! Where *are* you?"

Daddy got up from the chair and weaved toward me. He tried to hold me, but I fought him off.

He gave up and went back to the chair. He sighed, looked at me, and then he put his face in his hands and said so quietly, so very quietly, I almost couldn't hear him, "Well, shit." I'd never heard Daddy say a bad word in my life, and I almost didn't hear him this time. It was barely a whisper, no particular emotion, just kind of matter-of-factly. "Well, shit." It was like a surrender.

I saw my chance. I hauled myself off my bed on the couch, threw back the covers, and ran out to the street, half looking for Nanny's dead body.

As I took off toward Hollywood Boulevard, I kept glancing back over my shoulder, afraid he'd be after me, but he wasn't. I tore up the street in my underwear, screaming her name, clutching the Bible to my chest, covered in chicken pox, heading straight for Penney's. She had just reached the store when I caught up with her. Jack Robinson.

She didn't look surprised when she saw me. I was as happy as I had ever been in my life. She took me home, and he hadn't moved.

I knew I had hurt him.

I can still picture him in that chair, after all these years, with his face buried in his hands.

When it was time for us to go out to the movies, Nanny would make herself feel better by saying, "Get thee behind me, Satan." In hardly any time at all we'd hit the boulevard headed for the show, and make it just before they could hike up the prices.

She sure liked to get dolled up. She'd put in her teeth and put on her makeup, and in about ten minutes she'd be looking pretty good.

She was crazy about bright colors, especially red. She wore a lot of it. On her face, too. Apple red lipstick and bright rouge. She'd open up the tube and run it across her bottom lip and then smack her lips together. Her top lip looked like the bottom one when she did that. Then she'd dab on a little bit of rouge, before she tackled her hair. She complained that her hair was getting thin, and I'd get a laugh out of her when I'd ask her what it had been like when it was fat. She was always getting real frizzy permanents at the beauty parlor, and the curl was never tight enough to suit her, so she'd go back again and raise enough hell until they'd fry it all over again—for free. When she started getting gray, she began coloring the frizz. Sometimes it would be blue, sometimes purple. I told her I liked the gray better.

"You're nuts," she said. "Nobody likes gray. Gray is old. Don't ever have gray hair, and don't ever tell anybody how old you are. Men don't like it."

She made me promise never to put how old she was on her tombstone.

"If you do," she said, "I'll come back and haunt you."

I promised.

* * *

Sometimes, when they left me alone in 102 to go to the store, I'd turn on the radio and dance all around the room. I'd get on the furniture and jump from the couch to the bed to the chair, leaping and twirling the whole time. Then I'd fling myself on the floor and writhe to the music, like Maria Montez dancing for the sultan, who wouldn't cut off my head after all because I was such a swell dancer.

One of the only places I was ever really, really alone was in the bathroom. I liked it when Nanny went down the hall to Mama's because she'd use the bathroom there, and it would give me more time to hole myself up, soaking in the tub. I could've stayed that way for hours, floating and singing, and pretending to be the Little Mermaid, who had the most beautiful face and voice in the whole mysterious underworld beneath the sea.

Nanny and I hardly ever went to a first-run movie because it cost too much, but I loved hanging around Grauman's Chinese Theater, where all the movie stars put their hands and feet in wet cement and signed their names. People came from all over the world to stand in the footprints and see how big or little their idols' feet were. And all Nanny and I had to do was walk a few blocks, and there we were. I'd usually stand in Betty Grable's square (she even had one of her legs outlined in the cement) or Linda Darnell's—another favorite of mine. Betty and Linda had tiny feet.

Sometimes we'd hit the boulevard and head for the premieres that were held at the Chinese, or the Egyptian, or the Pantages theaters.

The beams from the huge klieg lights would shoot up into the sky, announcing the opening of a new movie—a musical, or an adventure, or a love story—and the arrival of the stars. Bleachers stood on both sides of the entrance to the theater for the fans, so that they could scream and cheer (and sometimes faint), when the big cars pulled up to the curb, and out would pop Lana Turner, Tyrone Power, Robert Taylor, Barbara Stanwyck, and everybody else you'd ever been crazy about. I was always disappointed we didn't get to sit in the bleachers because that's where the best view was, but you had to get there at the crack of dawn to get a decent seat, and Nanny said her kidneys wouldn't hold up for all that time. But sometimes we'd worm our way to the front of the ropes that would be strung up around the block (usually guarded by policemen), and that way we could catch a glimpse of a tuxedo and some sparkles in the back seats of the cars that had slowed down or even stopped, waiting for their turn to pull up to the front of the theater, where they'd make their entrance. The radio announcer would blare out the names of the movie stars as they stepped out of their cars. They'd smile and wave to the crowd, and the mob would go crazy, screaming and shouting for autographs. Nanny and I would lean as far out as we could over the ropes, and if we were lucky, we might catch a glimpse of somebody with platinum hair in a white sequined gown being whisked (like a fairy-tale princess) toward the lobby doors, with flashbulbs lighting the way like exploding stars.

One night we were hanging over the ropes at the Pantages when I spotted Linda Darnell getting out of her car halfway down the block. She was headed our way! Her car had been waiting in the long line, and she had just gotten out and was walking the rest of the way to the entrance . . . just like a real person. And there wasn't a policeman around anywhere. I couldn't believe it. I had cut pictures of her out of movie magazines and pasted them on the walls of 102, and here she was, right before my eyes . . . life size. She was the most beautiful live human being I had ever seen in my life, and she was from Texas, too! That's what *Photoplay* had said.

She was about to pass us when Nanny reached out and grabbed her by the sleeve of her purple dress. "Linda! Linda!"

Linda Darnell stopped, looked at her sleeve and then at Nanny. "Yes?"

"Linda, we're from San Antonio! Fellow Texans!" Nanny wouldn't let go of her. "And this little child is your biggest fan . . ."

Then Linda Darnell looked down at me, and I began to wilt.

Nanny went on. "She has pictures of you plastered all over the place, so give her your autograph . . . here." Nanny released her and shoved a piece of paper and a pencil under her nose.

Linda Darnell looked down at me again and smiled. Her teeth were brighter than the klieg lights. "Thank you . . . ?"

"Carol. Sign it 'To Carol,' " said Nanny.

Linda Darnell kept smiling and said, "Why, I'll be happy to."

I thought I was going to cry.

While she was signing the scrap of paper, I looked up at her and stared. It was the first time I'd ever noticed that people's nostrils aren't the same shape. The left one is different from the right one. I'll be darned. But hers were the most glorious nostrils I had ever seen.

She handed the paper to me, and I whispered, "Thank you."

"You're welcome." She headed for the theater, and the fans in the bleachers went nuts when they saw her.

"Thank you, Linda!" Nanny was beside herself. "Well, how about that? We met Linda Darnell!"

I fell asleep that night with the scrap of paper under my pillow.

I saved that autograph for years.

I can still duplicate her signature.

I'd work the faucets and the rubber stopper with my toes, keeping the water piping hot. With the shaft window closed, the little room steamed up in five minutes flat, and I'd make-believe it was the ocean fog engulfing me after I'd been washed up onshore, and any minute, I'd be discovered by the handsome prince, who would carry me to his castle, where I'd grow a pair of legs. By the time I stood up to dry off, I was withered and dizzy.

The other place I liked to go was up to the roof. There was a corner I could sit in where nobody could see me, and I could look all around Hollywood at the buildings and the mountains and then lie down and stare up at the clouds. Sometimes I'd be there for hours, daydreaming away. I'd usually be jolted out of this reverie after five o'clock, when people would be getting home from work and head for the toilets. The sudden sound of all that flushing would shoot up through the air shafts leading to the roof, and I'd come to, and remember where I was.

I started nosing around the kitchen. Nanny wasn't too thrilled about it, but I wanted to experiment. I wanted to learn how to cook pound cake and pumpkin pie and enchiladas. We were rationed during the war, and Nanny said she wasn't about to let me "experiment" with her ration stamps.

It was okay to whip the pound cake batter and lick the bowl clean when she had poured it into the cake pans, but when it came to mixing stuff, she drew the line. Mama said Nanny wasn't that good a cook anyhow.

I liked it, though. Everything chicken-fried . . . black. Then I'd sop up the grease and sorghum molasses with a slice of white bread.

I looked forward to a piece of pie and a cup of hot Ovaltine for breakfast, and then I'd get to school and fall asleep at my desk in the mornings.

It made Mama mad. She was always talking about salads and fruit and vegetables, but Nanny and I weren't too interested, so she finally quit pushing it.

Anyhow, I lost interest in learning how to cook. The kitchen was always a mess anyway. It got so I used the oven only when I wanted to dry my hair.

I don't know whose idea it was, but I was sent to a dentist. I was nine, and I took the streetcar and transferred to the bus and got out somewhere on Wilshire Boulevard in Santa Monica.

He was waiting for me in his office. I gave him the slip of paper I got from Nanny, who got it from the Relief Lady. He looked at it, made a face, and pointed to The Chair.

I climbed up onto it, and he started to drill. There was no Novocaine.

Nine fillings later I got on the bus, transferred to the streetcar, and went home. Since then I've brushed my teeth about eight times a day, and I haven't had a cavity.

My tonsils were yanked a year later. This time Nanny and Mama went with me. We took the streetcar in the other direction to downtown L.A. We walked into a big hospital building and presented the relief lady's slip of paper to a woman behind a desk. She looked at us as if we were there for a sale.

We were sent to a room, where I changed into my pajamas we'd brought from home. Nanny had them in a grocery bag. Then we went into a hallway, where there were a lot of other kids in their pajamas, too. They were standing in a long line. I got behind the last one. One by one they were disappearing through some double doors way down at the end of the hall. Nobody was saying a word.

A few minutes of silence would go by, and then a body would be shot back through the doors on a cart, past the rest of us, looking deader than a doornail. We'd all move up one.

It was my turn.

This was it. I'd be the next dead kid on the cart. I grabbed a last look at Nanny and Mama down at the end of the hall and waved good-bye. They waved back. I felt a hand in the middle of my back push me through the dreaded double doors. Up close the doors were a yellowish green and the paint was chipped. I'd never been so scared. The lights inside blinded me for a few seconds. And then I saw the doctor. He was waiting just for me, and he looked exactly like that dentist.

He pointed to The Table, and I climbed up. I stared right into the ceiling lights, figuring they were the last things I'd ever see, when somebody stuck something in my face. It looked like a black baseball glove, and stank.

A voice said, "Count back from a hundred." I hit ninety-three and died.

I came to on a cot. I checked out the kids in the beds on either side of me. As far as I could tell, they'd gone on to heaven. I was surprised I hadn't. Then I wished I had. I started to throw up in a white pan. Nanny and Mama took turns holding it and my head. It was awful, and I swore I'd never let another mean old doctor touch me again, even if it was for free.

When I was feeling a little better, Nanny and Mama washed my face and dressed me.

As we were leaving, the other two kids were throwing up in their pans.

We took the streetcar home.

I didn't take to the ice cream, but I kept the enchiladas down.

Ever since I could remember, Uncle Parker hated Nanny's guts. And she hated him right back. They seemed happy with the arrangement, but it wasn't a lot of fun being in the same room with them when the family got together. I think that was when I first began to understand the definition of the word "tension." Even though he joked with me and called me JoJo (after my daddy), I wasn't exactly comfortable with him, with or without Nanny.

For one thing, he used to like to tell the one on me where I had "doo-dooed" in his best blue velvet chair. Evidently I'd been propped up in his favorite antique, and when left to my own devices and the call of nature, I had let go, and the diaper didn't catch all of it. I'd been potty-trained for years, but he would still tell it at every single family get-together, as if none of us had ever heard it before. And everybody would laugh—even me. But I wanted to sock him in the nose.

He and Nanny spoke only if it was absolutely necessary. I heard him tell Mama and Aunt Dodo that their mother was, without a doubt, the meanest woman in the world," and there wasn't a truthful bone in her body: "Every time that woman opens her mouth, out pops another windy." Nanny wasn't around when he said it. Mama laughed, and Aunt Dodo looked grim and her skin got tight.

Uncle Parker and Mama got along okay. They'd have a drink and joke. She said he was a good guy, and she was happy that "Sister had given me the big brother I never had." That always got Nanny's goat. He worked in the furniture business, and when they moved from Texas to California, he opened up the Vance Furniture Company on Pico and Crenshaw.

It was loaded with old, used stuff. It looked like a bunch of junk to Cuz and me.

But we had fun in the store. He'd let us come there and play. We'd go into the windows and pretend to be mannequins, and we were absolutely convinced that we fooled every busload of people on Pico who pulled up to the stoplight. We'd pick a position and freeze. We got so good at it we could hold our breaths for a whole minute. Then we'd howl with laughter and change positions and wait for the next load of suckers.

I kind of liked Uncle Parker those times. He was okay. Then it would change again at the next get-together.

The worst was Christmas.

We'd take the bus clear over there to their little house on Alcott, around noon, Nanny, Mama, and me. Everybody would smile, and there'd be ho-ho-hoing and Merry Christmasing, and Mama would say "bullshit" under her breath and head for the kitchen to pour herself a drink. Nanny and Dodo would bury their heads together and talk in whispers, and Mary Lou would be in and out of the house all day, and Uncle Parker would go into the bedroom and not come out until the turkey. Nanny would act as if he'd insulted her, and Aunt Dodo's mouth would get smaller. I'd eyeball the presents under the tree that "Santa" had left for Cuz. We weren't fooled. We knew St. Nick was bull. Their tree was tall, but it looked as if someone had decorated it by throwing the ornaments over his shoulder. Still, it was a *tree*. The one we had in 102 was a twig as far as I was concerned. Under the twig, on Christmas morning, was a small package (about the size of a bracelet) that had my name on it. I couldn't wait to tear into the wrapping paper. It turned out to be a white patent-leather coin purse that Nanny and I had seen on sale at Thrifty's. I hated it. I didn't even open it. I knew it would be empty.

Looking at Cuz's presents under their tree made me hate that ugly coin purse even more. She had a new dress, a Storybook doll, and a dollar. I couldn't wear my purse, I couldn't play with it, and I didn't have anything to put in it. Dammit to hell.

Endless hours went by, and somebody finally would say, "Supper." Uncle Parker would come out of the bedroom and sit at the head of the table. Mama would be feeling no pain, but Aunt Dodo looked as if she were feeling plenty.

Mary Lou was bored, and Nanny stared straight ahead and sucked in her cheeks. "Pass the gravy" was about the most anybody said. Cuz and I would try to break each other up, silently, by staring at each other without blinking and opening our mouths as wide as we could before we'd swallow our food. After dinner came the Christmas carols. Nanny would play, and everybody was supposed to sing and be merry. Uncle Parker would go into the bedroom, and Mary Lou would disappear again.

The notes were too high, but Nanny and Dodo would go for them anyway. Mama would undercut them by singing down the octave. Even with "Jingle Bells," she sounded like a nightclub singer in a smoke-filled room, right out of a Warner Brothers movie.

"Joy to the wor-llldddd . . ." I looked around, but I couldn't see much joy anywhere.

It would all peter to an end, and my stomach would start to churn from a combination of all the grease I'd eaten and the thought of the bus ride home.

4

Goggy came to California. To stay.

It meant we weren't ever going back home to the old house. I knew that much.

She moved in with Cuz. They had more room, and Aunt Dodo was crazy about her. Mama said that "Dodo loved Grandma much more than she loved Nanny . . . and with good reason." I didn't exactly get it, but in a way I understood because I loved Nanny (*my* grandmother) more than I loved Mama. Maybe it ran in the family.

Then, one day, Goggy ate a sandwich and "slipped away." That's the way I heard them tell it.

I hardly got a chance to play a few games of checkers with her before she "went to the Great Beyond, to meet her Maker, where there was great rejoicing in heaven." Aunt Dodo cried the most at the funeral.

I missed her.

The man who did all the talking asked us to "remember her."

I remembered how little she was, almost as little as I was. And boy, did she ever love God. Not talking on Sundays, for goodness' sakes. The other days, when she did talk, her voice was so light I could barely hear her. I remembered her cotton dresses that went clear to the floor, and the shawls she wore—which she crocheted. She taught me to crochet. I remembered her sunbonnet. It made her look like those old ladies in the cowboy movies who rode on the covered wagons and patched up bullet wounds. I thought about her long, long silver hair. I remembered it went all the way down to her waist, when she undid it.

I remembered the times she'd make me lie down on the floor in the parlor of the old house during a norther and slap a wet handkerchief over my whole face, so the dust storm wouldn't choke me to death.

The checkers games. Shelling peas on the porch. Tickling her. The firefly jar. The look on her face when she thought about her boy Hubert, who was whisked to heaven when he was fourteen, to be with God.

They said she had been eating a sandwich at the kitchen table and "quietly and simply slumped over, never made a sound. It was as if she didn't want to disturb anybody."

"A saint," they all said.

Mama and Aunt Dodo didn't look too much like sisters. Dodo had blond hair and dark brown eyes, and Mama had dark hair and light blue eyes. Mama said she took after their daddy, Papa Bill Creighton, more than Dodo did. But Dodo always said he had loved *her* more than he did Mama. Mama didn't like to hear that. She'd say that her sister was just jealous because Mama had been the baby and looked just like him.

Nanny said that Eudora (Aunt Dodo) had just about killed her when she was born because she weighed at least thirteen pounds. Mama had come into the world, four years later, "small enough to put in a teacup." She had been early. Nanny said that was the end of the trouble with Dodo and just the beginning with Mama.

When Nanny wasn't around and Mama and Aunt Dodo were alone together, they got along pretty well. But sometimes they'd go for weeks not speaking to each other at all. It was usually after Nanny had told Mama something nasty Dodo had said about her behind her back. Mama would hit the ceiling and have a few choice words about her sister and slam out of the room. Then Nanny would pick up the phone and call Dodo to tell her what Mama had said about her.

Then Dodo would get all riled up at Mama, and the freeze would be on. Nanny would be the only one they'd both talk to, and she seemed to like that setup.

After a while it all would die down, and they'd start speaking to each other again.

That's when Nanny would begin to get fidgety because Mama and Dodo usually put two and two together and figured out that the whole thing had started with her.

"You just can't stand it when Eudora and I get along, can you?" Mama would say.

"What's the matter with you, Louise? I don't know what you're talking about." Nanny would snort back. Whenever Nanny felt trapped about something, she'd snort and sniff and get a spell.

"Oh, you don't, huh?" Mama'd press on. "Well, *Eudora* told *me* what *you* said *I* said about *her,* and you know damn good and well I never said any of those things! *You* are the one who said them, not *me*!"

Nanny would put her fingers on her temples and rub them and begin to gasp for her breath.

"I did not! You know how Eudora can twist things around, and besides, you agreed! And I told you what she said about you!" She'd reach for some aspirin.

Mama would be screaming by now. "Don't start! Look who's talking about twisting things; you never told the truth in your whole life! You hate it when Sister and I are friends. You're so damned selfish and scared of being left out of anything that you lie through those goddamn false teeth of yours and say anything to keep us apart! You don't even *know* what the truth *is* anymore!"

Nanny would be on the bed by now. "That's what I get for loving you both and giving up everything for you." She'd reach out for me to hold her hand. I'd run over and take it.

Mama's face would go red. "Don't hand me that! You're a *liar*! And you know it, and so do I, and so does Eudora."

Nanny would moan and say, "You'll be the death of me, Louise."

And Mama would say, "Who're you kidding? You'll outlive us all. You're too mean to die!" Then she'd leave.

On my birth certificate my name was spelled "Carol" in spite of the fact that Mama had named me after Carole Lombard.

She liked the plain way better. She said she hated cute and coy stuff. Of any kind.

Nanny liked the *e*. And *"That* was the way to spell it."

Mama said I was *her* daughter, and *she* had the right to spell my name any damn way *she* wanted to. *She* had me, *she* named me, and that was *that*.

They went 'round and 'round with that one.

So, whenever I wrote my name out, I wrote it like this:

Carole

I loved looking at the old family pictures in Nanny's scrapbook. Everybody looked so funny. And old. Nanny looked older when she was younger. She was round and plump and had puffed-out cheeks. Her dresses were long, and she wore her hair piled on top of her head. The men wore high-neck collars and had tight, little mouths. And they all looked as if they had stiff necks. Nanny said that every man she had ever met had "wanted" her.

I thought she looked a whole lot better now. For one thing, she was thinner, and when she felt like fixing herself up, people would say, "Mrs. White certainly is a handsome woman. Must be where Louise gets her looks."

I never understood where they got that "handsome" bit. Men were supposed to be handsome. Women were supposed to be pretty.

Mama said her daddy, Papa Bill, was very good-looking and Nanny had no right taking all the credit.

My daddy was good-looking, too. So was Mama, and so was Nanny. I'd stare in the mirror and wonder why I wasn't even close.

5

The cops didn't even wait to see if anybody was going to answer the door. They knocked two times and kicked it in. It wasn't locked.

I was alone in 102, sitting on the couch, drawing. Mama had gone down the hall to her room for a minute, and Nanny was at the store.

They were after the extra phone we had in the kitchen. Mama had made a deal with a bookie. He gave us a few bucks to set up a number in our apartment. Sometimes she and Nanny took bets over the phone. I didn't know it was against the law. I was just told to keep my mouth shut.

I thought the cops were going to shoot me.

Mama came running back down the hall, scared to death. She started to cry about how poor we were and that she needed the money to feed her "eight-year-old baby" (I was around ten, so I stayed seated). Nanny came in, saw the commotion, and began to have an attack.

Mama spilled all the information she had on the bookie, and they let us off, with a warning. They yanked the phone out of the wall and left. The lock was broken, and Nanny was really mad at Mama: not for what she did but for getting caught.

Mama hung a saying on the wall next to the autographed pictures of the movie stars she had interviewed. It was rust-colored and made out of tin. The lettering was very fancy, as if it had been written with a quill pen:

> For when the One Great Scorer comes
> to write against your name—
> He writes—not that you won or lost—
> but how you played the game.

She just loved that.

Mama was a soft touch. Sometimes we'd get our relief checks and be broke before the month was out. Usually it was because she'd lend a couple of bucks to friends.

"Thanks, Lou. God, you're a lifesaver. Pay you back as soon as I can . . ."

Mama would say, "Oh, that's okay . . . whenever."

They'd pocket the bills. "Lou, what can I say? You're the best."

And Mama would cock her head and smile.

Then Nanny would find out and go haywire.

I stole something once from the dime store, and I made myself take it back. I wasn't as ashamed of myself as I was terrified of getting caught and sent up the river.

It was a ruby red lipstick from the makeup counter. I ran all the way home with it hidden in my pocket.

I slammed the door to 102, locked it, and hugged the wall. The apartment was empty, but I checked under the bed anyway.

I went into the bathroom and closed the door. My hand shook when I reached in my pocket for my loot. I was just about to unscrew the tube when there was a loud knock on the door. It sounded like a gunshot.

"Why is this locked?" It was Nanny.

I shoved the lipstick back in my pocket and opened the door.

"I'm sorry!" I cried as I ran right past her, heading back to the store where I had committed the crime. I got there just as it was closing. I banged on the front doors, begging them to let me turn myself in.

The manager let me go since I was ten and this was my first offense.

I felt cleansed—kind of like Claire Trevor getting out of the big house.

When Nanny bought me my new $2.95 oxfords at the beginning of the school year, we'd bring them home from Karl's or Thom McAn's and spread the *Citizen-News* all over the floor. I'd put them on and walk back and forth on the newspaper to break them in. It would take a couple of days. If they pinched or rubbed a blister anywhere, we could take them back to the store and show the salesman the clean soles to prove they hadn't been worn. That way we could exchange them or get our money back without a lot of hassle.

Of course, not too many people could argue with Nanny when it came to money. Or would.

I bought my first pair of shoes, shoes that actually fit, when I got on *The Garry Moore Show* in New York in 1959. I had never known it, but I wore a 7½AA. The salesman said I had an "expensive foot." I took them back to my New York apartment and spread the *Journal-American* all over the floor. They cost over forty dollars, and they fit me to a T. They felt like butter, and I couldn't wait to wear them outside.

But I walked on the newspaper, back and forth, for two whole days . . . just to make sure.

Whatever money Nanny could save would wind up in a sock. She sewed the top of the sock closed and safety-pinned it to the underside of the mattress on Murphy. And every night, before she went to bed, she'd check to make sure it was still there.

It came in handy when they raised the rent on us. It went clear up to thirty dollars a month. "Dear Lord in heaven," she said, "a whole dollar a day just for a roof over our heads."

One night Nanny and I went to the Admiral to catch *Citizen Kane*. I thought I was going to die. It lasted forever, and I didn't get what was going on one bit. I don't think Nanny did either. Wednesday nights were keno nights, and she was hoping to get a row of numbers on our cards and win five bucks. We didn't win that week, either, and we sat out the movie. I wanted to go home, but Nanny said, "We paid, so we'll stay." I know she was as bored as I was. Nanny liked her love stories, and this wasn't her idea of a light romantic comedy. When it was finally over, and we got up to go home, the manager told everybody they had to stay because Los Angeles was right in the middle of a blackout. We had a lot of these air-raid drills, and people weren't supposed to be on the streets when they were going on.

So we sat down again.

I kept wishing Orson Welles would turn into Betty Grable.

I met Orson Welles when I was grown up, and I told him about that night all those years ago. He said he thought a lot of people probably would've liked to see him turn into Betty Grable.

I loved the neighborhood blackout drills (when I wasn't stuck watching *Citizen Kane*). They were scary and exciting. The whole city would go "out." Shades would be pulled down, and maybe a candle or two would be lit. Sirens would scream away, and I'd peek out through the little rip in our window shade and look up at a black sky filled with brilliant searchlights zeroing in on pretend Japanese planes. I wondered how far away Pearl Harbor was and if the rumors were true about some people spotting subs off the Santa Monica pier. I was never *really* scared, though.

The war was one giant movie we all were starring in.

Sometimes I was Veronica Lake, the brave nurse, in *So Proudly We Hail,* who blew herself up with a live hand grenade hidden in her shirt, taking a whole squadron of enemy soldiers with her, thus saving her own battalion. At other times I chose to be Claudette Colbert in the same movie . . . because she lived.

Every day after school, and on Saturdays and Sundays when we weren't at the picture shows, the neighborhood gang—Asher, Malcolm, Bobby, Jean (his dad owned the French cleaners on Cahuenga), Ilomay, Norma, and I—would head for the vacant lot that was up on a hill, just off Cherokee, a block away. The lot was in the process of being dug up. A hotel/motel was going to be built there someday.

In the meantime, the churned-up dirt made absolutely perfect trenches and foxholes. The guys were into the Robert Taylor, *Bataan* bit, while the girls would pretend to have been sent overseas with Bob Hope's USO troupe, to cheer up our fighting men with our rendition of "Don't Sit Under the Apple Tree with Anyone Else but Me," à la the Andrews Sisters. Since the whole thing was my idea, I got to be Patty, the one in the middle. For us, World War II was what Hollywood showed us. We rooted for John Wayne and bled right along with Robert Walker.

There was no way I was going to kiss Malcolm.

It was my eleventh birthday, and the ice cream and cake had been dished out and polished off, the tail had been pinned on the donkey, and for some dumb reason we were playing spin the bottle.

Mama and Nanny were down the hall in 102, and I was having my party at Mama's. The gang was all there: Ilomay, Norma, Bobby, Asher, Malcolm, plus Ralph (who was a little older), and Joanne. Joanne had a big crush on Ralph and had brought a couple of her girlfriends along. Spin the bottle had been their bright idea.

Each couple went into Mama's closet when it was their turn to kiss. It was dark in there. Nobody else could see them, and they couldn't see each other. The older kids (around twelve and thirteen) seemed to be having a good time. I was kind of interested, but I would've been just as happy with hide-and-seek, and Asher and Malcolm (who were ten) were acting like real jerks. Every time a couple went into the closet, Malcolm and Asher would throw themselves on the floor, kick their legs wildly in the air, scream with laughter, and yell out things like "Stick it to her!" Then they'd howl some more. They were disgusting.

Bobby and Norma had just come out, and I was hoping I might get a crack at Bobby the next time around when Malcolm said, "I want to spin! I haven't had a turn!"

Ralph chuckled, handed the empty Coke bottle to Malcolm, and he spun it. It finally stopped and was pointing straight at me. I felt as if I'd been shot right through the heart.

Malcolm was up on his feet and headed for the closet. "Well, c'mon! Let's get at it!" He really was repulsive.

Some of the kids started to laugh, and I shot every one of them a dirty look. Their look back at me was saying, "We *dare* you!" I followed him into the closet. The door closed, and it was pitch-black in there. I felt him reach for me, and one of Mama's dresses swung and brushed across my face. I almost jumped out of my skin before I realized what it was. I thought, *Never!* I'm not gonna kiss that toad. I had to get out of there fast. I whirled around and bolted for the door.

I made a wrong turn and ran right into the wall.

I came to in the living room. I was lying on the floor, and when I opened my eyes, I saw Mama leaning over me. She was putting a cold rag on the bump on my forehead. I had knocked myself out. I heard Ilomay's voice screaming, "She's alive, everyone! She's *alive!*" Nanny was giving Malcolm holy hell, and Malcolm was saying, "I didn't even *touch* her!" And I was thinking, "What a crappy party."

Mama would say things about herself like "Goddammit, Lou, but you have one hell of a voice!" and "Christ, I can sing! I have a perfect ear . . . lissen, lissen now, Carol." She'd be sitting at the kitchen table, strumming her ukulele and pouring herself another shot of whiskey. She'd throw her head back and run her fingers over the uke strings, and her eyes would be half-closed in ecstasy. "God*damn!* What a chord! Carol, take the lead. Mama, you sing third. I'll take second. Now, *don't let me down!*" After she had issued her instructions, Mama, Nanny, and I would all start singing "Carolina in the Mornin'," "I'll Get By," and "Louise" (Mama's song).

I'd make-believe I was Patty, and they were Laverne and Maxine. I just loved it. Those were the times they didn't fight. In fact, they even laughed and enjoyed each other. Mama would brag about her "good ear," and Nanny would remind her where it came from. And it made me feel closer to Mama. I liked hearing her sing in that bluesy voice as much as *she* did. I looked forward to these kitchen sessions because most of the other times I got the feeling that Mama was mad at me for something.

She'd make sour faces and call me "Nanny's little darling." And Nanny would shoot back and say it was Mama's own fault that I loved Nanny better. Sometimes Mama would get so mad she'd take off one of her house shoes and throw it clear across the room.

I'd make myself scarce and go outside to play war with Ilomay and the rest of the gang. I don't remember being told or even the moment I knew, but it was around this time Mama was going to have a baby.

Tony was a good-looking-Italian-sometimes-actor Mama was head over heels in love with. She had been nuts about him even before Nanny and I had left San Antonio. She wrote about him in her letters to Nanny. And when we moved out to Hollywood, Mama was going out with him a lot.

I used to love to watch her get ready for a date with him. She'd plan on having enough time so she wouldn't have to hurry. She had a large red strawberry birthmark on her right temple, and her hair had to be fixed "just so" to cover it. She'd put setting lotion on her fingers and fashion a wave on that side of her face, setting it with two bobby pins. While she was letting it dry, she'd put on her makeup. She'd apply her red, *red* lipstick right from the tube and then smooth it out with her little finger. Then came my favorite: the mascara. It was in a little rectangular box with a brush, and it was black. She'd spit into the mascara and squish the brush around and sweep it up under her top eyelashes, which were pretty long to begin with.

She'd be humming to herself, sitting there in her slip. When her hair was dry, she'd take out the bobby pins and kind of fluff the wave with her hands. She'd look at her face in the mirror and smile and rub her teeth with her little finger, to get off any lipstick that showed. She looked real good.

One time he got there early, and I was embarrassed because he saw her in her slip. She carried it off very well, I thought, as if there were nothing wrong with it. She didn't even bother to put on her robe. She went about her business and put on a frilly dress and her very high heels, grabbed her purse, and off they went. They looked nice together.

I thought he was okay. He didn't bother me at all.

He bothered Nanny, though, because he was married.

Even though Nanny bragged that she had never really loved a man, it looked to me as if she sure enjoyed being around them. It didn't matter how old she was or how old they were. She loved to flirt. And she was real good at it.

She had very pretty legs and liked to show them off. She wore her

skirts shorter than Ilomay's grandmother and shorter than all the grandmothers in all the movies I ever saw. Whenever she was complimented on
her lovely legs (by a man), she'd lower her eyelids, kind of giggle, sit
down (if she wasn't already sitting), and hike her skirt up an inch or two.

She told me about her three husbands: Mr. Creighton (my grandfather), Mr. Melton, and Papa John White. They'd been crazy about her.
She talked about all the beautiful jewelry she'd had and didn't have now.
She said she had been much prettier than both Mama and Dodo; her
daughters couldn't hold a candle to her when she was younger. "Too bad
I couldn't have come to Hollywood in my heydey. I'd have shown 'em all
a thing or two."

One time I asked her if she hadn't loved at least one of her husbands,
just a little.

She replied, "What for?"

Mama talked all the time about how much she loved Tony. She said she
didn't know what love was until she met him. Nanny would say it was
too bad Tony's wife felt the same way, and 'round and 'round they'd go.
Mama would say he was going to get a divorce as soon as he could, and
Nanny'd look as if she'd smelled something rotten and say, "Louise,
when are you going to come to? Bill Burgess is your only hope!" Then
Mama would call her a dried-up old bitch, and Nanny would storm out,
slamming the door behind her. I'd follow, close at her heels. I could hear
Mama crying behind the closed door.

Tony had broken his leg and had to use crutches for a while. He'd
come over, and Mama would cook dinner for him in her apartment. It
drove Nanny nuts, wasting good food like that.

One night Nanny and I were coming home from a movie, and she
walked right past the entrance to the building and up to Mama's window.
It was on the first floor and faced the Yucca Street side. Anybody walking
by could look right in if the shade was up. Mama had pulled the shade
down, except for about an inch at the very bottom. One dim light was on
inside. Nanny put her nose up to the pane and peered in, through that
one inch. Whatever she saw made her start sniffing and snorting, and
clearing her throat, and poking her fingers into her chest, and feeling her
pulse—the things she usually did when she was having an attack or doing
something she knew she shouldn't be doing. Then she pushed me up
against the side of the building and told me to keep still. She stood next

to me, her eyes glued to the lobby door. It dawned on me that we were going to wait outside. For Tony.

She didn't let me in on it, but I knew it anyhow. I just didn't know why. And I wasn't about to ask her.

After a while it started to get cold, and I was sleepy, but she wasn't budging. He finally came out of the building, hobbling on his crutches, and headed in the opposite direction. When he reached the corner, Nanny called out to him. He stopped and turned around. He sure was good-looking. She told me to stay put and marched up to him and started screaming at him.

I remember rocking my body back and forth against the cool concrete of the building, right below Mama's window. I could've peeked in, too, if I'd stood on my tiptoes, and then maybe I'd've known why Nanny was raising so much hell. I couldn't make it all out, but she was wagging her finger at him and saying things like she bet his wife would be interested in knowing what was going on, and he ought to be ashamed of himself, and he'd better not hurt "that little child over there," turning around and pointing at me. They both looked at me, and I looked down at my feet. I stared at the grooves in my shoes my roller skates made where I screwed them on with my skate key. I made a go at pretending I was somewhere else, some*body* else. I was glad now we'd waited outside and not in the lobby. I wouldn't have wanted the neighbors in on this. A drop of water hit the toe of one of my shoes. At first I thought it was rain, but it wasn't. I was starting to cry. I hated this whole thing.

Finally she was through.

He didn't say much, just kind of nodded and turned and hobbled around the corner. Nanny came back to me, yanked my hand, and we went inside.

I don't remember ever seeing him again.

After a while Mama started to get a big stomach, and she'd sit in the corner of the couch and cover it with a pillow whenever anybody came in. Then she'd go for walks late at night, when it was dark.

Ilomay and I were kite flying up on the lot, and Malcolm and Asher thought it would be funny to mow down our kites with little rocks. I was wearing my brand new Thom McAn shoes, against Nanny's orders. They were *for school only,* and I wasn't supposed to play in them because they cost $2.95 and had to last me the whole year. One of the rocks sailed into my foot, and I felt its sharp edge dig right into my arch. I looked down at my ripped shoe and saw little drops of blood oozing through the canvas. I let go of my kite string and took off after Malcolm and Asher. Malcolm made a clean getaway, but Asher wasn't so lucky. He was a lot bigger than I was, but I was older and madder than hell. I grabbed him by his collar and jerked him around.

"Take off your glasses, Asher." I had seen Gable pull that on somebody in a movie.

"No." He was shaking.

"I *said,* 'Take off your goddamn glasses,' Asher."

"You can't make me."

I pulled them off his face and socked him in the nose. "You ruined my brand-new shoes!" I had also just lost a brand-new kite.

He started to cry. "I didn't do it! Malcolm did it! It was his idea! I'm going to tell on you!"

It was my turn to get scared. I'd never hear the end of it from Nanny. A brand-new pair of Thom McAns.

I ran all the way home praying nobody would be in 102.

When I got there, it was empty. Thank you, God.

I took off my shoe, and for the first time I noticed how much the cut was hurting me. I tried frantically to wash the blood off my shoe with some soap and a rag in the sink. It didn't help at all, and the canvas was starting to stink, and my foot was starting to throb. I heard Nanny's voice in the lobby, so I dived under Murphy, taking my shoe with me. Just in time. She came into the room. She started puttering around, sniffing, coughing, and clearing her throat—her regular routine.

I was starting to doze in my hiding place under the bed when Asher's mother knocked. "Mrs. White! Are you home?" I watched Nanny's feet walk to the door. She opened it, and there was Asher's mother, livid and yelling. Nanny asked her what she wanted.

"Carol knocked Asher's glasses off his face and beat him up!"

"What for?"

My mouth was completely dry. I proceeded to roll myself up into a ball.

"She's beatin' up on Asher when it was Malcolm!"

"What happened?" Now Nanny was screaming. If I hadn't been so scared, I'd have laughed.

"Malcolm was throwing rocks, and one of them hit Carol in the foot and cut her shoe, and she took it out on Asher."

Oh, Lord.

There was a pause. I took a quick peek and ducked back. Nanny snorted, cleared her throat, and made her neck real long. "Well, Asher's big enough to take care of himself, and if Carol hit *him,* you ought to be ashamed of yourself making that moose hide behind your skirt. Can't be doing him any good." And she shut the door. I heard her go into the bathroom.

I figured I'd have to make an appearance sooner or later, and my foot was killing me, so I crawled out from under the bed, ready to face her hissy fit over the $2.95 down the drain.

All she ever said was: "I *told* you not to wear your new shoes to play in. You know we don't have that kind of money, so you're just going to have to wait until your toes poke through the tops before you get another pair." She stuck my wounded foot in a pot of hot water and cleaned the cut. I couldn't put my shoe back on, so she got me a sock to wear, and we went to Thrifty's for a vanilla soda. While we were sitting at the counter, I put my head on her shoulder and she put her arm around me.

I don't remember a time when I wasn't waiting for a scab either to grow or to fall off my knee.

It probably *had* been Malcolm who cut my shoe with the rock. I think I knew it deep down all along, but Asher had just been too slow in making his getaway.

Malcolm was "forever causing mischief" in the neighborhood (according to the neighbors). The grown-ups branded him "no good and headed for the hoosegow, without a doubt."

Mama liked him. She thought he was good-looking, talented, and spunky.

He lived with his mother, Dixie, in a corner room on the second floor. I liked Dixie. She reminded me of a plump Betty Boop with red hair. Dixie would come down to Mama's, and the two of them would sit in the kitchen and gripe about men. After a while Mama would tell me to get lost, and they'd start telling jokes. I'd open the door and let it slam so they'd think I'd left. Then I'd tiptoe back toward the kitchen and lean up against the wall, so I could hear. I heard, all right. And I didn't think any of it was as funny as they did.

I remember Dixie telling the one about "this man and this woman who were going at it hot and heavy, and the man, right in the *middle* of it, says, 'Kiss me, honey, quick!' And she says, 'Oh, no! I shouldn't even be doin' *this*!' " I thought Mama would bust a gut. The next day I asked Malcolm if he'd heard the one about this man and this woman, etc., and he laughed as hard as Mama had. I didn't let on to him how much it irritated me that he got it, because he was a whole year younger than me.

Dixie had a job, and Malcolm was alone most of the time. He was forever playing hooky and hanging around Hollywood Boulevard. When he got bored doing that, he'd run up and down the halls in our building, yelling and banging on Old Mrs. Wolff's door in the middle of her afternoon nap. He'd usually wind up on the roof, throwing garbage down the bathroom air shafts. Sometimes he'd light matches with his thumbnail, blow out the flames first, and then toss them at Ilomay and me. One Sunday the fire department was called, and they found two old mattresses smoldering in the basement. Malcolm swore he didn't do it, but he was blamed anyhow.

I think Mama liked him because he was musical. She always said she could forgive anybody almost anything if he was musical. Malcolm could drum. His idol was Gene Krupa. We'd set up big cardboard cartons on the corner of Yucca and Wilcox, and Malcolm would haul out his drumsticks and beat away. Ilomay and I would sing. She'd be Frances Langford, and I'd be Ginny Simms. If Norma joined us, we'd be the Andrews Sisters. It wouldn't take too long before he'd get bored and wind up poking holes in the boxes with his drumsticks. Then he'd storm out in another direction and be gone for hours. "Looking for trouble," Nanny would say with a snort.

In the late 1970s I was filming *Friendly Fire* in Northern California, and I got a phone call from him.

"Carol?"

"Yes?"

"Malcolm."

We arranged to have dinner. He was living right there in Stockton. It was well over twenty-five years since I'd laid eyes on him, and there I was, standing in front of the hotel, waiting for the Terror of Yucca Street to pick me up at 7:00 P.M. Malcolm.

Malcolm the Terrible. The Toad. The Jerk. The Delinquent. The Jailbird. I felt kind of funny. Maybe because deep down I couldn't picture him still alive.

It was a hot summer night, and I had on a sundress with a full skirt. Seven o'clock. He was on time . . . and on a motorcycle.

Good old Malcolm.

He handed me a helmet (a grown-up thing for Malcolm to do), and without hesitating, I put it on, hopped on the back of the cycle, and threw my arms around his waist. We were off and running, tearing through the Stockton streets with my billowing skirt maybe slowing us down just a little. I wouldn't have recognized him. He was so much older. And he was better-looking than I remembered. Mama had been right.

We stopped, suddenly, in front of a house in a quiet neighborhood. A house. Malcolm had a house. We went inside, and he introduced me to his wife. Malcolm had a wife. He told me about his work. Malcolm had a job.

Dinner. Talk, talk, talk about the old days . . . "Whatever happened to . . . ? Remember the time . . . ?" Then we'd laugh. Later, in the living room, we talked about his mama, Dixie. She was dead. I filled him in about my family.

There was a silent moment.

"Well."

"Huhummm . . . Lord, that was a long time ago. . . ."

His wife tried hard to look interested.

Every so often we'd all stare at the floor.

After one of the pauses, I asked him if he remembered the rock-throwing incident up on the hill, "You know, with Asher? . . . When my shoe got cut?"

"No."

"Oh, well . . ." I told them the story.

Malcolm owned up to the fact that he probably *had* thrown the rock and let Asher take the rap.

We all laughed at that for a little bit and stared at the floor some more. Time.

It was time to go home.

He dropped me off in front of my hotel. I handed him his helmet and kissed him on the cheek.

He gave me a little good-bye wave as he roared around the corner.

Everybody was rationed during the war, so I thought I'd do the patriotic thing and grow a victory garden. Our building didn't have a real back-yard, but there was about a three-by-five-foot patch of rock-hard dirt right below our window.

I dug it up the best way I could with a tablespoon and sprinkled in the vegetable seeds. Because our building and the Mayfair, next door, were right next to each other, the sun hit my garden only a hot four minutes a day.

The radishes thrived. Everything else died or stayed put. Nanny hated radishes, and I didn't like them much either.

They turned Mama's stomach, but then she hadn't felt like eating much of anything lately.

Sometime after midnight, December 12, 1944, Mama and her best girl-friend, Lucille, walked the block down Wilcox and got on the Hollywood Boulevard streetcar, headed for downtown L.A.

That afternoon Lucille came back alone and told Nanny and me that I had a little sister. I remember being delighted. I got the feeling that Nanny was just glad it was done with.

The big cover-up was over, and it crossed my mind that now they were going to have to explain this brand-new person. Mama couldn't cover her up with a pillow anymore, the way she covered her stomach.

The whole time she was waiting for the baby, I never heard them tell anyone about it in front of me. It was as if it weren't happening. The whole world knew it, but nobody said anything. I'd overhear bits of conversation between Nanny and Mama when they thought I wasn't listening, enough to know that Tony was involved and Daddy wasn't, that Mama was a "disgrace and a damn fool." Then Mama would cry and say she didn't care because "Dammit! This is the one thing that's really *mine,* and nobody's going to take it away from me!"

Then there were the times they'd agree. They'd talk about how no man was ever worth it, how "the whole thing is overrated," and how "they'll screw you every chance they get."

All I knew was that I should be ashamed of what was going on and keep my mouth shut.

I was, and I did.

I don't know how they explained Christine.

Mama named her Antonia Christine. The "Antonia" was dropped. Nanny didn't like it because it sounded too much like "Tony." The birth certificate read, "Antonia Christine Burnett."

She looked like "Antonia" to me. Black hair. Great big dark brown eyes, with feather-duster eyelashes. She was beautiful. Mama said she was the most beautiful baby she had ever seen, and she wasn't the least bit disappointed she didn't have a boy.

"All the glamour gals have girls," she said.

And now she had one all to herself. For the first time in a long time Mama looked kind of happy. For a while even Nanny couldn't rile her up.

Mama had her very own little girl, and I had my very own little sister.

And I adored her.

They let me hold her and feed her and change her.

After a while I didn't adore her quite so much. It got so they wouldn't let me go out to play until I had put her down for her nap. She'd take forever to nod off, and I'd blow on her eyelids to force them to close so she'd finally give up and conk out.

And it took hours to burp her.

I used to pray she would learn to let go like Nanny.

Nanny liked her sherry. She didn't drink like Daddy or Mama, but she did like her sherry.

She would buy the little bottles and put one in a small brown paper bag. The bag would go in the large purse she carried. She would zip it closed and safety-pin the end of the zipper to the imitation leather strap. She said the robber would die of old age before he could figure out how to open *her* purse. We would usually stop at Thrifty's on the way to the movies to have a vanilla ice cream soda. She'd pick a time when it was real crowded and the waitresses were frazzled. Nanny would put her purse in her lap, unpin and unzip it, and open it wide. She always kept an old dishtowel in there. Then, when no one was looking, she'd put her arm on the counter and in one swift move sweep the knives, forks, and spoons into her purse. Sometimes salt and pepper shakers would go in there, too.

She'd quickly tie the four corners of the dishtowel together, so the loot wouldn't rattle around. Then she'd zip the purse closed and safety-pin it again. We'd pay up in a hurry and make a beeline for the exit. I never saw her leave a tip.

She would open up her purse in the dark safety of the movie theater, take out a soda cracker, and eat it. She'd wash it down with a swig of sherry. She'd close the purse most of the way, leaving just enough room for the top of the bottle to stick through. Then she'd unscrew the cap, and keeping the bottle in the paper bag and the paper bag in her purse, she'd lift the entire purse to her mouth and drink. It smelled like cake batter. She'd belch softly and lock everything up again.

When it was time to leave the theater and go home, we'd go to the bathroom, and she'd empty all the toilet paper dispensers, sheet by sheet. And we'd be set for another few weeks.

I couldn't breathe.

I thought I'd swallowed a pin.

We were having dinner at Thrifty's and Nanny was busy at the counter when I pulled at her sleeve. I couldn't speak, and the tears were running down my cheeks as I began to choke. I remember thinking if I lived through this, I'd never eat another piece of fish, ever again.

But then I saw the expression on Nanny's face when she looked at me, and I figured I wouldn't have to worry about it. I was a dead duck.

She began pounding me on the back, and the waitress said I should drink some water. A lady came up from behind and told Nanny to shove some bread down my throat. I was seeing spots when the manager of Thrifty's screamed at Nanny to get me to a doctor . . . fast.

She jerked me out of the swivel seat, and we bolted for the door. I heard a kind of rattle sound, and it was coming from my throat. I heard a clanking noise, and it was coming from Nanny's purse. I remember thinking she hadn't had time to tie up the dishtowel.

She dragged me down Hollywood Boulevard, looking for a doctor, and she was saying to me, "You'll be all right, you'll be all right, I'm knowing the truth . . . there is no error . . . there *is no bone*! You're fine . . . you are God's image and likeness . . . Dear God, we never should have ordered that fish! I hate fish! They *told* me it didn't have any bones! I'll sue them for every nickel they've got!" I was starting to pass out. There was no way I could exhale.

And I'd inhaled all there was.

She hit me on the back again, and I began to throw up. It made it worse. I started choking on what was coming up in my throat.

She stopped dead, grabbed me by the shoulders, and looked into my eyes . . . hard.

"Breathe!"

I coughed. The bone started to come out. Nanny reached way down in my throat with her fingers and got it. Air!

It was about an inch-long sliver.

I finished throwing up on the curb, and she wiped my face with a Thrifty's paper napkin she had tucked away in her purse and she wrapped up the bone in another one from the stack she had stashed next to the silverware she had pilfered.

We headed back for Thrifty's.

"Just *look* at this! That fish was supposed to be *boneless!*" Nanny was showing the bone to the manager. He happened to look in her purse as she pulled out the bone to show him. For some reason she didn't sue but settled for two free vanilla ice cream sodas.

I remember the first time Daddy came to visit us after Christine was born. For a wild second I thought Mama would sit on the baby or try to stuff her behind the couch pillows—hide her some way—but she didn't. She was holding her in her arms. Daddy reached out to Chrissy and let her wrap her little fingers around his thumb. He looked sad.

I figured I'd better go out and play.

He was still there when I came back. He said he had waited for me because he wanted to tell me something important.

We went outside and started to walk around the block. He didn't say anything until we turned the corner at Cahuenga.

"She's a real little doll, isn't she, Punkin?"

I nodded.

"You love her a lot, don't you? Your mama says you're real good with her."

"Yeah." I felt funny, as if I should have more to say, but I didn't know what.

He was quiet again, until we hit Hollywood Boulevard.

"You know, none of this is her fault."

I looked up at him. "Whose?"

"The baby's. It's nobody's fault, really . . . but it's especially not hers."

"Uh-huh." I was looking down at my feet. I took two steps to his every one. His legs were miles long. We were getting near Wilcox, and I knew we were in the home stretch. I wondered if he'd finish telling me something important.

"You should always love your little half sister. Someday you'll both be everything to each other. She's not my little girl, but I love her, too. I'm glad she's here for you. . . ."

I didn't exactly get it, but I knew that was the important part and that he was being awfully nice about something. And he wasn't drunk that day either.

I never heard him tell anyone else that Chrissy wasn't his little girl, so I never said anything. In fact, I never heard anybody (outside the family) ever say anything about my little sister's real daddy. I saw Nanny tear up and throw out all the snapshots Mama kept of Tony. They had quite a row over that one.

After a while nobody said much of anything about it.

And Mama started drinking again.

I loved to draw. I still have a big bump on my right middle finger from holding a pencil. For the longest time I wanted to be a cartoonist when I grew up. I dreamed that someday I'd have my own comic strip. So I drew "The Josephson Family." My main character was a perky teenage girl named Jody. Her dad was Joseph, her mom was Josephine, her kid brother was Joey, and the dog was Jo-Jo. The perfect family, the way I wanted it to be in real life. All the characters were named after Daddy in one way or another. I drew them completely in profile with unfinished noses.

Like this:

Most of what I knew about the Burnett side of the family came from Nanny, and none of it was very good. She said the whole clan wasn't worth a toot. Daddy was the youngest of three brothers. He was born in Texas, in 1907, to Nora and John Burnett. They named him Joseph Thomas, but everyone called him Jody. Grandpa Burnett was a heavy drinker, and so was the firstborn, John. The middle brother, James, was the only one Nanny didn't say too much about because he "at least" could hold down a job. Daddy drank hooch instead of milk from the day he was born, according to Nanny. He was always high as a kite. And Mama had been a fool to marry him. Useless. That's what the Burnetts were. Useless and worthless.

Uncle Parker said Nanny was full of it. He and Daddy had been school buddies, and he said there had never been a guy as "okay" as my daddy.

"Everybody loved Jody in school. He was real popular and smart as a whip, too. Sure, he drank a little, but we all did . . . and he was never a mean drunk . . . nosirree, never had a bad word to say about anyone, and nobody ever had a bad word to say about him—except that grandmother of yours. Yessirreebob, Jody was aces." I liked it when Uncle Parker talked about Daddy.

Daddy's yearbook listed him as "Joke Editor of the school paper, good sport, roofhound, best dancer in the '24 class, President of the Jeffersonians, and the first boy in school to roll his socks." He was a tall, good-looking senior when Mama entered the ninth grade at Breckenridge High in San Antonio.

"They made a swell-looking couple," Uncle Parker said. "Your mama was beautiful, even then, and Jody fell hook, line, and sinker. They were nuts for each other and fun to be around."

I'd try real hard to picture it.

We didn't see much of Daddy anymore. Mama said he had TB and he'd better quit the booze or it would be curtains, because he had always been too skinny to be so tall.

Uncle Jimmy, who was the middle of the three Burnett brothers, lived in Los Angeles and worked at an airplane plant. He picked me up and drove me over to his house a few times, and I got to know the Burnett side of the family a little bit. He was the rich one because he had a regular job. There was his wife, Aunt Inez, and my two older Burnett first cousins, June and Bud. I remember that they all ate dinner together and talked without yelling. I liked Uncle Jimmy. He wasn't tall and rumpled like Daddy. He had a little mustache and was kind of spiffy, and he moved a lot quicker than Daddy did. He reminded me of a rooster.

He'd tell me about how much he loved his kid brother (Daddy) and how he'd cut off his own right arm for him if only he'd straighten out. He was sorry Jody and Lou couldn't work it out. He talked about how he had put them up in his apartment when they first got married—on a mattress on the floor in the living room.

"They sure were in love, your mama and daddy."

He even had nice things to say about Nanny.

I wished I could visit them more often, but I didn't get to.

I didn't know how old Iney was, but she was six years younger than Nanny, so she had to be up there. Aunt Ina was Nanny's only sister, and I thought she was swell. She was the most cheerful person in the whole family. Every time I saw her as I was growing up, she was smiling and laughing about something. She liked bright colors, like Nanny, but that was the only way they were alike. Iney never got sick. She bounced around a lot, and she reminded me of a ball. Her husband was dead, and her son lived in New Mexico. I looked forward to her visits because she'd spend most of her time playing with the gang and me up on the vacant lot.

She'd help us fly our kites and even play war with us, crawling around on her stomach in the dug-up trenches. It never bothered her to get dirty.

All the kids were crazy about her.

"I swear, Ina, people are gonna think you're cracked. Why don't you act your age?" Nanny would say.

Iney would chuckle. "Age? Why, Mae, I thought you, of all people, didn't believe in age."

"That's not what I mean, and you know it. You act like you're simple or something."

"I am simple."

"Stop that! I mean, it's not right for a grown woman to behave the way you do. People will talk."

"What're they gonna say?"

"That you're *cracked*!"

"Bull, I'm happy."

We stayed in touch and saw each other off and on during the next several years, but by the time I was grown up, Iney was pretty much a loner. She lived about two hours (by bus) south of Los Angeles, and she seldom called anyone in the family. She didn't want to disturb anybody. I'd have to call her and swear we wanted to see her. I'd offer to pick her up or send a car, and she would always say, "Oh, honey, thank you so much, but you know that's not necessary. Tell you what, I'll let you know." Then she'd pop up unexpectedly, after a long bus ride, spend thirty minutes visiting, and then bolt to catch the bus back without allowing us even to feed her, let alone drive her home. A four-hour round-trip for a brief "howdy." I got the feeling that she was afraid to use up our oxygen. She was acting more and more like Goggy, her mother, who had always seemed embarrassed by the space she occupied, too. My last clear memory of Iney was in 1972, shortly before she died. She came to see one of my shows, but true to form, she hadn't let me in on it. My secretary, who had met her previously at my house, just happened to spot her leaving with the crowd when the taping was over (probably on her way to catch the bus) and brought her back to my dressing room.

We hugged each other, and she was so frail. I thought back to the times, about thirty years before, when she had played with us kids on the lot, when we thought she was so old. She had been in her fifties then.

"Iney! For God's sake, why didn't you let me know you wanted to come to the show? You know I would've—"

"Honey, I know how busy you are, and it was no trouble really. I like the bus."

It was no use. I introduced her to some friends who were in the room, and one of them pulled up a chair for her.

"Here, Iney." I took her by the arm. "Now you just sit down and stay awhile. I'm not letting you get away so fast."

"No . . . I don't want to bother the chair."

8

Asher used to sit on the couch in the lobby and read comic books. Even though he wore those thick glasses, his face would be hidden by the covers of the books. I had him thinking I was twins for about two days. He was younger than I was and a cinch to fool. One day after school I walked past him and into 102, which faced the lobby. I said, "Hi," and he said, "Hi." I shut the door. Nobody was home, and I was bored. I changed my clothes, grabbed the old suitcase we had, climbed out the window, ran around the back of the building to the front, and walked into the lobby again.

I had thought up a way to entertain myself. It was inspired. I asked him, in an English accent, where Mrs. White and Carol lived. He looked up from *Batman*, and did a double take. He pointed to our door, and I opened it and walked in before he could say anything. I had a loud conversation with myself behind the door, making sure he could hear every word.

"Oh my god! You're here! You look wonderful!" Lots of shrieks and screams. "How long can you stay? Oh, I've missed you!" Back and forth it went, and all this time I was changing my clothes and getting back into "Carol" and trying to sound like two different people. After I'd changed, I ran out into the lobby and told Asher that my sister, "Karen," had just this minute arrived from Canada.

By now he had put down his book and found his voice. "Gosh, I never knew you had a *twin*!"

"Oh, yes. We were separated at birth. For years and years we didn't know about each other."

"How come?"

I looked down at the floor as if it hurt too much to talk about. "Asher, please . . . don't ask me any more questions. I—I've said too much as it is. I'd catch holy hell if Nanny and Mama found out I'd told you this much . . . please." There was a silent moment, and I seized it to run dramatically out the front door of the building, leaving him to think I might be headed straight into traffic. I ran around the back of the building again, and this time climbed back *into* the window of 102. I changed my clothes and became "Karen." I waited a couple of minutes and then opened the door and looked around the lobby. Asher's mouth was still open.

"Excuse me, but have you seen Carol?" He just stood there and stared. I was beginning to wonder if he'd ever blink again.

Finally he said, "I didn't know Carol had a twin."

I stared back at him with the most pained expression I could summon up, made my chin quiver, and slammed the door. I sobbed just loud enough.

Back into Carol. Out the window. Around the building and into the lobby. I was beginning to get a little tired.

Just as I was about to say something to him, Nanny walked into the lobby. She'd been making a run to the liquor store for Mama. Before Asher could talk to her, I screamed, "Nanny! Have I got a surprise for you! Close your eyes and come with me!" I motioned to Asher that if he spilled the beans, he was a dead man. When I got Nanny inside 102, I tried to explain to her what I was up to. She mumbled something about my being nuts and went into the bathroom.

I spent the rest of the afternoon changing my clothes and accents and running around the building. He bought the whole thing, and I had me a swell time. I let Ilomay in on it the next day, and she helped me out by telling Asher that she had known about "Karen" for a long time, but it was a dark family secret and he'd better keep it to himself or else.

He even crossed his heart and hoped to die. Ilomay and I howled with laughter, and I couldn't wait for school to let out so I could get at it all over again. That afternoon was pretty much a repeat of the day before. I had him going in circles.

But after a couple of hours of climbing in and out the window and running around the building, I got a little careless. Instead of completely changing my clothes, I put an old chenille robe over what I was wearing as "Karen." Asher spotted what I had on underneath. I had forgotten there was a big hole in the sleeve of the robe. I tried to bluff my way out, but it was all over. It was just as well. I was exhausted.

A few years ago, Asher got in touch with me and brought his wife and kids to a taping of my show. It was a kick to see him. I'd have known him anywhere. And I was glad to get the chance to apologize for all the things I had done to him.

* * *

When Chrissy was a few months old, there was a whole bunch of stories in the newspaper saying that some people had predicted that the world was coming to an end . . . soon. I got scared. Then I heard it on the radio, and it terrified me. Nobody else paid any attention to this awful turn of events. I was the only one. I tried bringing the subject up once or twice, and all I got back was: "Don't be silly."

A date was announced. I started counting my heartbeats.

Dear God, why isn't anyone else *listening*?

"The day" arrived, and Nanny and Mama decided to take in a movie that night and leave me alone to look after my baby sister. As they were going out the door, I wanted to scream, but I didn't make a sound. I followed them out to the front of the building and stared real hard at their backs as they walked around the corner at Wilcox. Nanny's hose were bagging a little. It was the last look I'd ever have of them. I went back into 102, picked up Christine, and crawled under Murphy. I blew on her eyelids so she'd close her eyes and go to sleep. I settled down on the floor to die.

Nanny and Mama were screaming my name. They woke me up. I knew it was late. They had come home and thought we were missing. I crawled out from under the bed with the baby. She was starting to fuss.

Mama said, "What the hell's the matter with you?"

And Nanny was feeling her pulse.

I came to and looked at the clock.

It was after midnight. We were still here.

By now Mama, Nanny, and Chrissy all were screaming.

I just stood there, grinning.

I remember how embarrassed I got when Nanny told Daddy I had gotten the "curse." Boys shouldn't know about those things, and fathers should be even more removed. When she told him, I looked down at the floor, and I wanted it to open up and swallow me. I had been taking one of my long baths, and Nanny had found the evidence in my clothes. I hadn't noticed it yet. She started to scream, "Good God! Get out of that water, *now*! Hurry! It's *dan*gerous to take a bath like that!" I didn't know what the hell she was talking about. I thought, at first, the building was about to blow up or something. I jumped out of the tub and started to dry off in a hurry. I knew *Nanny* hated taking baths, but she hadn't tried to stop *me* before this, so now I was scared.

"Are you out?" She burst through the door. "Don't you ever, ever get in the water when you're in this condition! You know better than that!"

I understood. And I was scared to death. They had talked about how unsafe it was to take a bath at that time of month, but I just didn't know it had happened to me yet. I felt very dumb and very frightened. Suppose I had harmed myself for life . . .

Daddy visited us later that day, and Nanny told him the whole story in great detail. I was staring hard at the floor when he said, "Well, I think it's terrific. Up to now you've been a little boy running around in a dress."

Daddy had sobered up.

He was living with his mother, my Grandma Nora, in Santa Monica in a tiny place that looked kind of like a lean-to, right off Tenth Street, behind a sporting goods store.

I started to visit him on weekends. Every Friday, after school, I'd take the red streetcar from Hollywood to the Beverly Hills end of the line, and he'd meet me there at the station. Then we'd transfer and ride the bus the rest of the way into Santa Monica.

Sometimes Ilomay would come with me. We'd bunk together in a little space that had a shiny curtain with flowers on it, separating us from the front room. We slept foot to head on a cot.

Saturday we'd walk the ten blocks to the beach and spend the day getting sunburned. At night Daddy would always say, "Who wants to see a movie? Anyone here want to see a movie?"

I'd shout, *"Me! Me!"* Then he'd take us to the early double feature, and we'd all share a box of popcorn. Then we'd go back to the house for dinner. Grandma Nora would be waiting, and when we walked through the door, she'd start to heat up the food on the stove. I loved the meals. She usually made enchiladas for us. This was the most I'd been around her. Mama and Nanny never had cared much for her. They said it was all her fault that Daddy was so "worthless." I liked her. And now that Daddy wasn't drinking anymore, he wasn't in the least bit worthless. And Daddy even said that he had sworn off the hooch for his mama's sake.

And mine.

No, I liked her. She was okay. When she got sick, she never talked about it. She'd just go lie down and get better. But sometimes, at night, I could hear her moan in her sleep.

On Sunday morning Grandma Nora would go to church, and Daddy would ride back on the bus with us to the Beverly Hills station and put us on the streetcar for Hollywood. If he'd had a good week selling coupons, he'd give me a couple of dollars. I'd turn them over to Nanny as soon as I got home. She'd quiz me about the weekend, and I'd say it was just so-so. It seemed to satisfy her. I didn't say what I really felt. Those were the best weekends. I loved them. I didn't even mind the bus. Daddy was so wonderful and handsome. I'd never seen him walk so straight before. And his eyes were bright and clear—no more red. We had fun together, and I was proud when he told people I was his daughter. He looked just like Jimmy Stewart.

Folks said I looked like my daddy. I was getting tall, fast. One time he had an argument with the movie theater manager over how old I was. Daddy had bought me a child's ticket, and the manager insisted I was at least fourteen. I was eleven. I was glad I was tall and lanky. Like my dad.

I think it was the happiest I had ever been.

It lasted a little over a year.

I was growing up, almost twelve, and I guess I was starting to get over being scared of being separated from Nanny.

As long as I was doing the separating.

He showed up at 102 the day Grandma Nora was buried.

He was drunk.

I had almost forgotten what it was like to see him weaving and his eyes out of focus.

He smiled at me and said, "Well, Punkin Kid, she's gone to heaven. . . ."

I stared up at him.

He spoke so carefully that the words came out of his mouth like slow motion. "Only one little beer, Punk, to steady my nerves . . . y'know?"

My body went heavy.

Why? I couldn't understand it. He had loved our weekends as much as I had, hadn't he? And even though he didn't make much money, he must've been proud to hold down a job, wasn't he? Didn't he like the way he could put one foot in front of the other and not bump into anything? Didn't he like the way he looked? And the way I looked at him?

Didn't he love me?

I tore out of the building and started running up the street. Ahhh, dammit. *Dammit!* What'd he have to go and spoil everything for? God, why? Dammit! *Damn him!* I felt the tears go in my ears while I ran. I hated him.

I hated him so very much.

It was dark when I walked back into the building.

I opened the door and went into the room. The lights weren't on, and I could barely make out the furniture. Nanny and Mama and Chrissy weren't home. I didn't know where they'd disappeared to. I flicked on the light switch and saw him. He was sprawled out on the floor—as still as could be. At first I thought he was dead. I heard him say something, but I couldn't make it out, so I bent down to him. "Daddy?"

He opened his eyes, and all I could see were the whites. His pupils were lost back in his scalp somewhere.

And then I socked him square across the jaw.

He mumbled something, but I could tell he didn't even know I was there. He hadn't felt a thing. I went nuts. I hit him again . . . and again. I couldn't stop. I even kicked him. I straddled him and began to slap him across the face and yell at him, "Goddamn you! *Look at me!*" For a second I thought I'd knocked him out, and then he half opened his eyes. "Look at me!" He did, and I said, "Why don't you just go ahead and *die!*" The neighbors ran in to see what all the commotion was.

It took three or four of them to drag me off him.

There were no more weekends in Santa Monica.

The room started to move. My heart popped right into my throat. I threw down the covers and jumped off the couch before I was even awake. Nanny was already at the foot of Murphy, heading in my direction, screaming my name. We grabbed each other and took shelter under the doorway, the way they told us to do it over the radio whenever there was an earthquake. She held on to me as tight as she could. She was in her old long underwear with the drop seat in the butt, looking sillier'n hell, but I felt safe.

Don't you die, Nanny, don't you ever die on me.

9

I hit the vacant lot with the gang just about every day. It was my set for acting out whatever, and whoever, I wanted to be.

Jungle Girl was a big favorite of mine. I was always Sheena or Nyoka. I bossed Ilomay around a lot when it came down to who we were going to be, and she let me get away with it. We'd mark off certain areas in the dirt with a stick, which was where the quicksand was supposed to be. If we ran over that line when the natives were after us, we were in grave danger. The one who wasn't caught in the bog would have to lasso the one stuck in the muck and pull her from certain death to safety. I had found a five or six-foot-long piece of cord in Nanny's closet to use for just such an emergency. It didn't take us long to give up on that idea because neither one of us could even come close to our target.

Ralph was a year or so older than the rest of us, and he was nuts for animals. Not dogs. Not cats. Ralph loved lions and tigers and elephants . . . and snakes. Since there was no way he could get any of the first three into his apartment in the building, Ralph talked his mama into letting him collect snakes. He gave Nanny a couple of old pillowcases, and she made some snake bags for him. He'd go to the desert and "bring 'em back alive," like Frank Buck, the Great White Hunter.

We all waited, breathlessly, for Ralph to come home to the building after each of these safaris. One day he came back with quite a catch: a king snake. One by one Asher, Malcolm, Ilomay, Norma, Bobby, and I peered into the wiggling pillowcase. I thought I was going to die from the excitement. We sneaked around to the side of the building, and Ralph lifted it out of the bag . . . very carefully. It was a thousand feet long. As far as we were concerned, Ralph *was* the Great White Hunter. He allowed us to take turns holding the king. I remember its wrapping itself around my arm. I stepped out from the shade of the building and stuck my arm into the sun. The snake began to squeeze, and my entire arm turned white, tingled, and went numb. I pulled back into the shade, and as the snake relaxed, I watched my blood come back. I was Sheena.

After the king came a blue-eyed racer. It was skinny and silver, with marble blue eyes, about a foot long, and mean.

One day it slithered out of its cage and got loose in the halls. We all frantically tried to find it before anyone else did because Ralph had been warned by the manager not to keep these dangerous creatures in his apartment or he and his folks would wind up on the street right along with his treasures from the desert.

It was bad news when we heard Old Mrs. Wolff's screams coming from her room. We ran behind the manager into her apartment, and there was Old Mrs. Wolff, jumping up and down on top of her couch, out of her mind and hysterical. The manager had no idea what she was yelling about, but we sure did.

Ilomay and I were casing one side of the room, and Ralph and the others covered the rest. We spotted a sliver of silver cowering in the corner behind a chair, its bright blue eyes glistening. While the manager was trying to calm the screaming, incoherent old Mrs. Wolff down, Ralph casually bent down and, with great care and skill, grabbed the little streamlined snake behind its head and hid it behind his back. We all gathered around him as camouflage and bolted for the door.

I looked back, and the manager was having a tough time holding Old Mrs. Wolff up. She seemed to be fainting dead away. Her eyes were rolling around, and her mouth was wide open.

Poor Old Mrs. Wolff.

Adrienne Lenore Weingart was in the sixth grade with me at Selma. I never saw her again after we graduated from grammar school.

We went to different junior highs.

Adrienne Lenore Weingart.

I loved her name; I thought it was one of your all-time great names.

About thirty years later I used it in a sketch with Harvey Korman on my show. After it was aired, a woman called our office long distance from Las Vegas. My secretary answered the phone: "Miss Burnett's office."

Caller: "Excuse me, but I'm wondering—"

Secretary: "Yes?"

Caller: "I was watching *The Carol Burnett Show* last night, and I just about died."

Secretary: "Oh?"

Caller: "I mean, she said *my* name in that skit."

Secretary: "Really?"

Caller: "I mean, it's not my name now, but it was. I mean, it was my maiden name, Adrienne Lenore Weingart, and I was—"
Secretary: "Oh, yes! Is this Adrienne Lenore Weingart?"
Caller: "Yes, I am! I mean, I was."
I had told my secretary where I'd come up with the name, so she said: "Oh, tell me, did you go to school in Hollywood?"
Caller: "Yes, I did."
Secretary: "Did you attend Selma Avenue Grammar School?"
Caller: "Yes."
Secretary: "Well, Miss Burnett went to school with you!"
Pause.
Caller: "I don't remember her."

People were screaming and yelling and jumping up and down in the streets.

The gang and I tore up newspapers in tiny little pieces, put them in grocery bags, ran onto the fire escapes of the building, and dumped them all over the neighbors below, who were singing and laughing on the corner of Yucca and Wilcox: "We gave 'em hell! Yow-ee!" All that meant to a bunch of twelve-year-olds, growing up one block north of Hollywood Boulevard that summer of 1945, was that there would be no more diving under desks during practice air-raid drills in school, no more rubber and tinfoil drives, no more blackouts, and no more war movies. That big game was over.

But for weeks after that Old Mrs. Wolff was still crying and hugging everyone in sight. Even the gang.

We were about to graduate from Selma Avenue Grammar School, and I was sad. There were about ten of us big-shot seniors, and we'd all soon be lowly seventh-grade "scrubs" at a new school. I wasn't only sad but scared about going to a bigger school. I would miss some of my class-mates, who would be going to Bancroft Junior High because they lived in that district. I was glad Ilomay and I would at least be together at Le Conte. I figured we could face all those strange new kids together.

I didn't like the idea of different teachers for each subject either. I wanted my sixth-grade teacher, Mrs. Ernst, to be with me the rest of my life. Mama said I should "grow up."

I felt grown-up. I felt very grown-up, because the thing that bothered me the most was my breaking heart. Eddie Garunian was going to go to Bancroft. I had loved him ever since the fifth grade.

So had every other girl. He was the most popular boy in school and president of the sixth-grade class. I once got a feeling he kind of liked me when I was walking home with Ilomay and he came up behind me and snatched my sweater from my shoulders, threw it up a tree, shoved me a little, and ran off. As far as I was concerned, it meant only one thing: He loved me, too. Ilomay agreed wholeheartedly. I happily climbed the tree and retrieved my sweater from the branches.

I figured this encounter made Eddie and me a "couple." Then I saw him do the same thing to Aura San Juan the next day.

It was probably just as well, I thought later. After all, he was the shortest boy in class and I *was* the tallest girl.

"Nanny, who're you looking for?" It got so I asked her that just about every night, for the fun of it. She'd be on all fours looking under the bed, as always, before she'd get into it and turn off the light. She used to say she did it to make sure some man, who might crawl out in the middle of the night and murder us or rob us in our sleep, wasn't hiding under there.

Now she said, "Randolph Scott. But if he's not there, I'll take Nelson Eddy."

And I'd just howl.

What went on between men and women was a secret—a deep, dark secret.

And it didn't seem to have a happy ending, in real life anyway.

Nanny bragged that she'd never really been in love. Mama had been stung by Tony. Daddy was called "worthless." And Aunt Dodo and Uncle Parker looked mad at each other most of the time.

I'd pick up bits about the sex part here and there, but I couldn't quite figure it out or put it together. Grown-ups had the annoying habit of whispering and clamming up around me.

All I knew was women were cursed and were the ones who "always had to pay the price"—whatever that was. Ilomay didn't know any more than I did, and I wasn't about to ask Ralph or Malcolm or Asher.

For some reason, I never knew why, our family referred to the "private parts" as Roger (the male) and Suzy (the female).

The "monthly curse" was just that.

* * *

At first I had liked getting taller. But now it was a royal pain because the boys only came up to my neck. The boys *I* liked anyway. And they liked the short girls. The short girls were also getting round. Even Ilomay was sprouting two hefty-looking bumps on her chest. My best friend—how could she?

Nanny said that the way most girls "got titties" was by fooling around, which meant they were bad girls. I was positive Ilomay was a good girl, and I told Nanny so. Then she explained that sometimes you can make them grow if you rubbed cocoa butter on your chest. I tried it a couple of times, but it was too greasy, so I gave up.

Cuz was beginning to blossom, too.

I asked her if she fooled around, and she said she'd never do that, and she couldn't understand why anyone would want to, especially after what her mother had told her. I was all ears. I was about to find out what "fooling around" really meant. Cuz said that she had asked Aunt Dodo all about "it" one day, right out of the blue. She said Dodo had looked as if she were going to pass out at first but sat down and blurted it out as fast as she could: "The man sticks Roger in Suzy."

Cuz had said, "That's im*poss*ible."

End of explanation.

I figured Cuz had had success with the cocoa butter.

Le Conte Junior High School was huge. Too huge. There were a million kids, and they all belonged to the same club—a club I wasn't in. I was terrified.

And to top it off, Ilomay and I weren't in the same homeroom because her last name started with an *S* and mine started with a *B*.

I had a different teacher for everything, and they were all spread out in different classrooms. I kept getting lost the first week. I hated it. Ilomay and I would huddle together during the lunch hour and wish we were back at Selma with Mrs. Ernst.

She was my favorite teacher. If our sixth-grade class had been extra-good that week, she'd spend the last hour or so on Fridays reading to us. She was a wonderful actress, and she threw herself into the stories and became all the characters—accents and everything.

I remember when she read *The Yearling* to us. It was the story of a young boy, Jody, who lived in the backwoods of some southern state with his parents a long time ago. It was a story about his love for his pet, a wild fawn named Flag. It was a story about growing up and learning to shoulder responsibility, Mrs. Ernst said.

When she got to the part where Flag had to be shot, she "became" Jody, and she started crying real tears and screamed the way a real little kid would. She turned into him right before our eyes.

I thought that was a swell thing to be able to do.

I was gangly and skinny. All bones and no meat.

A true "Burnett," according to Nanny and Mama.

I also had the famous "Burnett lower lip." It meant I had no chin. Andy Gump. Gopher Girl.

Ugly.

It didn't make sense to me. Daddy was good-looking. Grandma Nora didn't have a Burnett lower lip. Daddy's brothers, Uncle John and Uncle Jimmy, had chins. Didn't look like a Burnett trait to me.

It was a trait that was mine, all mine.

Mama backed down a little when she said I probably got the buckteeth from sucking my thumb so much. And she thought she made me feel better when she told me, "It's great that you can draw so well 'cause no matter what you look like, you can always be an artist."

I just ate up fairy tales.

All kinds.

When I was in the sixth grade at Selma, I illustrated a few of my favorite ones in watercolors, and they were picked by the Hollywood Public Library to represent my class.

I was very proud. So were Nanny and Mama.

My favorite was "The Princess and the Pea," by Hans Christian Andersen. I had drawn the princess trying to get to sleep on top of all those mattresses, with a tiny wicked-looking pea peeking out from under the bottom one. I used a different color and design for each and every one of the mattresses. It took me hours. I emptied the water glass for the brushes dozens of times.

Fourteen years later I played that very same princess in a musical on Broadway.

Daddy came over every once in a while.

He looked okay, but I could tell he was back to drinking.

There wasn't too much to say.

He asked me about my new school and any new friends I might have made. I'd show him my papers and my grades. And he'd say how proud he was that I was doing so well in school. He said he just knew I'd whiz by " 'cause my punkin kid has always been so smart."

At least he didn't show up falling down drunk, but I could tell he'd always had a couple.

It mattered to me, and it didn't . . . at the same time.

I guess I had kind of closed myself off.

I'd wheel Christine first in her baby buggy and then later, when she got bigger, in her stroller up and down Hollywood Boulevard. Sometimes I noticed people on the street giving me funny looks. They'd shake their heads and go, "Tsk, tsk." I knew they thought I was her mother. "Isn't-that-awful-why-she's-no-more-than-a-kid-herself" kinds of looks.

She sure was beautiful. She was the kind of baby who made people stop and turn around. They'd say, "Why, look at those big, brown, beautiful eyes! Where did *those* come from?"

I knew where they came from. And I didn't care. As far as I was concerned, she was my full, real, whole, honest to God baby sister. I was crazy about her. Sometimes I almost felt I *was* her mother.

During the first year at Le Conte there was a ten-minute break in the morning between classes. It was called the nutrition break. The more robust kids were allowed to run around the field and bounce balls off each other.

We skinny ones, by orders from home, sat on the benches and were doled out graham crackers and watered-down milk, to beef us up. It was paid for by the state.

I was itching to get out on that field.

I was a fast runner, and since I wasn't so hot in the looks department, I figured I could attract some of the cuter guys with my athletic ability.

My regular PE class was all girls, so this nutrition break was cutting into any social life I might be able to drum up. Time was passing me by. I had to take some action. I rummaged around in 102 one night and found my old toy holster and gun under some grocery bags in the closet. I wore them under my too-big dress the next day, along with some rocks in my pockets.

The school nurse weighed me, said I was a solid little thing, and sprang me from the bench group. That extra couple of pounds did it.

I didn't tell Nanny because she would have been mad at me for blowing a free meal.

Ilomay and I started palling around more with Norma. We called ourselves the Three Musketeers.

Norma was pretty good-looking, and sometimes we'd all put on makeup and walk up and down Hollywood Boulevard, pretending we were older and flirting with sailors. The minute a trio would turn around and look as if they were going to follow us, we'd scream and run like crazy and ditch them.

Our big crushes were Peter Lawford, Farley Granger, Lon McAllister, and Robert Walker. We never missed a movie they were in.

But my idol was James Stewart.

He was special. He always had been, ever since I first laid eyes on him. The first time I saw him I cried. But it wasn't a sad cry. I felt good about it. I remember staring at him up there on the screen, and all of a sudden, out of nowhere, I was bawling my eyes out. People were turning around and looking at me. Nanny poked me on the arm and whispered, "What the heck's the matter with you?" I couldn't tell her. I couldn't tell her because I didn't know what it was myself. It's just that when he talked, it was to me. When he smiled, it was at me. He was my friend, and he'd never, ever let me down. Nanny thought I was nuts, but I didn't care.

He was a "well" daddy. He was just like my daddy could've been.

But my real-life crush was Tommy Tracy. He looked like his name. Perfect.

I fell in love with him in the seventh grade, and it was to last clear through our graduation from Hollywood High.

The most I ever got from him was a "Hi, Carol" when we passed in the halls.

I didn't know if he knew the misery I was in or not. He was friendly enough and nice enough. And it was hell.

I would've killed to be beautiful.

I would sit in class and practice signing my name "Carol Tracy" on scratch paper. I made up names for the children we'd have someday: "Stacy Tracy" and "Dick Tracy." He was the main reason I didn't drop the "Burnett" and become "Carol Creighton" (a catchier stage name, I thought) when I joined Actors' Equity a few years later. If I ever got famous, I wanted Tommy to know it.

Judy was the cheapest girl in school, and she also had the biggest bosom. She was in the same science class with me. If Mr. Gamble happened to be late, Judy would march up to the front of the room and pull her sweater up to her neck, so she could show her bra to the whole world.

The boys would howl and whistle, and the girls would look down at the floor and giggle.

Mr. Gamble's science class had taught me that cocoa butter had nothing to do with the size of anything. But I still wondered about the other half of Nanny's theory because there was no doubt in my mind that Judy fooled around. What Aunt Dodo had told Cuz about "it" was the truth, even though her information had been sketchy at best.

I was grateful to Mr. Gamble for clearing up a lot of the mystery. He was the most popular teacher at Le Conte, not only because of the subject he taught but because he would reward us on Fridays, too—just the way Mrs. Ernst had, in grammar school—with stories.

Except he didn't read books to us.

He acted out gory, horror stories in great, gleeful detail. He'd pull down the shades, light a candle, and set the scene. He'd tell about chopped-off heads and torn-off limbs and pickled hands and stomachs being sliced open and guts falling out all over the place . . . and he'd do the sound effects and the screams. Then he'd fall down and die, in the most perfect agony. And he scared us to death. He was some actor. We all loved him.

I started thinking that was not a bad way to get noticed.

Nanny got a job.

It was a secret, because if the Relief Lady found out, the checks would stop coming. We had to keep mum. I helped her out.

We were cleaning ladies in the Warner Brothers office building on Hollywood Boulevard and Wilcox, a block away from home. We worked nights.

We emptied the wastebaskets and threw out the cigarette butts from the ashtrays, while we pushed a big old cart down the aisles between the desks. I would empty, and she'd take a swipe at the dust with a rag. It was the most I'd ever seen her clean anything.

I liked it.

I liked it because we cleaned out the offices where the artists drew all the posters and billboards that advertised every single Warner Brothers movie.

I was in hog's heaven with all those pencils and pens and brushes—thin bristles, thick bristles—ink, every color of the rainbow, and all of them used to illustrate *the movies.* Paradise.

The artists were wonderful. Their drawings would be spread out on huge architect-type tables, and I would pore over their sketches and concepts as long as I could until Nanny would yell at me to help her empty some trash from another room down the hall.

There were drawings of Errol Flynn in tights and Bette Davis in shadows. Humphrey Bogart, looking dreamily through lowered eyelids and cigarette smoke at Ann Sheridan. It was all so fabulous I never wanted to go home.

I decided to get discovered.

One night I left a sketch of mine on the table of one of the artists. I would surprise Nanny with a job offer from the Warner Brothers art department the next day. I would be the youngest person ever to hold such a position. We'd be rich and famous, and the relief lady could just go to hell.

I couldn't wait to go back the next night and read the message from the artist telling me when and where to report for duty.

At school the next day I kept drawing Joan Crawford's mouth all over my notebook.

That night I could hardly contain myself while Nanny took her sweet time with the huge ring of keys and finally unlocked the office door. She switched on the naked neon, and I flew past the thousands of cluttered desks and trash cans into the cubicle where I had left my drawing. I looked on his desk. He had left a note. He asked that his office be cleaned . . . "period." And please don't mess with his pencils.

10

Girls who peroxided their hair, wore a lot of makeup, and chewed gum in class were easy and headed for ruin. Girls who owned felt skirts, full enough for twirling, *real* saddle shoes (from the Broadway department store), angora sweaters with shoulder pads to pin inside, and bobby socks to match were rich.

Girls who wore glasses, no makeup, collected the homework, and weren't athletic usually got the best grades. Just like the movies.

And then there was me.

Our social studies class was in the middle of a test. The only sounds you could hear were the ticking clock on the wall and Mrs. Vorachek's heels clicking as she walked up and down the aisles between the rows of desks, her eyes peeled for any sign of hidden notes in our laps or answers written in ink on the palms of our hands.

I was sitting directly behind Bob B. Most of the teachers sat us alphabetically. Bob was blond, cute, and popular. I sat at the desk behind him in a lot of my classes, and he hardly ever said hello, but I knew every hair on the back of his head and whether or not he'd missed a spot washing behind his ears in the mornings.

Vorachek was at the far corner of the room, with her back to us, when Bob slowly turned his head, looked over his shoulder, squinched his mouth to one side of his face, and whispered something to me. I knew if she caught us talking, she'd flunk us, but I was so thrilled that he had acknowledged my existence that I took the chance and whispered back, "What?"

He mumbled again.

I still couldn't make it out. I sneaked a peek at Vorachek. We were still safe. "What . . . I can't hear you!"

He let out a frustrated sigh, raised his voice a notch, and this time I heard him. "I said, 'What's the answer to number fourteen?' " He turned quickly and faced front. I looked down at my paper. *I* was already on number 25, and I had never been accused of being a brain. I checked out my answer to number 14, and it was a long one.

He was losing patience. "Well?" Vorachek must've had her hearing aid turned down. I knew she'd catch me if I tried to tell him the whole paragraph I'd written, and there was no way to slip the page to him without her seeing me.

I leaned forward in my seat and lied to the little fuzz on his neck. "I don't know."

He slowly turned around one last time, looked straight at me, and said, "Jesus, I always knew you were a dumb cluck."

Except for math, my grades were pretty good. I didn't study much because there wasn't anywhere to go to do it. My teachers were okay, and they seemed to like me without going overboard.

It was the same way with boys. They seemed to like me without going overboard.

Mama talked a lot about how smart she was and how sometimes she wished she weren't because the dumber you are, the happier you are. Mama was smart. She had the answers for everything, but in the rare instance she was stumped, she'd pick up the phone and call the Los Angeles *Herald-Express* or the Hollywood Library. After a while the people on the other end of the line got to recognizing her voice, and they'd have some pretty good chats and laughs. Mama was smart and pretty and funny and sexy and all those things. All those things I wasn't.

There were two beautiful, *beautiful* sisters who went to Le Conte Junior High, Barbara and Madeline. They had an older sister who was already in high school. The three of them had appeared on the cover of *Life* magazine as the three most beautiful teenagers in America.

I didn't know Barbara and Madeline very well because one of them was a year ahead of me and the other one was a grade below. But I passed them in the halls every single day, on the way to my locker.

They had long, thick, wavy chestnut brown hair that framed their perfect faces. They wore something different to school every day, and they were always color-coordinated. For six long years, through Le Conte and later Hollywood High, I prayed every night that I'd wake up the next morning, look in the mirror, and see either one of them (it didn't matter which one) staring back at me.

I slept in pin curls, with the bobby pins sticking into my ears every night, hoping that what little curl they gave my limp mouse brown hair would hold up through at least first period. I'd imitate them. I tried to slink through the halls on the way to class, balancing my books on my hip, stretching my neck as long as it would go, and smiling to myself as I passed the other kids—as if I were keeping some kind of mysterious secret. While I sat at my desk, I would press my finger against the tip of my nose, hoping that I could eventually persuade it to remain upturned.

About twenty-five years later, a bunch of us from our television show were in Chasen's restaurant in Hollywood, celebrating an Emmy win. I looked across the room and spotted Barbara at a table with a group of people. She was as gorgeous as ever. I broke into a cold sweat, and I found myself pressing the tip of my index finger against the end of my nose. I even started to suck in my cheeks. I was thirteen all over again.

As we were leaving, we had to pass her table. We were just about out the door when I felt a hand on my arm. I turned around and looked into her big, wide-set, beautiful eyes, which were framed by nonfalse thick dark eyelashes and perfectly arched eyebrows. She smiled at me, revealing her straight, even pearly white teeth. Her neck was as long as ever. She was very gracious, and she congratulated me on winning. Then she said something like "I don't know if you remember me, but we went to school together."

11

Bill Burgess still hung around Mama. He'd bring booze and groceries and sit in the kitchen looking gaga at her. He'd drink with her and laugh at her jokes and listen to her sing. Nanny and Chris and I would eat the food. Bill was always welcomed with open arms. I felt kind of sorry for him.

When school got out at three o'clock, Ilomay and I would walk the long blocks up to Sunset Boulevard and race the red streetcars home. Sometimes we'd stop to rest and lay a penny on the tracks and wait for a streetcar to run over it. Then we'd run into the middle of the boulevard and pick it up. It would be flat as a pancake and quite hot.

I'd kill as much time as I could, but sooner or later I'd have to go home.

Nanny would be lying down on Murphy with a cold rag on her head, and Mama would be taking a nap, and Chrissy would be waiting for me in the lobby.

I'd come in, and throw my books down, and pick her up and twirl her around.

We'd go into 102, and if Bill wasn't coming over, Nanny would give us some money to go to the grocery store to buy stuff for dinner—usually chuck and a can of peas or potatoes. Sometimes she fried up some salmon balls and we'd have french fries and lots of ketchup. We could always con her into making pound cake with lemon or vanilla sauce. Then we'd fight over who got to lick the batter bowl.

If Mama got up in time, she'd usually eat with us. She never had much of an appetite, though.

Once in a while Mama would be in a good mood and decide to do the cooking. I loved it when she did. She had a way of making things taste better. She said she had an "ear for cooking," just the way she did for music. She'd say to Chris and me, "Your old lady's got talent she's never even used!" Then she'd pour herself a shot, grab her uke, sit down at the kitchen table, and chord away. "And I can do the same thing with a piano, too. And I never, ever had a lesson." She'd shoot Nanny a look. "My problem is I'm just *too* versatile!"

And Nanny would shoot back: "Oh, is *that* what it is?"

Mama would ignore that one and start singing:

> Nothin' could be finah
> Than to be in Carolina
> In the mor-or-or-nin'. . . .

Ever since I could remember, I could leave my body if I really wanted to. Or at least it seemed like it. I'd look in the mirror and stare real hard at my eyeballs. I wouldn't budge, and I wouldn't blink. Before too long I would "leave" and kind of float up and hang around behind the right shoulder of the kid who was standing there, frozenlike, staring into the mirror.

Sometimes I would be there for thirty seconds or more before I'd pop back in.

It was a terrific game, and I played it a lot. I got so good at it that I stopped doing it when I was around fourteen because I was scared that one of those times I might not get back in.

Anyhow, it seemed that way to me.

There was one area where I could outshine the rest of the girls at Le Conte: I could run.

Our gym teacher, Mrs. Foal, had even written Nanny a note, asking permission to coach me after school. Nanny had refused, saying she didn't want me running because it was bad for the heart. There went my career in the Olympics, I thought.

It didn't stop me from challenging anyone and everyone in school to a footrace. I got a little bit of attention at first, but after a year or so my fleet-footedness became old news. Most of the girls had reached the conclusion that the way to catch a boy was to hold still, look pale, and act helpless.

As much as I thought I wanted to be able to do all those things, I couldn't pull it off. So I kept on running.

There was a new boy in school, a ninth grader, Joey. He was Italian, and he made the girls drool. The guys liked him, too, because he was a sensational athlete. Even though, in my heart of hearts, I still loved

Tommy, I developed a side crush on Joey. Norma was nuts about him, too.

His dad owned a liquor store in Burbank, and sometimes on Saturdays Norma and I would take the bus (as much as I hated it) and hang around talking to him all afternoon, watching him bag merchandise. We found out his phone number and called him every night until his mother answered it one time and told us to cut it out.

He started to pay a little more attention to Norma in school, and I became desperate.

I challenged him to a footrace. That would make him look at me all right. He would fall in love with me and ask me to run through life with him, hand in hand. At last he would have found the girl who could keep up with him.

At first he thought I was kidding, but I kept bugging him to meet me after school. He finally said okay. There was an alley right next to the athletic field where a lot of the guys and Judy, with the big bosom, hung out around three o'clock every day and smoked cigarettes. It was a block long and perfect for a race.

Norma, Ilomay, and I showed up around two minutes after the three o'clock bell and tried not to stare too hard at the bad kids, who were already lighting up in the alley. They cleared the way when Joey showed up. "Hey, what's goin' on?" Judy took a deep drag and eyed Joey up one side and down the other. She looked like Ida Lupino in *Road House.*

"Don't ask *me,*" Joey said. "This is all her idea." He looked at me and then through me. "C'mon, let's get this over with. I gotta get home."

Ilomay said, "All right . . . *get ready . . .*"

There we were, side by side—Joey and me—bent over, touching shoulders. . . .

"Get set . . ."

My neck was throbbing. I pictured a perfect photo finish and him hugging me and saying, "Hey, you're *really something!*"

"Go!"

He tore up the alley like Superman, and it was over. I was left way behind, eating dust. He never even came back. I guess he ran right to the Burbank bus.

A couple of weeks later he asked Norma to go out.

Most of the kids at school made a stab at trying to do the Tarzan yell, but none of them could even begin to throw their hips out of their sockets like I could. My Johnny Weissmuller was, hands down, the best, and I was the only one who possessed a double-jointed hip. During recess I'd take requests, sometimes doing both tricks at the same time.

By the time I hit the ninth grade, I had a lot of boyfriends. Boy-*friends:* Jimmy, Lee, John, Alan, Buddy. At lunchtime Ilomay, Norma, and I would hang out on the field with them, and we'd all slap each other on the backs, tell jokes, and see who could hold their breaths the longest—general messing around. We were buddies, pure and simple, and that was all there was to it.

But when it came to the school dances in the gym, our "buddies" didn't know we were alive. They'd knot up together under the basketball hoop and stare at the floor, and the girls would wind up jitterbugging with each other. It really didn't matter that much to me because none of those guys could dance worth a toot anyhow.

Aunt Dodo had enrolled Cuz in Sheehy's Dance Studio on La Cienega Boulevard, where they taught ballroom dancing to "young teens." The studio was near their house and Cuz's school. Sheehy's had real dances every Friday night, so the pupils could show off for the parents, who wanted to see for themselves that the Saturday afternoon lessons were worth it. I got to tag along a couple of times as Cuz's guest. I liked it . . . a lot. The boys were gorgeous and actually *danced* with the girls . . . *slow*-danced. A boy would put his hand right up against the small of your back and press. His left hand would take hold of your right one, and like magic, you'd wind up moving together at the same time and in the direction you both wanted to go . . . without stepping on each other's feet. To music. Fred and Ginger.

Cuz had always been beautiful, and now she looked like a baby Lana Turner. She didn't even get pimples. Dodo, more than ever, was pushing her for the movies. Cuz, more than ever, couldn't care less. I didn't understand why Cuz wasn't interested because she was a born movie star. At Sheehy's the boys would be lined up clear out the door, waiting to cut in for even a ten-second whirl around the floor with her. Sometimes one would cut in to dance with me. I was sure it was because I was Janice's cousin, and if they didn't know, I'd tell them. I'd say, "I'm Janice Vance's first cousin." It seemed to be the best reason for me being there.

I wanted to be a pupil.

I would have traded in my Tarzan yell to be a pupil. *And* my double-jointed hip.

I pestered Nanny for weeks. I told her not to get me new shoes this year . . . anything, but *please, please* swing it so I could take lessons at Sheehy's, too. She came through. She took the sock out from under the mattress, unpinned it, and counted out the $5.50 for six lessons.

Now I could be a Sheehy pupil.

The following Saturday was my first lesson. I wore a powder blue wool suit Nanny had made for me the year before and caught the La Cienega bus. The studio was closed when I got there around noon. I was an hour early. I walked up and down the block for a while to kill some time. It was starting to get hot, and I could feel the perspiration beginning to roll down my sides and into the waistband of my wool skirt. There was a tiny amusement park across the street for little kids, so I walked over and bought some candy and ate it. Nanny had safety-pinned a dollar bill to the inside of my jacket in case of an emergency. This was an emergency. I was seeing spots, so I figured I'd better eat something and get into some shade. I polished off the Baby Ruth in nothing flat, but I couldn't find any shade anywhere. I was dripping, and the armpits of my jacket were turning dark blue. I couldn't take it off, because I had only a dickey on underneath. Ten minutes to go. I needed a breeze. I bought a ticket for the airplane ride. The planes were scaled down to toddler size, so I had to scrunch up to squeeze into the pint-size seat. I strapped myself in and took off . . . around and around, in not-so-big circles. I felt a slight breeze on my wet forehead, and then the ride was over.

I climbed out of the little airplane, in sections, and looked down at my skirt. I was wet, clean through. I looked across the street. Thank God, the door to the studio had opened up, and I spotted some of the kids from the Friday night socials going in.

They looked cool as cucumbers in their summer cottons. I was beginning to wish I hadn't had that Baby Ruth.

I went inside. My eyes weren't used to the dark, and I bumped into one of the chairs lined up against the wall. I promptly sat in it. Somebody asked for my money, and I handed it over. Mr. Sheehy came in and greeted everybody. I was beginning to see a little better and feel a lot worse.

"Today we will *samba!*" Sheehy announced.

He got us all out on the floor, paired us off, and began to demonstrate. My partner and I started to sway back and forth to the music, and I knew it was over . . . I was going to be good and sick. I excused myself and tore out of there as fast as I could. I ran to the alley in back of the building.

As soon as I was up to it, I caught the bus back home. I didn't go back, and Sheehy kept the money.

But Nanny bought me my shoes anyway.

When John Anderson found out that I'd get sneezing fits if anybody so much as touched the bridge of my nose, he made it a point to try to push my face in whenever he could catch me. He'd chase me up and down the halls between classes. He got me one time and pressed his palm against my nose so hard Mrs. Nightengale made me leave choir and report to the school nurse because my sneezes were completely wiping out the alto section during our practice of "Toyland, Toyland." I was just as happy to leave. I didn't like Nightengale's choice of songs anyhow. I'd been spoiled by Mama in that department.

I remember coming home from school one day and finding Mama sitting on the toilet lid, her head sticking into the bathroom air shaft, singing "I'll Get By." She said the echo in the shaft made her voice sound even prettier. She was right. I wound up sitting next to her on the seat, with the two of us having a whirl at "That Old Feeling," wishing Old Lady Nightengale could've been in on this one.

I decided to join the Le Conte Junior High *News*. Mama was tickled pink. "Good girl! Be a journalist! Brenda Starr! You'll meet lots of important people that way." She pointed to her wall where she'd hung her autographed movie star glossies. "You'll travel . . . New York, maybe! No matter what you look like, you can always be a journalist!"

She'd said the same thing about drawing.

Brenda Starr, Girl Reporter was my favorite comic strip heroine at the time. I'd be a famous newspaperwoman like Brenda, have red hair, and fall in love with a mysterious man with a patch over one eye (his name in the strip was Basil St. John) and be forever thwarted because, as much as he wanted to, he wouldn't marry me since there was a trace of insanity in his family . . . way back. Mama used to say it never stopped any of our clan.

Reporting for the Le Conte Junior High *News* was one colossal bore. I wrote junk for the "Announcements" column. When I read what I wrote about the upcoming auditions for the ninth grade senior play, I decided I'd try out for it myself.

The tryouts were being held in the school auditorium.

Mrs. McNeil, who was really one of the English teachers, doubled as the head of the drama department. She also wrote plays. For the ninth-grade effort that year she had picked a play of hers.

It had a small cast. There was a father, a mother, a teenage daughter, her pain-in-the-butt kid brother, and a gum-chewing, wisecracking maid, whose main function in life was to sass them all back. McNeil said her play was about a "typical family."

I set my cap for the part of Musie, the Maid. It wasn't the leading role, but she had the best lines, and she didn't have to look good. I popped two sticks of gum in my mouth to get into character and headed for the auditorium to give it a whirl. It looked as if every single senior in the whole school was there to try out for those five roles. When my turn came, I walked up the steps to the stage, opened the script, and started to read. Then I made the mistake of looking out into the audience. I saw the faces of the rest of the kids waiting for their turn. And they were glued to what I was doing. One of my ankles started wiggling. It wouldn't quit. I heard a very high, unfamiliar voice squeak its way out of my throat and proceed to crack, followed by an ear-shattering, body-quivering heart-beat, which also happened to be mine. At that very instant I knew what stage fright was.

I would've given anything to have turned into Claude Rains in *The Invisible Man* right then and there (please, God). No such luck. I was stuck. I was stuck right up there on that stage, feeling naked as a jaybird, in front of the whole wide world, making a complete jackass out of myself. Why, oh, why hadn't I stayed put in my journalism class, where I was safe and snug, writing my "Announcements" column? Better to be bored to death than scared to death.

McNeil barked out a direction: "Chew the gum *harder!*"

I did.

"Faster!"

I thought I was going to dislocate my jaw. It could go with my double-jointed hip. She kept me up there for what seemed like days. I thought that woman would never let up.

I finally heard the blessed word "Next!" and I bolted out the back door as fast as my weak pins could carry me. So much for acting. Better to be in the background, anyway. Directing maybe.

The next day I got a call-back.

How about that? Come to think of it, it really hadn't been all that awful. Even the pros admitted to a little stage fright, every now and then. It was only human. The second time around was a lot better. I made it a point this time not to look at the audience. I pretended to be the character, kind of the way Ilomay and I always did after we'd seen a movie. I even had some fun. I made faces and got laughs. Not bad, not bad at all. The role of Musie, the Maid was finally narrowed down to two of us: Gordon and me.

Gordon was a boy. He wanted to play Musie in girls' clothes. I'd never heard of such a thing. It was just plain stupid. A gimmick, that's what it was. And McNeil was falling for it! It wasn't fair.

Besides, Gordon was a weird kid. Strange-looking, with skin like Snow White, and hair not only black as ebony but fuzzy. He was forever clowning around with the kids on the field during recess, trying to get laughs, and he was forever falling flat. He ate celery and a pear every day for lunch, folded up his brown paper bag very carefully, and saved it.

Sometimes he'd look real pitiful, and when you felt sorry enough for him to say hi, he'd stare right through you. But usually you'd try to avoid him because if he got the chance, he'd pin you to your locker and shove joke after dumb joke down your throat until you pretended to laugh, just to break loose.

For some reason, Gordon was a favorite of McNeil's.

There was no question in my mind. He'd get the part. I walked around in a glob of gloom for three days. I had cast myself in a private play of my very own, a tragedy, and I was the star. They finally posted the chosen cast on the main bulletin board outside the principal's office.

I got the part.

So did Gordon.

There were going to be two performances, and we'd each get a crack at it. I'd get to play the first one, and he'd get to close.

We had a full house the Friday night we opened. I did okay. In fact, I was pretty good. I cracked my gum like crazy, made faces, hollered out my lines, and got laughs. I followed McNeil's direction to a T. Mama, Nanny, and Chrissy came and said they liked it a lot. Chrissy looked sleepy.

Backstage Ilomay, Norma, and the rest of our gang said they thought I stole the show. I wished like mad I could play it the next night, but it was over for me. All my buddies agreed I'd been gypped. I'd hardly got my feet wet. Well, let Gordon have his shot. I could afford to be gracious. I was a hit.

We all were in the audience Saturday night.

Gordon made his entrance, wearing Musie's maid uniform. The kids

F. C. Jones and wife, Goggy
(my great grandparents)—
she always called him Mr. Jones

Nanny (in her twenties)—
"the Belle of Belleville"

Newlyweds Nanny and "Big Irish" (Papa) Bill Creighton
(her first husband), around 1906

*Nanny with Mama on her lap
and Aunt Dodo (1911)*

*Nanny, who hated water,
in a bathing suit (Texas)*

Mama — "a beautiful face"

Daddy around twenty-three

Mama

Daddy — "handsome and sweet"

Mama and Daddy—newlyweds

Me, three months old, San Antonio

*The old San Antonio house,
the hallway with the skate marks
still showing*

*Daddy and me in San Antonio
at the old house before he
moved west*

The old house today, with a face-lift

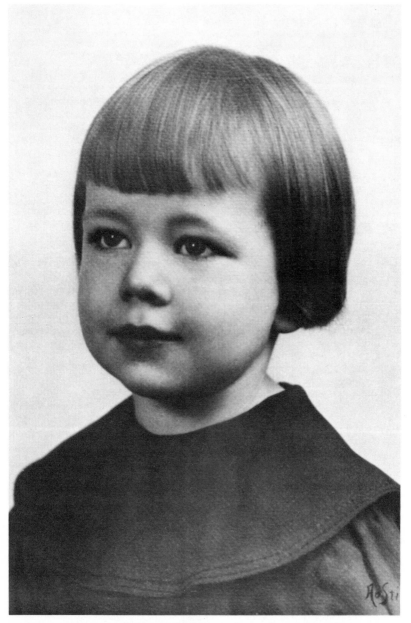

Me, around three, with the Buster Brown haircut I hated

*Four generations (left to right):
Mama, Goggy, Nanny,
me in front, around 1936*

*Cuz (right) and me (left) in San Antonio—
one of the few times Cuz wasn't
wearing her "pointy boots"*

This was the dress I hated, but Mama took my picture anyway (during the brief stay in Santa Monica, California). When I first saw it I tore it up, and Mama pasted it back together.

I liked the sidewalk photographers (San Antonio).

Me, seven years old, San Antonio street photographer

roared. Naturally. I mean, after all, he was a guy. The more they laughed, the less gracious I felt.

Then something started happening. He wasn't Gordon in girl's clothes. He was Musie. He wasn't "acting" funny. He didn't have to. He just was.

And he was wonderful. He was so wonderful I forgot what I was feeling about myself, and when he came out to take his bow, all of us in the audience stood up and clapped and clapped.

Gordon became the campus star.

None of us could get it through our heads why, just weeks before graduation, he shot himself.

His picture was in the yearbook. It had been too late to take it out.

I started dreaming about him . . . almost every night there for a while. I dreamed we both were playing Musie at the same time. We were different from each other, but we were the same person, in the same body. I was Gordon, and Gordon was me. I'd tell him how sorry I was I'd ever been jealous of him, and I'd ask him where he'd be going after graduation, and he'd smile at me. He'd never talk, just smile. Then sometimes I'd see myself in 102, holding a gun, and Mama would come in and say, "Good girl, be a journalist." Then the gun would disappear, and a whole bunch of people, who hadn't been there before, would stand up and clap and clap.

And then there'd be Nanny, lying down on Murphy, saying this was the worst day she'd ever had.

All of us ninth graders were getting ready to graduate.

High school was big stuff.

Hollywood High was big time.

And it just happened to be my high school because I lived in the right district. Selma Grammar School and Le Conte had only been the stepping-stones to this one. And this one could be, might very well be the last step for a lot of us. It was scary. Once you had completed all twelve grades and got your final diploma, there would be choices and decisions to make because you wouldn't be a kid anymore. Three more years of school. I was fifteen. I wasn't a kid then either. But I sure wasn't a grown-up.

Limboland.

What are you? Who are you? Those were the questions we all asked just about all the time now. Only I don't remember wanting the answers as fast as the rest of the kids did. I wasn't in that big a hurry.

Maybe because I didn't see any signs of things getting much better.

Buddy White, one of my boy(friends), asked me to go to one of the ninth-grade "senior farewell" parties with him. He was pretty popular at Le Conte, and I was flattered that he asked me. I think his girlfriend had a cold or something. I didn't mind. I was comfortable with Buddy. Also, he was one of Tommy Tracy's best friends. Maybe he'd put in a good word for me. Buddy didn't live in our neighborhood, so we agreed to meet each other at the party. Ilomay, Norma, and I walked over. It was at Barbara's house. She was the richest girl in school. Barbara had a swimming pool. I liked her, though, because she didn't "act rich." The whole class was there. I was the only one who couldn't swim. (Nanny had never wanted me to learn because she hated water.) Most of the afternoon I sat on the edge of the pool with my legs dangling in the deep end. I wasn't scared of being dunked because the guys did that only to the cutest girls. Later on there were hot dogs and Cokes and dancing to Frankie Laine records. Tommy was there, but he didn't ask me to dance. I had an okay time, though. Everybody was excited about going on to high school, and there was a lot of jabbering about who was going to major in what. The party broke up around nine, and a bunch of us walked home together, dropping each other off, along the way. Buddy and I saw Ilomay to her apartment, and then he walked me into the lobby of my building next door. We said good night, and he was headed outside when the door to 102 flew wide open, and there was Mama. Standing there. Drunk.

"Just what the hell is going on here?" She was swaying, and her shoulder hit the doorjamb . . . hard. She didn't feel it. Buddy was staring wide-eyed at her, and I looked down at the pattern in the dirty lobby rug, wishing I could be sucked into it somehow.

"Where have you been?" She looked like a wild woman, in her robe and nightgown. She was sweating, and her hair was sticking to her forehead. The red birthmark on her temple was throbbing. The robe wasn't tied, and I could see one of her breasts. I prayed that Buddy wasn't seeing what I was seeing. . . .

"Well? Answer me! Goddammit!"

I was swallowing so hard not to cry in front of Buddy. I know I tasted the salt. Without looking at him, I tore past Mama into 102, ran into the bathroom, slammed the door, and prayed to die. I heard her close the apartment door and fall up against it. I waited for God to take me. . . .

Okay, if I couldn't die, then I was never going back to Le Conte. I wouldn't graduate. I wouldn't go on to Hollywood High. No one would ever see me again. I would stay in 102 forever.

God, I hated that woman.

The next day, between classes, Buddy asked me about the drunk woman. "Was that your *mother*?"

"Lord, no!" I laughed. "She's this crazy neighbor of ours. Nobody in the building pays any attention to her."

Graduation. We were a winter class, so two weeks later I was enrolled in Hollywood High School right along with all the other kids in our district.

Three years to go.

And then the world would open up. Or maybe finally close in.

12

Hollywood High. Bigger'n life.

The most famous high school in the whole wide world. And all I had to do was get up in the morning and walk to it.

Lana Turner had been a student there when she was discovered at Schwab's drugstore, having a soda at the counter. That's how the story went. Joel McCrea was a graduate. So was Alexis Smith. God, real live movie stars had run in the same halls, maybe sat at the same desks as *me*. (Or did they ever truly run and sit like real people?)

Hollywood High, the great big . . . huge . . . beautiful, famous campus. And now it was *my* school. I was one lucky pup all right.

I was not happy.

I felt . . . lost. Stupid. Dumb. Outnumbered. Overwhelmed. Little. Insignificant.

Just when you start to get used to a place, maybe feeling a little comfortable even, *bang!* . . . it's yanked away from you, and suddenly you're outfitted in something way too big for you, something *else* you have to grow into. Like shoes.

How come everything gets bigger just when you think *you* are?

Crockett, Selma, Le Conte. I could never quite catch up, let alone feel I might even get a little bit ahead of the game.

The boys were taller now, and I couldn't outrun them anymore, and everyone who knew me at Le Conte was bored to death with my trick hip and jungle war whoop bits, and the kids I didn't yet know looked as if they wouldn't give a damn anyhow.

The first week was spent running for classes. Literally. It was the "tradition." You raced the other kids to the most popular teachers' classrooms to sign up for their particular subjects. Everybody but me knew which way to head. I kept bumping into people running in the other direction. I might as well have been in New York for the first time. I was always the last one to find my way to the rooms to sign up. Not a seat left. Then I'd get caught up in the piddling overflow and flushed into the classes taught by all the old fogies. Me and the rest of the losers.

The beautiful girls (including those sisters from Le Conte) belonged to a very special club called the Thetas. They wore burgundy-colored jackets, all alike, and dated the senior football players.

The tenth-grade counselor said we had to choose a major. I picked Spanish. (It was that or math or science.) I had entertained the thought of taking drama as my minor since I liked myself better when I wasn't me, but the teacher who had headed the department all those hundreds of years before I got there suddenly decided to retire just when I arrived, and Hollywood High School (of all the schools in this whole wide world) was to remain dramaless for the next three years. I wound up minoring in art and discovering I wasn't as hot an artist as I'd led myself to believe all my life.

It turned out there wasn't one single class I looked forward to.

I got allergies and sneezed even when nobody touched my nose. I started setting the alarm on Big Ben (still in the medicine cabinet in the bathroom) to go off fifteen minutes early in the morning, to allow me enough time to sneeze. Nanny and I usually counted around seventy-three of them before I was through. My skin got blotchy, and there was always a pimple somewhere. My hair just hung from my scalp, so Nanny gave me a Toni home permanent. I went to school with fried hair. I weighed two pounds and was seven feet four inches. Nobody in this whole wide world was as miserable as I was. And they'd never understand it even if I *could* explain it.

Besides, they all said life was just beginning.

Was all this only about school? Or was it what I was feeling about growing up? Because if that's what school was like, what about "life"? Was it *all* going to be just out of reach? The way it was with Mama and Nanny?

They'd be at it again.

"You go on about how smart you are all the time." Nanny had started round one.

"I *am* smart, goddammit!" Mama came out swinging. "I have more brains in my little toe than this whole goddamn family put together!"

"Then why don't you put that brilliant little toe of yours to tappin' out some use around here, so we can pay the rent? Or are you still waiting for Cary Grant to knock on the door so you can interview him and take over for Louella Parsons?" Then Nanny would shoot a look over at Chris and me. I was messing around with my watercolors, and Chrissy was playing on the floor with an old knickknack shelf that had fallen off the kitchen wall years ago. For some reason only her five-year-old mind could fathom, Chris had named the knickknack shelf January Pie. She had somehow turned it into a doll by wrapping an old blouse around it and managing, with her tiny fingers, to get all the buttons closed, camouflaging the two plywood shelves. January Pie looked almost human, in an eerie sort of headless way, and it was her favorite plaything. Nanny pointed at Chris.

"Just look at that . . . can't even afford a real toy for the baby." She paused just long enough and then snorted. "Thanks to you and the 'love of your life,' Tony the Rat, we've got *four* mouths to feed!"

I tried to find the right blue for the sky I was doing, so I mixed in a little white. Chrissy tied a red ribbon around January Pie's waist.

Then, coming in for the kill, Nanny wound up with "You don't give a damn about Christine, any more than you do about Carol!"

That was the below-the-belt blow that did Mama in every single time they went through this. "You really . . . are . . . a bitch . . . you know that? I love that baby more than my own life!"

"Then *do* something about it! Bill Burgess isn't gonna stay a chump forever, for God's sake!"

"All right . . . all right . . . *all right*! Just lay off me a *minute,* will you? Dear God, let up!"

In my head I heard the bell and saw them go to their respective corners. Nanny had definitely won that one.

I dipped my brush in the yellow.

There'd be silence for a little while. Nanny would get out her needle and thread and look through a pile of stuff she'd shoved under the bed months earlier.

Mama would pour herself a little Gallo, and then, in a whole new tone as if it were a whole other day, she'd say, "Y'know, sometimes I wish I *weren't* so smart. I'd be happier. I'm right, dammit, I know I'm right; idiots are better off."

Nanny would help herself to a little sip, start darning a sock on a dead light bulb, and chime in. "Well, you know, Louise, you inherited your brains from my side of the family. All the Joneses were brilliant . . . your musical talent, too. Why, we could play every single instrument that was put in front of us, whether we'd ever seen it or not."

"Ain't it the truth"—Mama'd nod—"and I can't even read music . . . perfect ear."

I would've loved to see either one of them tackle the tuba, but I knew better than to open my mouth at this point.

It was peaceful. And it was nice. After a little while Mama would pick up her uke and try to find some new chords to invent. Then they'd discuss who had the best voice, Alice Faye or Kate Smith, and Nanny would wonder if it was Eddie Cantor night or Jack Benny night on the radio. When the Gallo ran out, Nanny would make the run to the liquor store because she was usually the one who was dressed.

Mama would be a little tight. I liked her okay when she was a little tight because she'd act happy and be funny. It was only when she downed the next few she'd turn mean. Then round two would start.

I'd start another painting, and Chrissy would pile more clothes on January Pie. Anybody watching the two of us would think we were deaf.

Dingalingalingalinga!

Wake up. Get off the couch. Run into the bathroom. Open the medicine cabinet, and push the button down on Big Ben to shut him the hell up. Sit on the toilet, and sneeze for fifteen minutes. Brush teeth. Don't look in the mirror; you know you're still there. Reach up, and push the clothes hanging from the shower curtain rod to one side of the tub. Reach down, and turn on the faucets. Heavy on the hot, it takes awhile. Quick bath. Pick out a dress. Doesn't matter which one. The other one will be there for tomorrow, and the one today for the day after tomorrow. Stagger into the kitchen vowing never to stay up so late again, listening to the radio.

Nanny'd been fast asleep, the night before, and *Big Town* was one of the great shows in this world. I'd turned it on real low, and put the right side of my face smack up against the portable. My ear covered the little speaker. She never budged. I did it every night. There was always something good on, something just too good to miss. Sometimes Nanny would stay up with me, and we'd play cards, high, low, jack, and the game, and catch *Burns and Allen, First Nighter, Edgar Bergen and Charlie McCarthy*—lots of good stuff. When she got sleepy, though, all bets were off. And so were the lights. I'd wait in the dark and listen for the steady breathing. I'd click on the dial, and the orange glow from the little radio would light up 102 way into the night. I never wanted to turn it off. It meant going to sleep. Going to sleep meant getting up. Getting up meant school. Here it was, another dawn.

Finish dressing.

Go into the kitchen. Nanny's up. Says she never batted an eye all night. Hasn't for years. The hot Ovaltine feels and tastes good. So does the slice of pumpkin pie. Looking forward to a cold enchilada tomorrow morning. Mama promised she'd make enchiladas for dinner tonight. Hope she can hold her head up. Ilomay and Norma are at the door. Time to go. Grab binder, homework, and books. Kiss Nanny three times. Has to be three; three's her lucky number. Chrissy's running down the hall in her nightgown to join Nanny in the lobby and wave good-bye to Ilomay, Norma, and me. She says Mama's out like a light. Chrissy wants to go to school with us in the worst way. I look down at her and tell her not to worry, she'll be old enough to go to school before she knows what hit her.

"Carol, do you know the answer to the third question?"

I popped my eyes open as wide as they'd go, bobbed my head a bit, and smiled brightly. I reminded myself of Harpo Marx. I'd been sound asleep, but I'd fooled her. My forehead had been propped up with my left hand (elbow firmly planted in the empty inkwell, on my desk, to prevent slipping), cleverly disguising the fact that my eyes were shut. From her point of view my entire being was completely concentrated on the homework page in my open notebook three inches below my nose.

"Did you say, 'third question'?" I intelligently inquired.

"Yes."

"Ah. Sorry . . ." I flipped a page. God, I hated this feeling, and it happened every day at this same time. I couldn't, for the life of me, keep my eyes open. I looked at the clock on the wall. I really didn't have to. I knew it was nine-fifty. I stifled a yawn and stretched it into a smile. I'd seen Joe E. Brown do it a hundred times in the movies. "Here we are"—I hadn't blinked since she'd called on me—"third question . . . the answer is 'seventy-five percent.' "

The class roared.

"This isn't your math class, and I'm not your math teacher. May I suggest you go to sleep earlier at night, so you'll know where you *are* during second period?"

I vowed to quit drinking Ovaltine for breakfast and to try to get to like coffee.

The Coke Sesh. That was the name of the weekly social event held in the gym every Friday night. There was Coca-Cola, slow dancing, and jitterbugging. Ping-Pong was available in the game room. The dress was casual. Lenny Mazola conducted his own student dance band. He also happened to be gorgeous *and* a football player. So it was no wonder the girls outnumbered the boys, three to one. Sometimes a guy or two would ask me to jitterbug, but nine times out of ten they were not only a foot shorter than I was but geeks to boot. Ilomay and I usually wound up playing Ping-Pong together before we gave up and walked home.

I joined the girls' drill team. I didn't know the first thing about football, but at least it got me a little closer to the players.

We'd all skip out onto the field during halftime, waving our red and white crepe paper pompons like crazy while our out-of-tune school band blasted "We're Loyal to You, Hollywood." There we were, marching (usually out of step) on the very same hallowed ground where the Magnificent Eleven had just dug up the turf with their cleats minutes before.

Unfortunately that year the Hollywood High girls' drill team had the reputation of being the *worst* in the entire Los Angeles high school school district. And it was, too. Everybody in the bleachers either laughed at us or booed, or both, when we did our routines. I dropped out before they started throwing things.

Next came the GAA, the Girls' Athletic Association. Every single one of the members outweighed me by a ton, and I was almost killed (by my own side) in our first after-school volleyball game. I resigned before they could get another crack at me.

Swimming was a requirement. You couldn't graduate unless you could do two laps. Nanny didn't like the idea of me and water, but she had no choice, so she signed the permission slip. I was in the shallow end for weeks. I kept sinking. I think the day I learned to float was one of the happiest days of my life. Next came the crawl. I was doing okay. Then came the diving lesson. There was no board. All we had to do was jump in headfirst off the edge of the pool. Our phys ed teacher demonstrated. Simple. We all lined up, and she gave us numbers. When she yelled out your number, in you went. I was 8. Charlotte bumped me in the nose just as my number was called, and I felt a sneeze coming on, mid-jump, two seconds before my head disappeared. There was nothing I could do about it. I finished the sneeze underwater . . . and my head exploded.

When I came to, I was out of the pool and laid out flat on my stomach on the wet, chlorine-smelling tile. There was a lot of squealing going on, and the head-splitting sound was bouncing back and forth, relentlessly, off the walls of the indoor pool. Some sadist was pushing me hard on the back.

I remember thinking, Lord, isn't there *something* I can get right?

13

The Hollywood Palladium hosted "teen night" on Saturdays. It attracted the same crowd from the Friday Coke Sesh, plus tons of other kids from neighboring high schools. We'd all cruise each other under the giant mirrored ball that hung from the middle of the ceiling. It was a sea of tight blue jeans, white T-shirts with the short sleeves rolled up over the shoulders, greasy hair combed into ducktails (the boys), flip or pageboy hairdos, powder pink or powder blue angora sweaters, full skirts over crinoline petticoats, and saddle shoes (the girls). That was The Look.

The Palladium was a world-famous dance hall that featured the top big bands in the country, like the Dorsey brothers, Harry James, and Freddy Martin. I had more fun there than at the school bashes (even though I couldn't afford The Look) because I loved the big band sound, and it gave me a chance to see people like Harry James in person. I kept hoping Betty Grable (Mrs. Harry James) might turn up and sing a song or two for us, but she never did.

There was a new young singer, Merv Griffin, with the Freddy Martin orchestra, who had a hit song, "I've Got a Lovely Bunch of Coconuts," that we all listened to on the radio and sang when we walked to school. He played the Palladium a few times, and all the girls would gather around the foot of the bandstand and swing and sway and swoon. We thought he was adorable, so I got the idea to form a Hollywood High fan club. It was my way to get to meet him.

"He was soooo cute to me!"—Ilomay was hanging on to my every word—"and look, he gave me his bio, his itinerary (for my newsletter to the new club members), *and* half a dozen glossies to get us started!" Ilomay squealed, and we recruited Norma right away. We weren't going to include the snooty girls on campus, only kids like us, and then our plan was to contact other kids around the whole nation, because naturally they would all want to be a part of the original Hollywood High branch.

The club bit the dust when it dawned on us we had to have stationery, envelopes, more photographs, and stamps to get started and nobody *we* knew could cough up the dues.

* * *

It just seemed that everything I did was wrong. Of all the ages in the world, fifteen had to be the worst—no question about it. I couldn't make a right move, and then I got this stupid rash on my leg. It was on my left calf, and it itched so much I'd wake myself up in the middle of the night, scratching my leg to shreds. Nanny told me to lay off it, but how could I help it when I was asleep? She tried to know the truth for me, but the rash wouldn't stop itching, and I couldn't stop scratching. It got worse and worse. She talked to the relief lady about it, and I was sent to some kind of charity medical building with a slip of paper to hand over to the doctor. There were hundreds of people waiting in the lobby, all with slips of paper. The nurse pointed to a chair. I sat down and waited and scratched. About three hours later she called my name. She pointed to a door. I walked into a small examining room. It was empty. There was a big table in the middle of the room, and the shelves on the walls were piled high with trays, bottles, scissors, adhesive tape, gauze, and other first-aid-kit stuff. I hated the smell. I went over to the window and stared at a tree. A few minutes went by. I was about to claw my leg off. I wondered if I'd have to wait another three hours in there. I thought back to the last time I was around doctors, the time I had my tonsils yanked. That *awful* smell. Who needs this? I was about to cut out when the door opened and in walked a movie star doctor.

"Well, hi there, little lady." He looked like John Payne, Robert Taylor, and Tyrone Power.

"Oh. Hi."

"Been waiting long?" He smiled. A little bit of Cary Grant, too.

"Oh, no."

"Well now, what seems to be the trouble?"

Trouble? I didn't know what he was talking about.

"Miss?"

I came to and managed to tear my eyes away from him, close my mouth, and point to my leg.

"Oh, I see. Well, hop up here so I can get a better look." He patted the table.

I would've hopped off the roof if he'd asked me.

"You've been scratching this a lot?"

"Yes."

"Well, you've got to stop doing that."

"Okay."

"I'm pretty sure I can fix what's ailing you."

I was sure of it, too.

He disappeared into a closet right next to the front door. "Do you know if you're allergic to penicillin?"

I'd never heard of it. Probably some kind of salve. "No." I looked at the rash. God it was ugly; how could he bear to look at me? I heard the closet door close, and he was standing there with a needle.

"I'm just going to give you a little shot. I promise I won't hurt you."

The only shots I'd ever had were the vaccination shots they gave you in school. I hated shots. But I knew he would be gentle, not like those school nurses. I started to roll up my sleeve.

"No, dear. We give this to you in the buttocks. Now all you have to do is lie on your stomach and pull your underpants down. It'll be over in a jiffy."

Oh. Oh, Jesus. Oh, God. Oh, no. He can't see me like that! No, please. I wanted to explain to him.

(You don't understand, I think I'm in love with you! But I'm . . . shy. Nobody has seen me naked since I was a baby! I don't even get undressed in front of the other girls in gym class, I'm too embarrassed. I go into the toilet stall to change clothes! I *don't want you looking at my bare butt!*)

I was on my stomach on the table. Oh, God, do I have on the pants without the holes in them? *Please,* let me have on my good pair. Oh, God, why did I have to keep scratching that damn leg, why did we have to meet like this? Why was I born?

"All done. That should take care of it, and here's some ointment to put on at night. That didn't hurt now, did it?"

I had adjusted my drawers and skirt and was up and off that table in two seconds, backing my way out of the room as casually as I could. My face was hot. I know I was as red as a beet. "Not a bit. Thanks a lot, Doc." Flip, that's it, act flip.

"Now remember, don't scratch it, and if it gives you any more trouble, you come back and see me."

(I'll never see you again, my beloved. Never . . .) I had on the pants with the holes in them.

I reached behind me for the doorknob. "Sure thing, Doc." I chuckled a little. "And thanks again for the shot!" I gave him a cute little salute, turned around, walked through the door, and closed it behind me.

I was in the closet.

14

I felt old. It had been a hundred years since I'd been in a really good mood. Ilomay and I were drifting apart. She had a boyfriend, a real one. He didn't go to Hollywood High. He was a little older, and I hardly ever saw her anymore.

The neighborhood gang had grown out of itself. The Hollywood Hawaiian Hotel/Motel stood where the vacant lot had been, and my roller skates were rusting, buried somewhere under God knows what in Nanny's closet behind Murphy, along with my Batman cape and Lone Ranger mask. It didn't matter. We didn't play those silly games anymore anyhow.

The only bright note, if I could call it that, was that I had made some kind of peace with my classes and was coming up with some pretty fair grades. I did my work the best way I knew how, turned it in on time, and didn't talk in class or chew gum.

A few of the other kids got into trouble. They'd get caught smoking, going off campus during lunch, cutting classes; some of the real bad ones got expelled for drinking Rheingold beer.

Not me. Nosirree. Unh-unh.

I was a good girl.

Don't make waves. I toed the fine line between being teacher's pet and still okay with the kids. I was able to have everybody like me. It was tricky, but I managed it. I got pretty good at being good. Good ol' Carol. Everybody's buddy.

Well, well, at last, something I could excel in—something that was mine, all mine: Likable, Trustworthy, Dependable, Organized, Honest, Can-Keep-a-Secret, Well Behaved. I might not be the prettiest, the smartest, or the richest, but I was the best at being good.

Sometimes it was as if I were two different people: the one who thought things and the one who said and did things. I couldn't, for the life of me, bring the two together. I don't know what I thought might happen if I did, but whatever it was, it scared me. Scared me enough to keep a wall up.

Mama called it my shade.

"Carol, sometimes you don't act like you're in there. When you pull that goddamn shade down, there's just no talking to you."

I took to saving a dime from my lunch money every day, so I could treat myself to something after school on the way home.

I'd walk down Hollywood Boulevard, toting my books, looking for a place to spend it. Most of the time the line at the Orange Julius stand was miles too long, and if it was hot, it wasn't worth the wait because my books got heavy, and it felt as if the sidewalk was scorching right through my cardboard soles. You could see the heat waves coming up from the cement.

Then there was Van de Kamp's, where I sometimes blew the whole dime on the gooeyest chocolate éclair in the display case. I'd wrap it in a paper napkin and head out into the heat, loaded down with my books, trying to eat it in one gulp, to keep the chocolate from melting and running down my fingers and onto my homework assignments. It was a losing battle. And expensive. Cokes were only a nickel at Biff's.

Biff's was inside and had a counter where you could park it and take a load off. Plus it was right across the street from where we lived. It made much more sense. I could stretch out my money. Two days for the price of one. I could sit down, drop my books on the floor by my feet, slip my heels out of my shoes, relax, cool off, and take my own sweet time, especially if I ordered a Coke with lots of ice. Good thinking.

It became a routine. Biff's was a popular coffee shop, and around three-fifteen or so it would be packed. Even if I was a little late, I didn't mind waiting for a seat. I was inside, where there was shade.

One afternoon I'd just finished sucking the very last bit of cola through the straw and was looking forward to another ten minutes of bliss, chewing the tightly packed crushed-drugstore-type ice, when a man who had been sitting next to me for a few minutes, said, "Are you in high school?"

"Uh, yes." I glanced at him.

He was staring at my notebook on the floor with the school stickers on it. His hair was heavy on the Brill Creme, and he needed a shave. "What grade are you in?"

I didn't like him. "Tenth." I looked around, and there wasn't another empty seat in the place. I started to chew. I wasn't about to give up my ice.

"That makes you, what, fifteen? Sixteen?" He turned toward me, and his seat swiveled and squealed a little.

I chomped. There was a pause. "Fifteen." I didn't want to be rude.

"Fifteen." He took a sip of his black coffee. "Hollywood High School, huh?"

What made me think I had to answer him? Why did I have to say anything at all? "Yep," I replied politely. "Hollywood High . . . tenth . . . grade."

He turned his seat and faced the counter again. For one happy moment I thought he was through. Then, without looking at me, he said, "Would you do me a favor?"

I was wishing I'd swung by Van de Kamp's. I was wishing I had appendicitis. I was wishing he'd do *me* a favor and drop dead.

"Sure," I said obligingly.

"Look down in my lap."

I froze. My heart started skipping beats so fast I could've given Nanny a run for her money. Then it simply ceased to function. My heart was not working anymore. But nobody would've known it that afternoon at Biff's. Nobody at all. I was still crunching my ice as I looked down at his lap. He was holding a tiny pair of scissors. He whispered, "Will you cut my fingernails for me?" He was staring straight ahead at the cook, who was busy frying burgers on the grill, three feet away. "Please." Nobody in the world would've known he was talking to me. Nobody. I wanted to scream.

What came out of me was a very easy "Sure."

He passed the tiny scissors to me, keeping his hands hidden under the counter. I took his right hand and began carefully to trim the nail on his pinkie. It was like a slow-motion nightmare. I did it slowly, so I wouldn't nick him. Suddenly my heart started up again. It scared me, and I almost jumped. It meant I was alive, but now the pounding was so loud I was petrified everybody would hear it and look at me, and see what I was doing. Nobody heard it but me, I guess, because nobody looked at me. He still stared straight ahead, not moving, like a goddamn statue. I never hated anybody so much in my life.

I finished the second finger and peeked at my Coke glass. The ice was water. All around us people were eating and drinking and talking, and not one single person was the least bit aware that I was trimming this man's fingernails right under the counter, right under their noses. I was about to pass out.

I courteously said, "I have to go. I think I hear my mother calling me." Wanting to stab him in the palm, I gently handed him his scissors. I retrieved my books very slowly and got up to leave, not touching the dime I'd left on the counter. He looked up at me, hurt. "I'm awfully sorry," I said.

When I got outside, I ran across the street, against the light, dodging the cars, with my feet still half out of my shoes. I was crying mad. At myself.

I hadn't gotten my nickel change.

I had cut the man's fingernails.

And I had actually apologized to the bastard.

15

I spotted her out of the corner of my eye just as I was walking by the Mayfair Apartments. She was running across the street, right smack-dab in the middle of all that Wilcox traffic, headed out to play with some other little five-year-olds who lived over on Cherokee. I dropped my books and tore after her. Dammit to hell! Doesn't anybody watch her when I'm at school? She could get killed, for God's sake!

I grabbed her by one of her pigtails and jerked her around. "Just what the hell do you think you're doing?" Her face went totally white, making her big brown eyes look black. "Don't you *ever* let me catch you crossing the street by yourself! Do you *hear* me, young lady?" She nodded, terrified. "Because if I *do* catch you at it again, I'll turn you over to the cops, and they'll lock you up and lose the key! I don't care *what* Mama and Nanny say! *Do you understand?*" She nodded and nodded.

We walked back to the Mayfair, picked my books up off the sidewalk, and headed home.

I knew Chrissy couldn't wait to go to school, and I couldn't wait *for* her to. At least she'd be off the streets a few hours a day.

Just a little while longer, and she'd finally be in kindergarten at Selma. God, time flies.

A couple of days after I'd pulled Chrissy up short about dancing around in traffic, Norma and I were on our way to a Jimmy Stewart movie when I saw baby sister at it again. I screamed her name, and she froze in her tracks. No question about it. I would have to keep my promise, my threat. She had disobeyed. After all, who else was there to look after her the way I did? What I was about to do could save her life.

I had her by the arms, and Norma was holding her feet as we carried her into the Hollywood Police Station. We had dragged her five whole blocks, and she'd been kicking and screaming and clutching at light poles and strangers all the way. The three of us were sweating when we came through the door. The sergeant looked up. We set her on her feet and hung on to her arms. She looked at the sergeant with those big, round eyes of hers and stopped breathing. I thought of Bambi.

"Sir, this is my little sister, and she was *jaywalking* on Wilcox. She *knows* she could've been run over, and she *knows* she's not supposed to cross the street by herself, but she did it anyway." And then I said (winking at him, hard), "You won't really have to throw her in jail, will you?" Chrissy started to shake.

He looked down at her. "Well, now this is a very serious offense." He picked up a pencil. "Just what is your name, young lady?"

"Chri-Christine Burnett."

It looked as if he wrote it down. "Have you ever jaywalked before?"

"No . . ." She looked up at me. I saw the tears start. "Well, just a little." I felt her arm go limp. She looked sick.

I wasn't feeling so hot myself.

The sergeant looked at me and winked. He was getting a kick out of it. "Tsk, tsk," he said, and reached for some handcuffs. Chrissy's legs buckled. Norma shot me a dirty look.

It had definitely gone too far. I hadn't meant it to go this far. "Officer," I said, "I'm positive she'll never do it again. Please, give her one more chance." (And please, God, get us out of here, fast.)

He paused. He looked up at the ceiling. He looked down at his desk. He looked at some papers. "Wellll . . ." He was milking it for all it was worth. I wanted to kill him. "I suppose, maybeee . . ." (Jesus, hurry *up*!) "Maybeee, we can let you"—he scratched his chin and closed his eyes, thoughtfully doing, I guess, what he thought was his best Judge Hardy—"we can let you go, this one time." (Thank you, God.) We all started to bolt for the door. *"But!"* (The son of a bitch was going for the Oscar.) "Just this once! Next time we won't be so easy on you. *Understand?"* Chrissy's eyes rolled back into her head, but somehow she managed to give him a little nod.

We thanked him a whole lot and ran like fools. I half carried Chrissy all the way home. She had her little arms around my neck, and her wet cheek was pressed against mine.

I felt awful.

Mama had, somehow, managed to salvage one little snapshot of her and Tony, in spite of Nanny's tear-up-every-single-photograph-of-Tony-raid, right after Chrissy was born. It was a picture of them in an open convertible, in happier days. Every so often she'd take it out of its hiding place and spend an evening with it. She'd sit at the kitchen table in her apartment, prop up the snapshot against a jelly jar, get out her uke, and sing "True Blue Lou" to it:

> She was a dame, in love with a guy
> She stuck to him, but she didn't know why
> Ev'ryone blamed her
> Still, they all named her
> "Tru-e Blu-e Lou-uuu."

It made Nanny furious.

Tony was the "family scandal," and Nanny got palpitations at the very thought of him, let alone the one Kodak reminder she had overlooked. I guess she figured as long as Mama could look at that picture, she'd keep on *not* looking at Poor Bill Burgess, who was our "meal ticket, for godsakes."

One night Nanny tried to snatch the photo while Mama was at the sink pouring another one. Mama caught her at it, grabbed the snapshot out of Nanny's fingers, and started screaming and crying.

It was a doozy of a fight.

"God*dam*mit! Can't you leave me with *some*thing? Do you think you own the whole friggin' *world*?" Mama clutched the picture to her stomach, and her face was beet red.

Nanny started snorting and clearing her throat. She always did that when she got caught at something. "I wasn't doing anything! I was just looking at it, Louise."

"*Looking* at it! Ha! That's a hot one! You know goddamn good and well you want to rip it to shreds the way you did all the other pictures I had of him! I'm just lucky you didn't find this one, or the baby never *would* know what her father looked like! Jesus Christ, you're a thief *and* a liar!"

Nanny puffed up like a pigeon. "Well, someone around here has to face the facts! The sooner you do, the better off we'll all be. He's gone for good, and he is *not* coming back! Forget it. He never really loved you, Louise, or he wouldn't still be with his wife!"

Mama looked as if she'd been shot. Nanny pressed on. "And you're not the least bit ashamed of yourself! *A married man*. Everybody is talking about it behind your back! They all laugh at you for being such a fool! It's a wonder you can show your face around the neighborhood! Why, I can hardly hold *my* head—" She never got the rest of it out. Mama took her by the arm and pushed her out the door.

"Get *out* of here! *Get out! You're* a swell one to talk about somebody's reputation! After all you put Eudora and me through, you have the nerve to criticize anybody? *Just get the hell out of here!*" It took her a minute before she realized she was yelling at the closed door. Nanny had gone back down the hall and was in 102. I'd heard her slam the door. I was just about to follow her when Mama started up again—this time at me. "That's right, run after your precious Nanny! You think she's so *wonderful* . . . well, I've got news for you, kiddo: When it comes to the *man department,* we can all take a back seat to my sweet mother."

I had no idea what she was getting at, but I stood real still.

She raved on. "Eudora and I never knew *who* we'd find waiting for us when we came home from school. There was a new man in her bedroom every time we turned around! The kids we played with never let up on us about her. 'Who's your daddy *this* week?' We were so ashamed of her we never wanted to go to school!" And she's got the *gall* to be embarrassed about *me!* The goddamn *hypocrite!*"

Mama was just about out of control, running back and forth across the kitchen, bumping into the chair, looking *at* me—*through* me—crying and wild-eyed. The best thing for me to do was to act like a statue. So I did.

She wasn't finished yet. "Christ, she goes around telling the whole world there were only *three* husbands!" When she saw the look on my face, she started to laugh as if she were crazy or something. *"You* bought it, didn't you? Didn't you?" Yes, I did. I nodded. She shot me a triumphant look. "Well, honey, lemme tell you here and now, she's worse than I could ever hope to be! Oh, she was married, all right"—she held up three fingers and began counting on them—"to my daddy, and to Herman Melton, and to John White—and *three others! Six,* baby, count 'em, *six!*" Now I was looking at six shaking fingers. "And God only knows how many others she screwed around with, for whatever she could get out of them! But she 'conveniently' leaves that part of her life out of the picture! Oh, she's an *original,* that one!" The way she said it made Nanny sound like an ax murderess. "And you wanna know the worst part of the whole thing?" I didn't, but I nodded again. "She brags that she never *loved* a single one of them! *Brags!* At least I loved your father and Tony . . . and they loved me, I know it . . . God, oh, God, oh, God, please, they loved me . . . she's the meanest woman in the world . . . oh, Christ, does she ever take the cake. . . ."

She wound down. I left her sitting at the kitchen table, looking at the snapshot. I opened the door and walked down the hall to 102. Chrissy was listening to the radio and trying to fit an old sweater around her knickknack shelf. Nanny was frying salmon balls for dinner. She sent me to the store for some ketchup and canned corn.

I never said a word to her about what Mama had told me.

When I came back into the building with the groceries, I could hear Mama down the hall, playing her uke and singing:

> Maybe somewhere in heaven above
> There's a reward for that kind of love
> Angels will blame her
> Still, they'll all name her
> "Tru-e Blu-e Lou-uuu."

Will I ever find
The boy on my mind,
The boy who is my ideal. . . .

The science classes showed the girls and boys (separately, of course) school-approved sex education documentaries. "ERPY CLASSROOM FILMS PRESENTS":

Everybody hated them. We nicknamed them *Urp*ies. They did a better job than Ovaltine when it came to making me nod off in class.

Mrs. Buchanan would ask one of us to pull down the window shades and turn off the lights. *Then* she'd go about trying to thread the projector, fouling it up every time, until she had to send for Mr. Naumann to fix it. First thing *he* did was turn on the lights so he could see what he was doing. When he got it working, he made a hasty exit, and we'd all giggle and clap. She'd shoot us a dirty look, and off went the lights again.

"ERPY CLASSROOM FILMS PRESENTS: FERTILIZING THE EGG" (!)

Groan.

We'd see a happy married couple smiling and doing happy-married things in their pretty little cottage: her washing and him drying, her picking posies in the garden and him watering the lawn, her knitting and him reading his paper and smoking his pipe. Then they'd look at each other and simply *beam*. Next, we'd be treated to some dumb animation about how the bees pollinate the flowers. And bang, before you know it, Mr. and Mrs. Happy are cuddling Hap, Jr., and "THE END" pops up on the screen. For all it let *us* in on, she could've picked the kid from their garden.

The lights would go on, and Mrs. Buchanan would go to a whole other subject, like photosynthesis. We never discussed what we'd just seen.

And it was the same damn dumb piece of film every semester.

When I didn't fall asleep, I found myself getting hot under the collar for some reason. Just wait a minute. Hold the phone here. There's a missing screw somewhere. You guys aren't telling it like it is. Sometimes, it just made me boil.

Fertilizing the egg, my butt.

Why don't they get Nanny up there and have her lecture on How to Get Your Man (or Men, in her case)? And Dodo. Boy howdy, she'd be a good one. She could talk about "Roger" and "Suzy" doing nasty things and then bow her head and pray. And _Mama_! How about _Mama_? She could bring her uke, and sing sad songs, and tell us all about how " 'It' (the big _it_) is so friggin' overrated it's pitiful." Then the three of them could close with a close-harmony trio: "I've Got Those True-Blue, Boo-Hoo, Why'd-It-Have-to-Be-You Blues."

Whatta show. And then the discussion: Face it, kids, things just don't ever pan out the way you plan 'em.

It's _not_ about eggs and flowers.

Maybe I didn't know what it _was_ about, but I sure as hell knew it wasn't about eggs and flowers.

And dammit, the reason I didn't know what it was about was that I just plain didn't _want_ to. Why should I?

After all, what _did_ sink in wasn't pretty or happy.

The only happy people I knew were in the movies. The movies _I_ liked anyway. They had their problems, but nothing that couldn't be fixed in an hour and a half.

Mama used to joke about the Hays Office and laugh herself silly. The Hays Office censored all the motion pictures. Nobody cussed. The bad guys always paid for their crimes, and if a couple went to bed in the movies, it was to sleep. Either that, or one foot had to be on the floor at all times. When they kissed, the film would go to black, and you'd either see skyrockets, ocean waves, or "THE END." Mama thought it was sillier'n hell.

Not me. I wanted it like the movies.

Maybe that's why I hated Erpy Classroom Films so much. They were selling the same bill of goods and passing it off as real life.

He was a short-order cook at Biff's. Mark. He was twenty-four, and I was almost sixteen.

He was friendly and awfully nice. I'd go in and have my Coke, and he'd ask me all about school, and we'd kid around. He hadn't been working at Biff's too long, but everybody in the neighborhood liked him. He asked me to go to the movies a couple of times, and it wasn't long before we started going out together a lot.

I remember becoming aware of the fact that this could be serious.

The picture Mama got to keep of her and Tony

Daddy (in his early forties)
on the wagon

Grandma Burnett shortly
before she died

Cuz in her recital outfit

Cuz at UCLA, Homecoming Queen finalist

On the corner of Yucca and Wilcox —
me, Jean, Ilomay and Norma with pooch

My new baby sister, Chris, and me in 102, early 1945

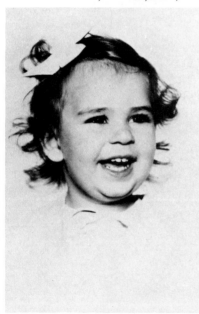

Chris, around two, and at four, a knockout

Chris and me: I felt (and looked) like her mama

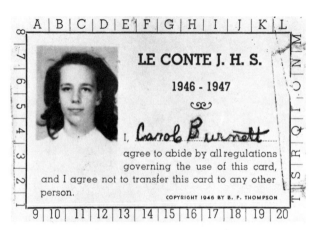

A not-too-thrilled seventh grader

As a Stumptown Player
The Torch Song That Went Wrong

Mark and me at my high school graduation
1951

Hollywood High yearbook — Nanny bought me the pearls from Kress's

The UCLA Homecoming Show (1953),
singing "Laura de Maupassant"
from Hazel Flagg

CLA, as the football coach in the varsity show
Love Thy Coach *(the year I left to go*
to New York, 1954)

Daddy at the Olive View sanitarium, the last time I saw him

From his point of view.

I don't know how I knew it, but I knew.

He was nice-looking and kind. And old.

Lots of times he would invite Nanny to tag along. She'd get all dolled up in red or pink, stick on the lipstick and rouge, put on her stockings and high heels, and try to do something with her hair. Mark would come calling, and we'd be off and running, the three of us. We'd parade down Ivar Street, him in the middle and me and my grandmother on either arm. He'd take us to the Ontra Cafeteria and to the movies. He'd buy us as much candy as we could eat, and more to take home to Chrissy and Mama. Nanny liked him a lot.

I had a part-time job at the Hoky-Poky ice cream parlor on Cahuenga, weekends, and he used to come in before he had to go to work around the corner at Biff's and sit at the counter and watch me scoop out ice cream for the cones . . . just to be near me. I could tell.

I didn't feel the same way about him, but I didn't want to hurt his feelings.

Most of the girls who came in would flirt with him because he was handsome and had a nice smile. Some of them would start talking to him out of the blue and move over a seat or two to be right up next to him. Others would just out and out stare at him.

But I was the one he paid attention to.

Instead of being flattered, I felt funny, awkward. That's what it was . . . awkward. I liked him a lot, even loved him in a way, but I couldn't help feeling caught. It was as if he might be the only one in this whole wide world who would ever want me as much, and I'd better not let him get away, or I'd regret it the rest of my natural life.

He gave me a surprise birthday party the day I was sixteen.

It was at the Hoky-Poky. His birthday present was a complete set of matching beachwear: beach towel, beach bag, and a one-piece bathing suit, all by Catalina. No question about it, Nanny said, Mark was a good catch, a perfect gentleman.

But he was so *old*.

Was Nanny right? Was all this love stuff the bunk?

Was Mark going to be my Bill Burgess? So soon? Like Ilomay? (Who was probably going to quit school and get married.)

He said he was willing to wait for me to graduate. Oh, Lord, he was talking about getting *engaged*, spending our *lives* together. Nanny sent out "nab him" signals right and left. "He makes good money, and he doesn't drink."

Who could ask for anything more?

God, wasn't there any other choice? Wasn't there something else? Somewhere? Or is this it? Nabbing somebody because he could buy you a bathing suit and your grandmother *dinner*? Spending your life with someone just because he was *nice* and you didn't want to hurt his feelings?

Wasn't there something I could cash in on? On my own?

Did I have to depend on somebody else, my whole life, to do it for me?

Yessirreebob. You sure as hell do. That's what they all said. Mama had tried it on her own, and look what it got her. And she was smart, ambitious, *and* pretty.

But wasn't there somewhere in me a talent for something? Something that I wasn't paying attention to?

A little voice from way down deep kept saying, "Yes, there is." But I couldn't, for the life of me, figure out what it might be.

And time was running out.

Mr. Thorpe was a small, wiry, thin-lipped man with tiny eyes. He wore glasses and a lot of brown. He talked only when he gave lectures, and he didn't tax his smile muscles any. He said hello by nodding.

He was my English teacher. He was also in charge of the sparse journalism class. The class was sparse because Mr. Thorpe was the most hated teacher at Hollywood High.

Mama wanted me to join the *Hollywood High News.* I tried to explain Mr. Thorpe to her, but she wasn't having any. "Christ, life isn't just a bowl of cherries, baby, and the sooner you learn that, the better." Ha.

I signed up, just as I'd signed up for cheerleading and the GAA. What's one more disaster?

We had to work after school, including Fridays. What the hell, I didn't have anything else to do.

Thorpe had not been put on this earth to put up with high school students, so he didn't. He never screamed or yelled or got flustered like some of the other teachers. He didn't have to. He was simply steely cold. He could do you in with one drop-dead look through those little bitty, beady eyes and those little bitty wire-rimmed glasses, without even saying boo. You'd feel as if you'd been thrust through the heart with an icicle. Worked like a charm. His English classes were cemetery quiet.

So were the journalism classes. The *News* staff whispered and walked on eggshells. He scared the hell out of us. We mapped out the pages, wrote the headlines, and put the paper to bed, tiptoeing and breathing softly at all times.

As a paper, the *News* was dull. None of the kids read it, and it was considered as big a joke on campus as the cheerleading team. I wanted out, but this time there was no play to try out for (as there had been at Le Conte) since there was no drama department and I'd exhausted all the other electives. I was stuck.

I was careful not to make waves. It was a good day when he didn't look my way. Blend in with the paint on the walls, kiddo. That's the way to survive.

But it bothered me. Inside. Down deep. I'd seen enough movies to know this was no way to run a newspaper, and I was beginning to get sick of blending. And mad . . . at me. Some of the things that went on in my head were 180 degrees from the way I behaved. There was another whole different person in there, and *she* had spunk, grit, sand, a personality, *courage*. But, oh, God, the outside me was a complete chicken. I'd have conversations with myself.

"C'mon . . . say something! Speak up!" *she*'d say.

"Are you nuts? Let's not rock the boat."

"What's the worst that could happen if you do?"

"He could kill me."

"Nah. You're not worth going to the chair over."

I did have an idea for the paper, though. A good one, too. I'd been nursing it for weeks. I dreamed about it. I even pictured its actually happening. But first I had to picture getting up the nerve to talk to Thorpe about it.

I got up the nerve.

By pretending to be Rosalind Russell.

Thorpe was sitting at his desk, meticulously cleaning his glasses with his ironed handkerchief. He was the first man I ever remember with clear polish on his nails. It was a late Friday afternoon, and the class was holding its collective breath, *living* for the moment he'd put the specs back on, fold up the handkerchief, return it to his breast pocket, take out the watch he carried in his vest, check the time against the school clock on the wall, lace his fingers together, clear his throat, and nod to us, meaning we were sprung till Monday. He finally nodded, and everybody got out as fast as tiptoes could go. Everybody but me.

I put down my pencil and pretended to check out my notes on an interview I'd done with Mrs. Jiminez about her trip home to Mexico during summer vacation. I glanced up at him. His little bitty, beady eyes were buried in some papers.

"Now!" *she* goosed. I jumped up and did a Hildy Johnson (the character Roz Russell played in *The Front Page*), star reporter, walk (long stride, determined chin) clear up to his desk . . . where I stood for eons. He didn't look up. It was the closest I'd ever been to him. I smelled some kind of cologne, not bad, and I could see his pink little scalp through the carefully combed sandy hairs on his head. I coughed. He looked up at me. The eyes were the color of gunmetal.

"Yes?"

(Roz, don't fail me now.) "Mr. Thorpe, I want to talk to Joel Mc-Crea."

"Excuse me?"

"Joel McCrea. The actor. See, it's an idea I've had for a long time, and I think our readers would really go for it. He, Joel McCrea, the actor, was an actual *student* here, *himself,* Mr. Thorpe! I mean, isn't that *terrific*? It could even be a feature series for the paper! *All* the famous people who went to school here! He's the first one to come to mind, and there are *tons* of others. It could put our school paper on the map. After all, this is *Hollywood High*! Mr. Thorpe, this is *the* most famous high school in the whole wide world! We deserve to pat ourselves on the back, to brag about what we've turned out!"

"Joel who?"

I thought I was going to die. "McCrea. Joel McCrea."

"Oh, yes." Pause. *"He* attended this school?"

"Yes." (YesyesyesyesYES!)

"Very well. See what you can do." He went back to his papers.

Dear God in heaven, I won the Academy Award.

How was I gonna make it through the weekend? I flew home to tell Mama. The shades were down in her room, and I could hear her snoring. Don't dare wake her up. Nanny and Chris were out somewhere. I wanted to shout it to the world: *"Joel McCrea! I'm gonna interview Joel Mc-Crea!"*

Oh, Lord. How?

"Call the studio," the other me said.

I did. I asked for the press department. Angle: Famous star grants interview to young journalist from alma mater, Hollywood High. Roz was cooking.

It worked.

I met him the following week after school. I took the bus to the studio and gave them my name at the gate. They actually had it written down!

He was too nice to be a movie star. He met me in his office, shook my hand, showed me to a seat, leaned back in his chair, and threw his long legs up on his desk. I stared at his cowboy boots. "Well, now, how can I help you out, young lady?"

My heart was in my throat as I probed, "How'd you get your start?"

He didn't hold anything back. (Refer to photo insert section.)

I swear Mr. Thorpe grinned a little when he read my scoop. He handed it back to me, looked up, and said, "Run it." His eyes looked blue this time.

I had Lana Turner set up two weeks later. The school principal called a halt to it when one of the other reporters snitched that I'd be cutting classes to see her at MGM. My series was axed after one interview.

Six years later I made my very first appearance on *The Ed Sullivan Show,* and I got a letter from W. H. Thorpe. He wrote:

Dear Carol,

It was very nice seeing you on television tonight. I have always felt you would make a career for yourself. I was a little surprised to learn you didn't pursue journalism. I'm sorry I was overruled by the principal the time you were scheduled to interview Miss Lana Turner. I think you would have given our paper another very good story. At any rate, I wish you every success in whatever you choose to do.

I was also a little surprised at how strong your voice is. Your legs looked very pretty.

Sincerely,
William H. Thorpe.

Mama had helped me with it.

I hadn't wanted Mama's help with the Joel McCrea interview, but she said I needed it. Even so, the whole McCrea idea had been mine. I had written most of it, and Thorpe liked the rest of my work enough to give me my very own column. It was called "The Roving I" and featured small bits of campus gossip, information and observations about events, fashion, advice, and all of it tongue in cheek. It was written anonymously (supposedly by a wet-behind-the-ears tenth grader), all in lower-case type with misspellings. Only Thorpe and I knew whose column it was. I loved the assignment. I could write dishy/funny things about everybody while they all wondered who the mysterious "10B Reporter" was. It was ideal. I could spill out what I thought, and nobody could get mad at me. Who could ask for anything more? My column became the first thing the kids read when the paper came out every week, and they'd laugh like crazy. There was great speculation about who was writing it. I felt like Wonder Woman, who had a secret identity. For the first time in my life I had a sense of power. I liked it.

Maybe I wouldn't even have to think about marrying Mark. Maybe there was another road for me after graduation. Maybe I had something I could do after all.

I wrote a poem for the Christmas column:

> i wisht i was a xmas star
> purched atop a tree
> folks wood see me from afar
> cuz of how brite i'd be
> i'd shine all nite
> i'd shine all day
> a lovly site to see
> and folks wood look at me and say,
> "we shoulda got a bell."

That last year in high school I almost went steady a couple of times with boys my own age. There was Leon. We liked each other an awful lot for a while there. He was blond, and we used to neck up on Mulholland Drive. He lived in Burbank, and his mother looked younger than he did.

The other one was Gerry. He went to Black Fox Military Academy, and he was gorgeous. I met him through Cuz. They had dated a few times, and suddenly, for reasons best known to himself, he started calling *me*. I couldn't get over it. On weekends he'd pick me up in the lobby, and we'd hike up around the Hollywood Dam, holding hands, and have long discussions about the meaning of life. I was overjoyed when he accepted my invitation to be my escort at my senior prom.

Uncle Jimmy took me to the Broadway, and as a graduation present he bought me a white nylon net formal that went all the way down to the floor. It had silver shoulder straps and a matching net stole. We hit the shoe department, and he got me silver flats with elastic ankle straps. I'd never owned anything so fine in my life. I hugged Uncle Jimmy so tight I almost squeezed the air out of him.

Gerry picked me up in full uniform and handed me a corsage. Gardenias. The net on the prom dress itched like crazy, but I didn't even notice. I felt like Cinderella.

When I got home that night, I put my gardenias in the icebox. They were brown around the edges from being crushed. As I was going to sleep on the couch, I thought if anybody could get me over my six-year crush on Tommy, it was Gerry.

But he transferred to a military academy out of the state.

We wrote each other for a while, and then it all petered out. Well, down deep I guess I had always thought he caught me on the rebound from Cuz anyhow.

Graduation was around the corner, and all of us seniors were expected to be ready and eager to get out there and "travel life's highways and byways." All it takes is a cap, a gown, a rolled-up piece of sheepskin, and bingo, you're an adult. We've been building up to this moment for twelve long years, and . . . *here it is.* We are now about to graduate into the real world, fully prepared to face the trials and triumphs ahead of us fearlessly, with our heads held high. We are the future, it is now in our hands.

Who, me?

"Yes, you." *She* was talking to me again, that other person in there, inside me.

Please. Give me a break.

I didn't know what I was going to do. I wasn't ready for the future. I could barely deal with what was going on now. Mark was still around, waiting for me to come to my senses. Nanny said if I wasn't going to grab him while the grabbing was good, I should get a job, save up for Woodbury Secretarial School, and go on the prowl for a rich husband in an office somewhere.

"You've got to look out for yourself in this life because nobody else will. I learned that a long, long time ago. I've said it before, and I'll say it again, 'It's just as easy to fall in love with a rich one as a poor one.' " And she'd say it again . . . and again.

"You don't want to do any of that," the other me said.

"I know, but I don't know what I *do* want to do."

"Yes, you do."

"What?"

"UCLA."

I applied.

The small Hollywood High class of Winter '51 collected its diplomas in the auditorium. Traditionally the June grads got to hold their ceremonies in the Hollywood Bowl because their class was always larger. The winter classes griped about this prejudice, but I liked graduating on campus. It was more personal. After all, we didn't go to Hollywood Bowl High.

Nanny, Chrissy, Mama, and Dodo were there. So was Mark. I got a telegram from Daddy: WILL BE THINKING OF YOU TONIGHT. LOVE, DADDY. He couldn't be there. He was sick in a charity hospital. Mama didn't look too hot, but at least she was able to make it.

I thought, "Maybe he went to the hospital to dry out; maybe he got the DTs so bad he'll never touch another drop as long as he lives, just like Ray Milland in *The Lost Weekend.* That would be some graduation present."

"Don't get your hopes up in that department," said the other me.

I looked at my diploma.

I couldn't believe it was over. I never thought the years would pass and now . . .

I was awfully sad.

I was saying good-bye to people I had known all my life. We ran around getting our yearbooks signed, pledging undying loyalty and friendship forever and ever. We hugged and kissed and swore we'd always keep in touch. We bawled our eyes out. Good-bye. Good-bye, Norma, Barbara, Beverly, Chickie, Yvette, Jane, Allene, Lee, Jimmy, Buddy, John, Alan, Lenny, Bob, Julius, and Tommy.

I missed Ilomay. She was married.

October 9, 1984

Dearest Friend,

I'm in a plane somewhere over the Atlantic, on my way to Europe, but my thoughts are with you. And my prayers. This year has been a reflective one for me. As I told you over the phone, I've been writing a lot about Yucca and Wilcox, Nanny and Mama, and all of us.

You have always been so dear to me. And lately you've been with me just about every day. I've been writing about our childhood . . . playing hooky, and jacks in the bathroom . . . Nyoka, Sheena . . . the first time I ever had borscht . . . your grandmother . . . oh, God . . . our beginnings. I'm so glad we found each other again and have kept in touch (at least over the phone) these past few years. But why not? The closeness has always been there. Maybe it's because we never forgot how we shared our secrets and dreams. Ilomay, if I could have a wish, a wish for you, it's that you will never be scared. I hate the thought of your ever being scared. I love you, and I cherish our childhood together. I'm grateful my best buddy was you. I hope you'll feel up to recording some memories . . . they're so personal . . . I'd love to hear what stands out to you.

I'll be in New York around the first week in November. I'll call you.

Know that you are loved.
Carol

November 28, 1984

Oh, God, Ilomay,

I just heard. I wanted so much to thank you for the tape. I love it so much. I wish I had called you as soon as I got back from Europe . . . my God, my God . . . how quickly it all happened. How fast, how rotten, and how blessed, in a way. My dear friend, I pray you didn't suffer. And oh, God, how I pray you are at peace.

I'm sending a letter to your family I wrote to you on a plane, over a month ago. I never mailed it, and I'm sorry. I think . . . I hope, it expresses how I feel and have always felt about you.

Your tape will always be one of my treasures. I'm grateful you did it for me.

I can't believe you're gone.

Ilomay, if there is "something" after all this, I hope we'll be swinging on vines and playing Betty Grable together again, somewhere in that big Pantages in the sky.

My love always,
Carol

October 19, 1984 Excerpts from Ilomay's Tape (with Her Son, Ira)

IRA: Okay, Carol, this is Ira, and I'm in town visiting Mom. We're going to try to get a lot of this done for you, and Mom's told me about how you're putting memoirs together for a book for the children, and we're figuring out the tape recorder here. Mom's not feeling real good, but I'm gonna ask her a bunch of questions, and hopefully that'll give you some things that maybe you don't remember . . . or just be able to share the experiences again. Here we go. When was the first time you met Carol?

ILOMAY: Carol and I met when she hit me in the stomach with a two-by-four. She thought I called her grandmother a nanny goat. Her grandmother's name was Nanny, who we dearly loved, but at the time I didn't know Nanny very well, or Carol, and we had this little encounter, and after that we became fast friends, in fact, best friends. We did everything together. . . .

I remember that day, years ago. I was furious with Ilomay. I thought she'd called Nanny a bad name.
"What did you say?"
Ilomay looked scared. "Nothing. I didn't say a thing."
"Oh, yes, you did. Repeat it." I was madder'n hell.
"No."
We were on the vacant lot. I picked up an old board that was lying on the dirt.
"I *asked* you what you said."
"Nothing!" She started to cry. "I didn't say it!"
"You called my grandmother an old witch, didn't you? I *heard* you!"
"No! Honest, I didn't!"
I whacked her across the stomach with the board.
Ilomay started to scream. I dropped the board and ran.
Nobody can talk about my nanny like that and get away with it. I'll kill 'em.
Later that afternoon, before dinner, Ilomay's grandmother dragged Ilomay over to 102 and showed Nanny the welt on Ilomay's stomach.
I felt awful. I wasn't really sure she had said it.
The next day we walked to school together, like always.
She had forgiven me. . . .

IRA: What school did you go to?
ILOMAY: Selma Avenue School in Hollywood. It was a nice school, we went all through Selma together, and then on to Le Conte Junior High, and then on to Hollywood High.
IRA: You said you guys used to play hooky or something?
ILOMAY: We used to play hooky and play jacks on the bathroom floor. It was ceramic tile, and it was the best surface for jack playing.

IRA: Just after you guys first met, what was the first thing you can remember that was a big deal after that?

ILOMAY: I don't remember in sequence. We did a lot of things together. We used to have lemonade stands at the corner of Yucca and Wilcox. There was a big pepper tree, and we'd set up our stand under it and drink up most of the profit.

IRA: How close did you live together?

ILOMAY: We lived on Yucca Street. Carol lived in one building, and I lived in the other. I lived on the third floor, and she lived on the first floor, so when I left home to go to school, I'd go out of the apartment and go downstairs, pick Carol up, so if we ever had a fight, it always seemed like it was up to me to make up because I'd be the one'd come by her apartment to go to school. I was happy to do it.

IRA: You guys used to climb trees and play and stuff like that?

ILOMAY: We used to play Tarzan. All these Tarzan yells that Carol does on TV were for real. Sheena . . . Nyoka. She was always the boss. But I didn't mind. We had a lot of fun. We used to swing from our legs and give our little Tarzan yells. We used to do all kinds of things. We used to play detectives in the apartment building. We were supposed to be baby-sitting her little sister, Christine; we'd make sure that she was okay; then we'd go around to the different apartment doors and listen in. We were detectives.

Ilomay and I were around nine or ten, and we'd sneak around the halls in our Batman capes and Lone Ranger masks, hoping to get the goods on any crooks we could find.

"Give *me* the mirror, *I* wanna look."

"Just wait your turn."

I'd try to angle it, just so.

We were spying on the neighbors. It was during the war, and we thought we might be able to capture us some traitors if we kept our eyes open. The newsreels in the movie shows told us to be on the lookout for spies, they're in our "mist." We'd take a small mirror and lie flat on our stomachs outside one of the apartment doors and hold the mirror up close to the crack in the bottom of the door. If you tilted it just right, you could see the whole room that way . . . or at least up to somebody's waist.

We never caught any spies, but sometimes we got an eyeful. . . .

IRA: Was one of the grandmothers more of a disciplinarian or a soft touch than the other?

ILOMAY: They were both soft touches. They were both sweetie pies.

IRA: You could really get what you wanted from them?

ILOMAY: We knew how to do it. They loved us. I think we were both pretty good instigators.

IRA: Did you ever go doubling or anything?

ILOMAY: I don't remember. We skated a lot together. On the sidewalks.

IRA: Did you go very far?

ILOMAY: We stayed in the area.

IRA: You couldn't go excursioning on your own too much?

ILOMAY: Not as real little kids. In fact, if my grandmother wanted me, she usually just leaned out the window and yelled, "Ilomay!" And throughout the whole neighborhood it was transferred from one person to another, and someone would say, "Ilomay, your grandmother's yelling for you." The whole neighborhood knew my name. She'd hang out the third-floor window. It was funny.

IRA: Now did Carol have any brothers or sisters?

ILOMAY: She's got one half sister.

IRA: That's who you had to baby-sit sometimes?

ILOMAY: Yeah.

IRA: What junior high did you go to?

ILOMAY: Le Conte. We used to take the trolley to go. Sometimes we walked. I don't remember how much it cost. A nickel? But we used to goof around and laugh. We were real cutups.

IRA: What about high school?

ILOMAY: Hollywood High. She and my girlfriend Norma were really good friends in high school. I mean, we saw each other, but it wasn't really close like it was in grammar school. I left Hollywood High and went over to Fairfax High.

IRA: Why was that?

ILOMAY: I don't know, I felt that the friends I had, not meaning Carol and Norma, but girls I was running around with weren't particularly the right kind of girls. They were a little rough.

IRA: Did you guys go steady with anybody at that time?

ILOMAY: I think Carol might have had a boyfriend, but I really didn't have a lot of boyfriends until I met your dad. He was my first really. . . .

IRA: Was he going to school also?

ILOMAY: No, he was out of school. He had quit school. . . . I remember one time we spent the weekend with Carol's father. He lived in Santa Monica, and we went to the pier. That was the only time in my life I'd ever been on a roller coaster. I'm the original coward. Carol and I had a lot of fun doing that.

IRA: When did she start doing all the stuff? Did she go to college?

ILOMAY: She went to UCLA. I got married, and that's when she started in with the acting and everything.

IRA: Well . . .

ILOMAY: It's funny that I should be in close contact with Carol at the beginning and at the end of my life. . . .

17

Bill Burgess finally got a yes out of Mama. She didn't look any too thrilled about it, but Nanny said she should be grateful. "So what if he's not the best-looking thing on two feet. At least he's got a job and can help out. He's better than nothing."

"I'm not in love with him." Mama said she loved Bill "like a brother," but it was not the same as "being *in* love."

Nanny looked up at the ceiling and said, "Lord preserve us."

Mama and Bill went to Las Vegas and took me with them. They got married in a funny-looking church with pink and blue neon lights all over its outside. Then we went back to the El Cortez Hotel, and Mama got hung up on the roulette table. She sure did love to gamble. I left her and Bill in the casino and went up to our room, put on my pajamas, and crawled onto the cot the hotel maid had set up under the window. Their bed was on the opposite side of the room. I felt weird being there. Honeymoons were for two people. But Mama had wanted me to come with them. And Bill would do anything Mama wanted. I tried to go to sleep. . . .

It wasn't the first time she had brought me to Vegas. Just a few months before, she said to me, "Kiddo, how'd you like to spend a whole weekend in Las Vegas, Nevada, with your old lady? Just you and me?" I don't know where she got the dough, but she was hot to trot. It might've come from putting her entire relief check on the ponies. At any rate, her ship had come in for once, and she was on a lucky streak she wasn't about to ignore. "And get *this,* baby: We'll *fly* there and back! Would you like that?"

Would I! The closest I'd ever been to a plane was the kiddie rides in the amusement park.

Nanny was having a hissy. "My God, Louise, you really *are* cracked. Why don't you just go flush it down the toilet and save yourself a trip? You never could hold on to a red cent! We need that money."

"There's more where this came from, and it's got my name on it! I'm *hot*! And we're going!" Mama was throwing stuff in an old cardboard suitcase.

"You just up and leave me to take care of Christine when you know I'm sick as a dog." Mama wasn't hearing any of it.

Nanny kept on, "And don't expect me to bail you out when you lose it all . . . and don't call collect either because I won't accept it!"

Mama shut the suitcase. "Well, don't you worry your pretty little head, Mother, dear, because if your phone rings, it ain't gonna be me. I'll be too busy counting my silver dollars, and if you're a good girl, I just might bring you back a present!"

Nanny snorted.

I stared at the propeller blades until they were going so fast I couldn't see them anymore. Up, up, and awayyyy. . . . I felt like Superman. Mama hummed and counted the money she was planning to win all the way, and I flew the plane. We both were in the clouds.

We landed and took a cab to the main street in downtown Las Vegas. It was almost nighttime, but I felt as if I had walked into an oven.

"Desert heat," Mama said knowledgeably. On the way we passed some pretty fancy hotels that had fountains and statues in front of them. The people going in and coming out were dressed like Fred and Ginger. The driver said we were "on the Strip, where the stars and the high rollers play." Mama promised we'd hit one of the big shows the next night. I couldn't wait. I never saw so many lights—more than the Hollywood Boulevard Christmas Parade. The sun had set, but it looked like daytime. The cab pulled up to our hotel, and we got out. Mama thanked the driver, paid the guy, and he smiled and said, "Thank *you*, lady!"

"I like to tip," she said to me. "Feels good." We were downtown. The main drag. There were even more lights on this street than on the Strip. The people didn't dress up, though. Most of them looked like cowboys. And there seemed to be one long, loud, continuous sound of slot machines, music, bells, and people yelling. It was wild. Mama was all lit up and cheerful, like the city . . . and she was sober. I hadn't seen her like this in a long time. The hotel was little and not like the fancy ones we'd passed, but Mama said their money was as real as the next guy's.

We went into the lobby, and she signed us in. On the way to the elevator we passed the roulette table, and she threw a dollar on number 36, in a kind of what-the-hell-why-not attitude. She didn't even watch the little ball go around. As she turned and bent down to pick up our suitcase, the man said, "And the number is . . . *thirty-six!*"

"What'd I tell you?" We both started jumping up and down and laughing like crazy. A month's rent. A whole month's rent, just from an off-the-cuff-toss on the way to our room! Rich. We were rich. Mama really was on a lucky streak. I couldn't wait to see Nanny's face.

They made me leave the casino because I was only seventeen.

Mama forgot all about going to our room. She told me to go on ahead and unpack. She'd be up in a few minutes.

I felt her shaking my shoulders. It was after midnight, and I had fallen asleep on top of the covers, waiting for her to come upstairs. "Wake up, honey, look what your mama's got!" It was a hundred dollars. Holy cow. I had never seen that much money in my whole life. She was grinning from ear to ear. She hugged me, and I smelled a little whiskey, but she was in pretty good shape. She went into the bathroom and closed the door. I could hear her singing "This Is My Lucky Day." She turned on the tap and called out to me, "Ohmygod! Have you had anything to eat?"

I hadn't. She had just reminded me I was hungry. It would be fun to go to a restaurant with Mama and order anything our hearts desired. All the restaurants were still open, too. She had told me on the plane that nothing ever closes in Las Vegas. I figured we could have a steak dinner and top it off with a hot fudge sundae together. Hell, we had enough money for a dozen steak dinners. I was having a swell time.

Mama came back into our room. She had washed her face and combed her hair, and fixed her makeup. I was all set to go out. She handed me seventy-five dollars.

"Keep this. Put it under your pillow or somewhere, but *hide* it . . . and don't let me have it—even if I get on my knees and beg."

I didn't like the sound of that.

"I'm going back. Can't quit now—bad luck!" Her eyes were sparkling. "You go get something to eat here in the hotel. There's a coffee shop next to the lobby. Don't lose that money. And remember, no matter *what I say,* don't let me have it. You're my *insurance,* baby."

I wasn't having such a good time anymore.

"Understand, honey?"

Yeah.

It was around five in the morning. She was having trouble unlocking the door. I heard her say, "God*dam*mit!" in the hall. I got up and let her in.

"Gimme the money."

"Mama, you told me not to."

"I don't give a good crap what I told you. That was then. This is now."

The sun was brutal. We were sitting on the grass in front of the depot, waiting for the train back to L.A.

Nanny had finally sent us a money order, or we would've had to walk home. It was high noon, and there wasn't a speck of shade or a breeze anywhere. We'd been there since 7:30 A.M. At first Nanny wouldn't accept the collect call. Then I guess she did, so she could hear herself say, "I told you so," to Mama.

There wasn't one red cent left. Mama was pretty hung over, so we didn't talk much during the long train ride home.

. . . Here I was again . . . with Mama and Bill on their honeymoon.

They were weaving when they came in after 3:00 A.M. I turned on my cot and faced the window. They got in bed, and I heard Bill say, "I sure do love you, Lou." Mama said something about being dog-tired, and not wanting to "disturb Carol." I heard a few little pleading noises, but it wasn't long before they both were snoring.

It was the second time she'd taken me to Vegas for insurance.

18

UCLA. I'd been accepted. The hitch was the tuition: forty-two dollars. Our rent was clear up to thirty-five dollars each and every month. Even before I asked the question, I could hear Nanny's answer: "Forget it. UCLA is out, period. No way."

Yes, there was. There was a way. I'd get to go. I didn't know how, but I'd get to go. I "knew" it. I "saw" myself on the Westwood campus. It would happen. In my mind it already *had* happened.

The registration period was almost over, but I wasn't at all worried. It was weird.

One morning I opened the door and looked across the lobby to check for mail in the pigeonhole slots next to the manager's desk. There was something in the 102 slot. I threw on my old blue chenille robe and scooted across the lobby.

It was an envelope, and it had my name typed on it. My address, too. It was stamped but not postmarked. Whoever sent it had just walked into the lobby and stuck it in the slot. I opened it very carefully, and a fifty-dollar bill fell into my hand.

A whole fifty dollars. On one little bill. I'd never seen one before. I'll be darned, President Grant. I looked at the envelope again. No other name on it but mine. No return address. I looked *in* the envelope. Nothing else. Who could've done this? Nobody I could think of. We didn't know anybody that rich. It wasn't Uncle Jimmy, he would've just said, "Here, kid, take it." Besides, I hadn't told him anything about UCLA, and anybody else in the family (even if he or she *had* managed to save up that much) would've made a big deal out of it. Not a single one of them would keep it a secret.

But here it was. My ticket to UCLA.

It had come true.

And after all these years, I'm still wondering who sent it.

Thirteen thousand students. Thirteen thousand. Count 'em. Bigger than Hollywood High, Le Conte, Selma, Crockett—a hundred thousand times over. I was scared, but it was okay somehow. It was different this time.

I pored over the curriculum book. UCLA offered no major in journalism. A class. One class. That was it. Oh, God, and all this time I'd pictured myself "majoring in newspaper." It had never occurred to me that UCLA wouldn't have a *journalism major!* All right. Calm down. At least you made it here. Just think a minute. Look through the book again. No problem. Simply major in English and join the *Daily Bruin.* Solved.

Except . . .

I found myself flipping through the Ts. Th-Thea-Theater arts. Lord, am I crazy? What am I thinking about? They'd all laugh me right off the face of this earth, especially Mama. I could just hear her: "Are you nuts? Who do you think you are, Helen Hayes?"

Me? A TA major? Don't be silly.

I registered as an English major and began my freshman classes. Five days later I started looking through the book again.

Flip, flip. Lots of choices in the TA department menu: "Theater Arts —Film," "Theater Arts—Theater," "Theater Arts—*English.*" Whoa. "Theater Arts—*English*" offered courses in *writing.* No squawk from Mama there. And Nanny wouldn't know the difference or care. She was still mad I hadn't taken the fifty dollars, gone to Woodbury Secretarial School, learned to take shorthand, and snared the boss. No, it would be okay. It wasn't too late. I'd be only a few days behind, and I could still join the *Bruin* and take that one class in journalism. All that *and* playwriting courses! I would tell Mama all about it, and Mama would approve.

When I told her, she mumbled something about getting around to writing a screenplay herself someday, and then she turned over and went on with her nap. She didn't even hear the part about the *Daily Bruin,* so I didn't bother to join. Nanny just said, "You'd better get yourself a job unless you're planning to walk to school every day."

What I couldn't tell either one of them was that down deep I wanted to be an actress. Not a reporter. Not a playwright.

An actress. I'd never said it out loud, and I still didn't. I could hardly say it to myself.

I thought about all the times Ilomay and I played Betty Grable and June Haver, Sheena and Nyoka, Brenda Starr, Mary Marvel and when Cuz and I were Tarzan and Jane, Nelson and Jeanette. I remembered pretending to be a whole radio show and belting away out the window in 102 trying to fool the neighbors next door at the Mayfair, making Asher believe I was twins, the times I'd dance and sing around the room, leap-ing from the couch to the Murphy bed (when nobody was home, of course), twirling around and around, dreaming I was in somebody else's dancing shoes. Those were the times I felt alive—not when I drew pic-tures and not when I wrote stories and columns for the school paper. No, I came to life the times I wasn't me.

UCLA wasn't just a new school to me. It was a new country. And it was gigantic. I never saw so many people in one place in my life.

The lecture halls were packed, and the professors didn't care if you showed up for class or not. There were sprawling lawns all over the place, and the red-brick buildings were right out of *Good News.*

I followed a map of the campus and made my way to the small clump of buildings that housed the theater department. The buildings weren't pretty like the others. They looked like army barracks, with tin roofs. They were temporary until the department could get enough money for real classroom buildings and a permanent theater (according to the book). Their major productions were performed in Royce Hall, which was the main auditorium for the entire university. I looked around. It was lunchtime, and tons of people were sitting on the lawn, soaking up the sun, eating sandwiches, talking, reading. Most of the TA students wore Levi's and old shirts and smoked. When they spoke, they stuck their chins up in the air and closed their eyes. They looked as if they practiced being serious. I sat down near a group huddled under a tree and eavesdropped. They were speaking fluent Shakespeare.

Oh, God, what have I done?

Maybe this wasn't for me after all. I was positive not a single one of them had ever heard of Carmen Miranda.

Mama wrote a song about Tony:

> Now I can see
> That you're not good for me
> And my friends all agree
> You're not the right sort,
> For you're not the one
> To find your place in the sun.
> I've got to forget about you.
> And the things that you do

Aren't becoming to you
And on top of it, too,
You're breaking my heart.
Oh, you're not on the square
You never did treat me fair.
I've got to forget about you.
I know we haven't a chance
To have a fine romance,
For you're not the lover type at all.
Oh, you drive me insane,
I wish that you would explain
Why, oh, why did I fall?
Oh, I shouldn't give in
Because I know I can't win.
Loving you is a sin,
And after we're through,
And all's said and done,
And you have had all your fun,
I'll never forget about you.

Bill Burgess moved out.

Chrissy had started school. Good old Selma Avenue. She still lived with
Mama in their apartment down the hall, but she started spending just
about every waking moment with Nanny and me.

Mama could get mean when she drank and then forget all about it
. . . and it was happening more often. It scared Chris because Mama
couldn't remember what she had said when she was drunk once she'd
sobered up. I used to call her Mrs. Hyde to myself. Chris stopped bringing her little playmates around after school because she never knew how
Mama was going to be or what awful things she'd say to them. Sometimes she'd be swell and joke around, but when she'd had a lot to drink
that day, it was better for everybody all the way around when she just
passed out cold. She'd sleep it off on top of the covers, and all the shades
would be pulled down. Chrissy would come home from school, peek in,
and check out the territory. If the room was dark, she'd run down the
hall, straight for 102 and Nanny—relieved as all get out. I could tell what
Mama's condition was when I got in from school by the way Chrissy
would fling herself at me.

Mama was crazy about her. But she was losing her, the same way she lost me.

This time not only to Nanny but to me.

All the TA freshmen were invited to Royce Hall to hear a welcoming speech from Ralph Freud (pronounced Frood), who was the head of the theater arts department. It was the same talk he gave every semester. The place was packed. Good Lord, did they all feel the way I did? Professor Freud got up and talked about what was facing us, going after a career in show business. I liked him. He didn't sound as if he'd given this talk before at all. He was telling us what he knew, period. He wasn't trying to discourage anybody, but he wasn't dishing out a fairy tale either. He was a gruff old bird, and you could tell he loved what he was doing. One thing he said really stood out to me: "It doesn't matter what anybody else thinks about you; it's what *you* think." I just thought that was terrific. I'd never heard anybody say anything like that before. Not to me, anyway. He talked about how the cards are stacked against you, and how maybe, just maybe, *one* of us in the whole audience that day might be lucky enough to earn a living in this crazy business. "But *you* just might be that one." I liked that a lot. He gave one piece of practical advice: "Once you're out of school and you're pounding the pavements, looking for that big break, give yourself a five-year limit. If you aren't successful by then, and 'successful' in this case means *earning a living,* not being *famous,* then it's time to wise up and go on to something else. And during those five years, if you last that long, make sure you have enough money for food and a roof over your heads. For those of you with a rich daddy, it won't be a problem. For the rest of you, I advise you to get a part-time job, doing anything . . . *legitimate,* of course." Laughter from assembly. "Be a waiter or waitress or what-have-you, but don't walk into an audition looking hungry. It makes producers nervous."

He wished us all luck.

When I walked out of there, I knew I had made the right choice.

Because I had changed my major, I was late in signing up for the acting class: Acting 2A. Because I was late, I turned out to be the odd one in class. By the time I reported, the students had already paired off and were busy rehearsing scenes to be performed in front of the teacher and the class in a matter of two days. I had to get cracking. My teacher, Estelle Harman, gave me two choices for my "solo" run: two typed monologues on five-by-seven index cards. One was from *The Country Girl* (the wife) and the other was from *The Madwoman of Chaillot* (the maid). I picked the *Madwoman*. It was shorter. I memorized and crammed like crazy, and Friday came very fast. I felt nervous but okay. I knew my words.

Mrs. Harman asked for volunteers to start off the afternoon. I was amazed at how brave some of the kids were. Hands shot up right away, and two by two they walked the plank and strutted their stuff. All of them acted up a storm, and I thought they all were wonderful. I clapped and clapped.

It was my turn. I was the only one left. I didn't feel so okay anymore. The stage in the tiny classroom was about six inches high, and I tripped stepping up on it. I turned around and introduced my presentation as "This piece from *The Madwoman of Chaylut.*" I got it out, and I was word-perfect. My homework had paid off in that respect, and I had added a personal touch to the character of the little maid by making small circles in the air with a clenched fist, so it would look as if she were dusting something. I returned to my seat, with my heart in my ears, thankful to God it was all over. I don't recall any clapping.

But it wasn't all over. Now came the critiques of each and every scene. I couldn't believe it. Nobody's feelings were spared. Teacher and class tore into each scene like hungry wolves. Then Mrs. Harman got around to me. Oh, Lord.

"Miss Burnett, did you read the play?"

"No." It hadn't occurred to me to read the play. I just figured she wanted me to memorize the five-by-seven card.

"I didn't think so." Then she skinned me alive. She wound up giving me a D minus. She explained to the class, "I'm giving Miss Burnett a D minus, because she at least had this piece memorized. However, it was an F performance." She dismissed us with "Now . . . choose new partners for your next scenes." Everyone left but me. I felt as empty as the class-room. I could quit or stay. It was my choice.

I decided to stay.

I had nowhere to go but up.

I was teamed for the next scene work with a guy named Dick DeNeut. He wore glasses and had big teeth—like me. (We were destined to become good friends.) We were the only ones nobody chose, so we were stuck with each other. We decided to do part of Noel Coward's *Red*

Peppers, a one-act comedy about an English music hall couple. This time I read the whole thing. We rehearsed every chance we got and even staged a short musical number from the play, "Has Anybody Seen Our Ship, the HMS Peculiar?" The class laughed. Lord, it was a good feeling, being up there and enjoying myself. Mrs. Harman laughed and gave DeNeut and me an A. The only thing I had done that was different this time was read the play and pretend to be Betty Grable with a cockney accent. I figured I had the answer.

Next time out I lost it. It was a scene from William Saroyan's *Hello, Out There,* and I couldn't get up the nerve to go for the serious stuff. I was embarrassed even to try to let go and cry. I was scared they might laugh at me the wrong way. Who did I think I was, Helen Hayes? I got a C.

For the rest of the semester I chose comedies.

Mama began to enter contests: radio contests, newspaper contests, name-that-brand contests—all kinds. That's how she was going to make her killing. She was so smart that sooner or later it was bound to pay off.

She burst into 102 one afternoon with the exciting news that all our money worries would soon be history. She had just mailed in the winning entry to the "Name Trigger's Brand-New Son" contest, being held by Roy Rogers.

"Bullet! It's Bullet! Get it? Trigger's little boy, *Bullet!*" She was practically hugging herself. "It's inspired!"

I thought it was inspired.

Nanny thought it was okay.

"*Okay?*" Mama screamed. "Okay? It's perfect!" All she had to do was be patient, and it wouldn't be long before Roy and his assistants got around to opening her envelope and she'd be crowned the winner. Hands down. Pay dirt. The waiting began. She checked the mail for weeks. When the announcement was finally made, she took it as a personal insult from Roy.

"Stupid! It's the goddamnedest, dumbest name I ever heard. Any stupid son of a bitch could've come up with a crappy name like that! I thought of it right away, and I threw it in the garbage can. Too *corny!* I figured he'd never go for something that *obvious!* Never! It's fixed. The whole goddamn *world* is fixed! *Trigger, Junior!* Took an Einstein to think up that one. What do they take me for, a jerk? Christ."

She got madder when, much later, they had another contest (which she

The publicity photo Nanny said I got "gypped on"

The Rehearsal Club Revue (1955)—we made Theatre Arts *magazine*

Don and me after I "got the ring"

Chris and Nanny in Hollywood

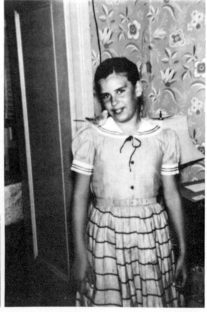

Chris and Tweetie, the alcoholic parakeet

The Paul Winchell Show, *1955*

Chrissy and me at her school in New Jersey, 1958,
after I'd kidnapped her

Dinah Shore Show (1958): *Shirley MacLaine, Pat Boone, Dinah, me, Bob Cummings (the week I moved Nanny out of 102)*

"*Princess Winnifred the Woebegone*" *from* Once Upon a Mattress

*Nanny in front of the Cherokee apartment building, around 1959,
after Mama died*

Nanny, me, Chris; New York, 1961

Pulling my ear with Nanny (1961)

"Princess of Monrovia" sketch (by Neil Simon) with Garry, around 1960

Last show with Garry, 1962

refused to enter) to name Roy's new dog, and the winning entry was Bullet.

Roy got his chance to make it up to Mama, and he did, but he never knew it.

Christine was around seven, and she had busted her leg, falling out of a swing at school. She'd been in a cast and on crutches for weeks. The holidays were coming, and Santa Claus Lane Parade on Hollywood Boulevard was a major event, not to be missed. It officially opened the Christmas season the night before Thanksgiving, and hundreds of movie stars rode on the floats and in convertibles and waved at the crowds. I loved it. Nanny and I had never missed one since we moved to Hollywood, and after Chrissy was born, she hadn't missed one either. The Santa and his reindeer float was always the grand finale, but it never did much for me. It was the stars I went to see. And they even waved at me.

I had always liked Roy Rogers, even though he did do dirt to Mama, and Chrissy idolized him. This year he was leading the parade . . . on Trigger. Bill and Mama were having a snort in the kitchen (poor Bill still hung around and brought booze and food, even though Mama had kicked him out) when Nanny said we'd better get going or we wouldn't be able to fight our way through the mob. Mama wasn't interested, but Bill, always eager to please, volunteered to carry Chrissy down the block to the boulevard so she wouldn't have to hobble on her crutches. Nanny grabbed a little stool from the kitchen and handed it to me. Bill gathered Chrissy in his arms while Mama poured herself another one and said, "Have fun."

As we walked down Wilcox, we could see that all four corners on the boulevard were beginning to fill up with parade watchers. Nanny picked up the pace and said to us, over her shoulder, "I *told* you!" We had to run to keep up with her. She never liked anyone getting ahead of her, anywhere. We got to the corner where the Warner Brothers Theater was, and she started pushing her way through a clump of people to get a better view. A man started to argue with her, and she said, "What's the matter with you? Can't you see we have a little girl here with a broken leg, who wants to see Santa Claus?" He shut up in a hurry when the crowd started to turn on him, and an aisle suddenly appeared. We wound up in a perfect spot, up against the ropes and not an obstacle in sight. Chrissy sat on the stool we'd brought, and Bill and I squatted down so we wouldn't be in anybody's way. Nanny craned her neck and stood on her toes, impatiently waiting for the parade to start. The crowd cheered when the switch was pulled and all the Christmas trees lining the boulevard lit up. It meant the parade was starting.

Everybody faced east.

It took a while for it to reach Wilcox. When it did, the people on our four corners started screaming and clapping. There was *Roy*! Leading the parade! On *Trigger*! Trigger was the most beautiful horse I had ever seen. Roy was beautiful, too. He rode tall in the saddle. He trotted past us and waved. Chrissy waved back at him.

Suddenly he held up his hand, and the entire parade came to a halt. He turned Trigger clear around and headed straight for our little group in front of the theater. I thought he was going to run over us. He stopped and got down off Trigger . . . and walked right up to Chrissy. Her eyes looked like Ping-Pong balls. Then Roy Rogers knelt before her and asked her how she broke her leg. I thought Nanny was going to faint. I thought *I* was going to pass out, too. Chrissy couldn't speak, and tears started to fill her eyes. He smiled and turned to Trigger and had him bow very low for her. Then Roy had him parade around in circles in front of the crowd —all for Chrissy. The next thing we knew, Roy took off his hat, put it under his arm, and bent down and kissed Chrissy on the cheek. Nanny squealed. He jumped back on Trigger, waved once more, and rode off into the night. Everyone went crazy.

I had never seen anyone as happy as Chrissy was at that moment. After that I never heard Mama say another bad word about Roy Rogers.

I tried out for every one of the "all-student-acted-written-produced-directed One-Acts" and finally got a small role as a hillbilly woman in something called *Keep Me a Woman Grown*. It was a twenty-five-minute comedy about a "mountain family," and it would run for three nights, along with two other original one-acts, in the same Quonset hut where Mrs. Harmon taught our acting class. I had two brief scenes.

I still didn't have the nerve to tell Mama *or* Nanny what I was up to, so I didn't ask them to come.

Opening night I was pretty nervous, but I got lots of laughs during the first scene I was in, using a kind of down-home Texas/Arkansas accent and walk, which was really an exaggerated combination of Nanny and Goggy. When I exited into the wings to wait for my next cue, I had the funniest feeling that the audience had come offstage with me, that they hadn't wanted me to leave, and I wasn't nervous anymore, just excited and feeling . . . wanted. I heard my cue, re-entered, and said the line that was written for my character, Effie, which was: "I'm back."

I couldn't get the next line out.

The audience started screaming, clapping, and stomping its feet.

At first I didn't know what hit me. I thought something had happened behind me, like maybe the scenery falling down, and I turned around and looked upstage. No, everything was the way it was supposed to be, but the audience kept it up. They wouldn't quit. Then it dawned on me. They were reacting to Effie. To me.

It began in my stomach: a feeling, a good feeling, a warm . . . something. What *was* it exactly? A glow? A light? Whatever "it" was, there were no words to describe the sensation. It quickly spread its way up to my heart and down to all ten toes, to my arms, my fingers, my head—all directions, all at the same time. I was a helium balloon, floating above the tiny stage. I was the audience, and the audience was me. I was . . . happy.

Happy. Happiness. That's what it was. Bliss.

I never wanted to lose it. And I knew then that for the rest of my life I would keep sticking my chin out no matter what, to see if I could *ever* feel that good again.

I got a rave in the *Daily Bruin*, and the next week dozens of TA majors were coming up to me on campus and congratulating me on my performance. Other student writers and directors were after me to audition for the next round of one-acts coming up. Several of the professors asked me to read for the upcoming major productions they would be directing. Some total strangers stopped me in the hall, and said they didn't remember the last time they'd had such a good belly laugh. I couldn't get over it. Nobody cared if I wasn't pretty, or smart, or rich. It didn't matter. *It didn't matter.*

At last.

That summer I landed a job at Warner Brothers Theater as an usherette. I was in hog's heaven: one block away from home, all the movies for free, and a whole sixty-five cents an hour. It would cover my lunch money and bus fare to school. And I had the whole summer to save up.

I'd clear about twenty-eight dollars a week for ten weeks. More than enough.

We wore outfits that were a combination of early Yvonne De Carlo and Buckingham Palace Guards. The pants were made of some shiny fake

satin material that ballooned out from the waist, fitting snugly around
the ankles. Mine were too big. I wound up tying the ankle part tighter
with shoelaces. The tops sported stiff gold braid and epaulets. My top
was too big on me. There was a hat, a Shriner-type hat. Mine was too
small.

Our manager was Mr. Claypool. He was a tall, thin gray-haired man
with a neatly trimmed little mustache. He was a spiffy dresser . . . and
a wolf. Anyhow, that's what the girls told me. He'd chase the pretty
usherettes around the balcony on slow nights.

He was also nuts.

He never gave us verbal orders. He gave us hand signals, his very own
personally made-up hand signals: "The Claypool Brand of Sign Language."

It wasn't that he couldn't talk; it was just more "efficient" this way.

He appointed me the "Spot Girl." This was the girl who stood in the
middle of the huge ornate lobby, bathed in an amber spotlight, announcing loudly to the customers as they entered the theater, *"Aisle two
straight ahead or the stairway to your right!"* He chose me because I was
the tallest and had the loudest voice.

When we reported to work every morning at eleven-thirty dressed in
our uniforms, he'd have us line up for inspection in front of the candy
counter. There were about six of us, at full attention: shoulders back,
chins up, stomachs in, eyes straight ahead. Claypool would review his
troops and then march clear across the lobby, do an about-face, and go
into his hand signal routine. He'd go from right to left, one by each and
every one of us. If he held up two fingers, it meant you were being
assigned aisle two, three fingers, aisle three, and so on. He'd make the
letter *C* with his thumb and index finger, meaning, "Go to the candy
counter." A tiny wave of all ten fingers meant, for some unknown reason,
"Report to the box office." Everyone was required to salute and march to
the designated areas, cutting square corners, where required. He usually
saved me for the last signal.

The Spot Girl position was indicated by his turning his *left* palm up,
facing the ceiling, and touching the middle of it with his *right* index
finger.

"Yes, sir!" I'd salute and march to my place in the amber spotlight. I'd
halt, turn, and look to him for further instructions. He was still a long
way off, about thirty feet, and he'd make a gun signal with his thumb and
index finger. It meant "shoot." (It reminded me of when Ilomay and I

used to play the Lone Ranger.) I'd wait for the second half, which would be a finger or two, telling me which aisle to "shoot" the customers to. If he wanted me to shoot them to the balcony instead of, or in addition to, an aisle, he'd turn his palm *down* this time and put his index finger *up* to touch the middle of his hand. Balcony. Yessirree. Got it. Salute. Face front. And stand there at attention for three hours at a time, shooting away. Perfect posture. Loud and clear.

It made for long days.

Every three hours he'd come up to me, slap his wrist, and hold up two fingers. Each one, in this case, meant five minutes—time for my ten-minute break. I'd salute, do my about-face, and march to the usherettes' locker room, cutting square corners all the way, because I knew he would be watching me like a hawk.

One time I was dying for a drink of water, and I got his attention as he was on his way to the office.

"M-Mr. Claypool?"

He looked at me.

"Mr. Claypool . . . could I p-please use the water fountain? I'm thirsty."

He came at me like a tank. *"Burnett!"* Lord. He's actually *talking.*

"Yes, sir?"

"Don't you ever do that again!"

"What should I *do?*"

He said, "You snap your fingers until you get my attention, and when you do, you open your mouth and point to the back of your throat!"

He was definitely certifiable.

A few weeks later I got fired.

It was Alfred Hitchcock's fault.

Strangers on a Train was playing, and I loved it. I absolutely loved it. Every chance I got, I sneaked in to watch a scene or two, even when I was on Spot duty. I was careful. I never got caught. I saw it so many times I had the dialogue down pat, plus an enormous crush on Robert Walker.

Late one weeknight, because it wasn't crowded, Claypool had signaled me to aisle two. I loved getting aisle duty because I could stand inside and catch my favorite bits in the movie. One of the best ones was the climax, where Walker and Farley Granger are in a fight to the death on a merry-go-round that's completely out of control. At this point a couple came in and asked to be seated. They had to be out of their minds. There were only ten minutes left, for God's sake. They could go to the bathroom, buy some popcorn, visit the water fountain—*anything!*—and by the time they got to their seats, the movie would be starting all over again from the top. I tried to explain it to them.

"We wanna sit down now."

"If you'll just wait a couple of minutes, it'll be over!"

"What for?"

"Well, it's the exciting ending. It would spoil the whole picture for you!" (You dumb jerks.)

She said, "My feet hurt."

He said, "You got a flashlight? We wanna sit down."

No jury would've convicted me. *"But it's Alfred Hitchcock!"*

The audience turned towards us and let out a loud "shush!" I ushered the offending couple up the aisle and out into the lobby, and while I was trying to explain the essence of Hitchcock suspense to them, Claypool came down the stairs from the balcony, straightening his tie and his hair.

"What's going on here?" Lord.

There was no explaining it. I was wrong, and the customer was right.

"You're fired, Burnett." He ripped off my epaulets. He actually ripped off my epaulets. I was drummed out of the corps.

A few years ago, the Hollywood Chamber of Commerce asked me where I would want my "star" put in the sidewalk on Hollywood Boulevard.

I said, "Right in front of where the old Warner Brothers Theater was, at Hollywood and Wilcox."

That's where it is.

Up yours, Claypool.

19

I couldn't wait to get back to school. The fall semester finally came.

I was having lunch with DeNeut on the lawn near the TA Quonset huts one day when a music major, Bill Beard, came up to us and asked me if I could carry a tune.

"Sure," I said. (Lord, if I couldn't, I'd have been beaned by Mama's uke long before this.)

"Would you be interested in trying out for the opera workshop class, in the music department? There's no credit, but it's great experience."

"Opera? Me?" I let out a Jeanette MacDonald squeak. DeNeut choked on his hard-boiled egg.

"Well, no, not exactly," said Bill Beard politely. "We're doing excerpts from Broadway musical comedies, and I'm directing one from *South Pacific,* and we're short a nurse."

The music department had nothing to do with the TA department. They treated each other as if neither one existed. I wasn't a music major, and this opera workshop/musical comedy thing he was talking about would cost me a lot of extra time for no credit.

That afternoon I found myself in the chorus of the "I'm Gonna Wash That Man Right Outa My Hair" scene.

Ellie Eby, who was a couple of years ahead of me, was doing Nellie Forbush. She was fantastic. She was beautiful, musical, and confident. I got so goosed by her enthusiasm I started belting like crazy when it was the chorus's turn and wound up drowning out everybody else. Bill pulled me out after the second rehearsal. I was too loud. I hadn't realized it. I'd just opened up my throat the way I always did when I used to do the Tarzan yell with Cuz or Ilomay and the gang. I apologized and swore to him I could tone it down, but he said no, that wouldn't be necessary. Before I could tearfully dash into the wings, he asked me if I'd do a scene with him from *Guys and Dolls.*

"*Guys and Dolls?* Me?"

"Yeah. I'm doing Nathan, and I've been looking for an Adelaide. You'll get to sing 'Adelaide's Lament.' You've got the perfect voice for it."

"Me? Alone? Sing?"

"Yeah. Why not?"

"My voice isn't pretty enough."

"Adelaide's voice isn't *supposed* to be pretty. She's singing about having a cold. She has a *cold* all the way through the show."

Ahhh . . . ha. In that case maybe I *could* do Adelaide.

Why not? Why couldn't I sing alone? As long as I was pretending to be somebody else and as long as I was making the audience laugh . . . on purpose.

Opening night I stood there on the stage and sang alone in front of an audience for the first time. I sang as loud as I could, just the way I used to out our window, the window I hid behind, when I pretended to be a radio show for the neighbors, way back when I was eight years old.

Only this time the people could actually *see* me, and there were lights, costumes . . . and a piano. There was actual musical accompaniment, and I wasn't hiding behind anything, except a comedy character who sniffled and sneezed all the way through the number.

And I was having a wonderful time.

The bliss hit me again, and this time the people laughed, clapped, and *stood up.*

I decided I would audition for the next batch of musical comedy scenes they were planning. I didn't care that the theater arts department and the music department weren't "compatible." I didn't care that I would get no credit, and I didn't care about the extra hours I'd have to put in.

Just tell me what to do, and point me in the right direction.

I lied, and told Nanny and Mama I was interested in choir. . . .

I walked into the music department tryouts, and *they* asked *me* to pick a scene. Any scene I wanted to do would be okay with them! They had loved the scene from *Guys and Dolls* and said they would be happy to have me be a part of every one of their productions if I wanted to. If I *wanted* to!

I felt like a star.

I picked a scene from Irving Berlin's *Call Me Madam,* an Ethel Merman hit, about a lady ambassador to a tiny country. One of the opera students, Lotfi Mansouri, was cast as the romantic European dignitary opposite the "hostess with the mostes'." He had a glorious voice and was also a wonderful director. The first half of the evening would be devoted to opera scenes, and the second half to the musical comedy portion.

It was time to let Nanny and Mama in on my life and finally admit the truth to them about my dream even if they thought I *was* nuts. I invited them to come to the opening performance.

We could hear the audience coming in. Ten minutes to go. I peeked through the curtain, trying to spot Nanny, Mama, and Chris. They weren't there, and there weren't too many empty seats left in the small auditorium. Had they missed the bus connection? Had Nanny had a spell? Had Mama tied one on tonight and not gotten out of bed? Or were they just a little late? There would be no way for them to get in touch with me, and it was too late for me to get to a phone, the nearest one on campus was a block away. I was nervous as hell. I wanted to be so good tonight. I wanted to prove myself to Mama and Nanny. I wanted them to be proud of me and say, "How about that? I never knew you had it in you! You were terrific!" I wanted them to hug me and tell me they believed in me. After five minutes had passed, I just wanted them to show up. Okay, Carol, calm down. You don't go on until the second half. They'll be here, they'll make it—but what if they do and Mama's *tight*? Oh, God, and I'd have to introduce her to my friends after the show. Oh, God. Maybe it's just as well they don't come. Forget it . . . better off . . . you'll be better off.

I peeked out again. There was Nanny, and I could see Chrissy behind her. Nanny was standing next to the end of a row, telling the people to move over so she could have an aisle seat. I knew she was warning every one of them about her claustrophobia spells. The whole row got up and moved over, leaving two aisle seats free. She and Chrissy promptly settled in. I figured Mama was simply out of it. The houselights were just dimming down when I saw the auditorium door open in the back and spotted somebody in a familiar old three-quarter-length red coat, standing there, looking around for a place to sit. It was Mama. She had probably just finished a cigarette outside. She headed down the aisle. I could barely make her out, but she seemed to be walking pretty straight, and she found an empty seat in the middle of a row toward the back. The houselights went completely out, and the piano overture began.

I realized I was a wreck.

"Oh, Sissy! You were the best one!" I swept Chrissy up in my arms, to kiss her, and had to put her down right away. She was seven but built like a ten-year-old. Nanny was busy introducing herself to everybody as my grandmother, and Dr. Jan Popper, head of the music department, was saying awfully nice things about me . . . to Mama.

All the performers and their friends and families had gathered in the audience immediately after the show. People were hugging and kissing and congratulating each other on another successful opera/musical comedy evening.

The *Call Me Madam* scene with Lotfi had brought the house down. And my *family* had been there. It had taken me awhile to get through the crowd to them. Nanny was beaming and blowing her nose. I hugged and kissed her. Chrissy was jumping up and down. I felt a tap on my shoulder, turned around, and looked down at Mama. I was surprised I had forgotten how short she was. I was wearing high heels, and I towered over her five feet two inches. (Funny, we so seldom stood up together at the same time anymore.) She had tears in the corners of her eyes, and then she *winked* at me. I hugged her. She had pulled herself together that night and looked better than she had in ages. She had come through for me, even if it was for only one night. I was so happy it scared me. She squeezed me back and whispered in my ear, "You really *were* the best one."

Why couldn't it always be like this?

At the end of my first year I won the theater arts department award as the "Most Outstanding Newcomer."

I brought the award home and showed it to Nanny and Mama. They thought it was nice.

20

A bunch of UCLA TA (mostly graduate) students formed their own summer stock group in 1952. They had found the ideal spot about fifty miles north of San Francisco, in the recreation hall in the Armstrong Woods State Park. They were calling themselves the Stumptown Players. They were the cream of the theater arts department and were actually going to *work* at their craft for the whole summer. They were the best actors, writers, composers, designers, producers, and directors the department had turned out, and all of us lowly undergraduates idolized them.

That summer I was working as a cashier in the box office of the Iris Theater, a second-run movie house, catty-cornered from Warner's (and the lovely Mr. Claypool), on Hollywood and Wilcox. I was saving every penny of the seventy-five cents an hour I got and putting it in a savings account for the next semester. For a while there I thought I might have to blow it all on an ear doctor. The manager of the good old Iris got a brainstorm and put the entire sound track of the movies we were showing directly over my head, smack-dab on top of the box office itself, figuring that the sound of the actual movie going on *inside*, blasting away at the sidewalk pedestrians *outside*, was a foolproof way of luring them into the theater. (Were all Hollywood Boulevard theater managers cracked?) This bullhorn effect didn't work. In fact, prospective customers made it a point to stampede across the street in droves, but our manager was undaunted. By the end of two weeks I knew all of *Ivanhoe* by heart. George Sanders, by far, had the best dialogue.

I thought I would really lose my hearing when we started playing the British movie *Breaking the Sound Barrier*. I dreaded . . . hated the scene where the pilot in his trusty airplane was going full force ahead, screaming time after time after time, *"We're buffeting!"* And all hell breaks loose. Our manager spared no decibels, and the sound reverberated so loud I thought the box office I was sitting in was going to cave in every time that scene rolled around.

The first time I heard it, I almost hit the deck. "Rattattattattt . . . boom-boom-boom . . ." Diving engines. Pulling out. "Screeeeech! Bang.

Crash." Actor screaming, *"We're buffeting!"* Then came "rattle . . . rattle . . ." and more "rattattattattttttt. . . ." The Iris was being attacked, no doubt about it. Either that or it was a box office-focused earthquake. And throughout it all I was supposed to sell tickets, make the correct change, answer the phone, and smile.

I had a thumper of a headache and was already tensed up and wincing at the thought of the *third* go-round of the dreaded buffeting scene late that same Saturday afternoon, when the call came.

"Good afternoon, Iris Theater." I knew I'd have to start yelling soon because I could hear the pilot revving up. It occurred to me I might be developing a tic.

"Carol?"

"Nanny?"

"I can hardly hear you. What's that awful noise?"

"They're getting ready to break the sound barrier."

"Oh."

"Why're you calling? You feeling okay?"

"My heart's been skipping beats. Somebody's trying to reach you from San Francisco or someplace. You know anybody up there?"

"No."

"What?"

The British were at full throttle.

It was time for me to speak up. "NO! I DON'T KNOW ANYBODY FROM SAN FRANCISCO! DID THEY SAY ANYTHING ELSE?"

"JUST SOMETHING ABOUT A PUP TENT PLAYER OR SOME DARN THING. . . . I COULDN'T MAKE HEAD OR TAIL OF IT. THEY WANT YOU TO CALL THEM. I TOLD THEM THEY'D JUST DARN WELL HAVE TO CALL YOU BACK. . . . WE DON'T CALL ANYBODY LONG DISTANCE. . . . LOT OF NERVE, IF YOU ASK ME. . . . WHO ARE THEY ANYWAY?"

My mind spinned. "Pup tent . . . pup tent . . . San Francisco? Pup tent player?"

Ohmygod.

The Stumptown Players! They're calling *me*!

"NANNY! LISTEN TO ME! GIVE THEM THIS NUMBER IF THEY CALL BACK, OKAY? OKAY?"

"WELL, WHO ARE THEY?"

"NANNY, PLEASE . . . JUST HANG UP. THEY MIGHT BE TRYING TO CALL BACK!"

"ALL RIGHT. ALL RIGHT! GOOD LORD, THIS CONNECTION'S AWFUL!"

She hung up. What in the world would the Stumptown Players want with me? I stared at the phone. C'mon, *ring*!

A couple of calls came in, wanting to know what time the prices go up. I resisted the urge to tell them they'd better bring earplugs. I talked as fast as I could, so the line would be free. I stared at the phone some more. Please let them call. Please. Please. It rang. "Good afternoon, Iris Theater."

"Is Carol Burnett there please?"

"This is her . . . *she*!"

"Carol, this is John Holden. I'm with the Stumptown Players"—as if I didn't know—"and we were wondering if . . ."

They wanted me to join them up north.

I couldn't believe it. All these glorious graduate gods wanted *me* to become a Stumptown Player. They were already halfway through their season and were planning to do a musical revue and a melodrama, and they'd love it if I could be with them for the rest of the summer. *They'd* love it!

When? How soon? Soon as possible. Someone would meet my bus in San Francisco, and we'd drive the rest of the way up to Guerneville in the Russian River area.

I wasn't working the evening shift that night. As soon as the six o'clock cashier reported, I totaled up the day's take, made sure my money tallied with the tickets sold, signed my report sheet, changed, flew up the block to Yucca, and was home in two minutes flat.

It took some talking, but Nanny reached under her mattress, unpinned her sock, and gave me the bus money to San Francisco. My box-office earnings would remain in the bank until school started again, in about five weeks. The Stumptown Players would provide room and board. I threw some things in our old suitcase and was on the bus for San Francisco the next day.

I never did see *Breaking the Sound Barrier*.

The bus took hours to get to San Francisco, but I didn't care. I didn't even get a little sick. It was the most beautiful ride, on the most beautiful day, in the most beautiful bus in the world. I was a Stumptown Player. I remember staring at the Pacific Ocean out the window as the bus bumped along up the highway, headed north. I hadn't been outside Los Angeles since Nanny and I came to Hollywood twelve years ago . . . except for the Vegas trips with Mama . . . but they didn't count, because this time I was alone . . . on my own.

Nanny was a wreck. I promised her I would write every single day and be very careful. I didn't know what I had to be careful of, but I promised. I told her I'd know the truth for her all the time and begged her not to worry about me. Christine wanted to come with me and started crying. I hugged her and kidded her, saying I'd bring her a redwood tree. Mama kissed me good-bye and said, "If you can swing it, bring me San Francisco."

I would be away five whole weeks. A lifetime.

Nanny had given me an extra five dollars for spending money.

I was on my way.

I worked my tail off. We made our own costumes, built our own scenery, lit the shows, struck the shows, and were in the shows. We designed and painted the billboards for advertising, distributed leaflets, and sold tickets. We never got enough sleep, but who cared? I learned to like coffee.

We all lived together in a big old house about four miles from the recreation hall, our theater. The girls slept upstairs in bunk beds (I was in an upper), and the boys slept downstairs in bunk beds. We shared our meals together and were assigned kitchen duty. It was a whole new experience: one big family, one big *happy* family. *Babes in Arms.* That's exactly what it was. It was five weeks of laughter, music, and hard work. I was the "baby," and all these extraordinary people were my big brothers and sisters.

The Stumptown Players was as dedicated to the theater as you could get, and not even Broadway could have been more professional in its attitude. We did well-known plays and original musical revues. The shows were mounted beautifully, and critics and real people came from as far away as San Francisco to see us, applaud us, and compare us favorably with little theater in the Bay Area. I was amazed at how each audience reacted differently to the same material. Some nights I'd lose a laugh and go crazy trying to figure out how to get it back the next performance. Usually I'd lost it because I'd pushed too hard to get a bigger laugh and had wound up turning the audience off. Then there would be the sheer joy of finding one where I'd never expected it.

There were unexpected emergencies, like the night something went wrong with the backstage lights and I had to find my costume and try to get dressed in the pitch-black dressing room. My number was next, a torch song called "Thank You, but I've Got a Dime." I frantically fumbled around in the dark trying to feel for my fishnet stockings, ankle-strap high heels, fake satin top, slit skirt, and beret. Somehow I managed to get them all on in about thirty seconds flat, grope my way to the stage, and lean up against the prop lamppost, far stage right, just in time for the spot to pick me up. Thank you, God. The light hit me in the face, and the piano started its bluesy introduction. This was one of the rare times I was given a serious song to do, and I was determined to give it my all. I belted out the first line without moving and then slowly and sadly began to take my time singing and slinking my way clear across the stage to the other end of the proscenium. I was really into it, feeling it, kind of the way Mama must have felt whenever she launched into "True Blue Lou." I even felt sexy. I had never felt sexy before. I liked it. I poured my soul into this mournful solemn tale of the down-on-her-luck, down-and-out gal with a heart of gold, who was singin' the blues about being down . . . down . . . down . . . I looked down, and the seams of the fishnet stockings I had pulled on in the dark were running up the fronts of my legs. I turned my back to the audience, which had begun to laugh, and finished singing the number over my shoulder. I haven't liked singing seriously since.

Every day I rode the company bike into town, picked up the mail, and sent a letter to Nanny. There was always a letter or two from her. I didn't have to open them to know what was in them. They all were the same: cheerless.

I loved being away. And I felt bad about that . . . because I *didn't* feel bad.

The Russian River and the giant redwoods made me feel like crying at times. It was the most beautiful spot I'd ever seen in my whole life. I was nineteen, and the largest stretch of dirt I had been around until now was the vacant lot where we had played Jungle Girl and had flown our kites. My feet were used to concrete.

After the second week I was asked to join the players permanently and come back full-time the following summer. They all had voted, and it was unanimous.

I had won the Oscar.

I fell in love.

He didn't make me feel threatened the way Mark had, and he didn't ignore me as my childhood crushes had. No misery. Ohmygod, no misery. I felt good about me. He gave me confidence. He'd tell me I could do anything and be anything I wanted. He believed in me, and because he did, I did. He was attentive, caring, and loving. He was handsome, talented, and smart. We all would go out to Skippy's, the local hangout after the shows, and he and I would always wind up together talking half the night, having wonderful conversations. Then we'd go home, and he would kiss me good night, tenderly, and I'd float up the stairs, eager to face the sweet dreams that always came when I fell asleep in my upper bunk. It was like June Allyson and Van Johnson in an MGM Technicolor love story that takes place in an exciting backstage show business setting: young, exciting, glamorous, and picture-perfect. It was a delicious and pure relationship.

But I began to want more. No more pure. For the first time I was willing to risk finding out for myself just what happens *after* the kiss and the fade-out. I wanted to know what "it" was like. Nanny and Mama had to be wrong. Loving somebody could be beautiful. It didn't always have to turn out rotten.

I gave him every chance, every opportunity. But our involvement didn't progress one bit. It stayed the same. Just like a movie . . . with the same reel playing over and over and over. He was still attentive, caring, and loving. And nothing more. I knew he cared. What was wrong? I thought I was going to burst.

One of my roommates took me aside and told me about homosexuals. I honest to God didn't know what she was talking about.

"You've got to be kidding," she said. "Where've you been living, in a convent?"

Hardly.

I flashed back on Mama talking about "that old queer" Mr. Byrd, who had lived in our building for years on the third floor with his poodle. She and Nanny would go on and on about him, but I didn't pay them any attention. In fact, I kind of liked him.

But what did that have to do with this?

Nothing. Everything.

What the hell was the matter with me anyway? Why couldn't I see it? *Why didn't I know things?*

Why did I have to hear it like this and be so hurt and embarrassed?

Embarrassed. Conned. Rejected.

I was so very angry and . . . god*dam*mit! It's not just about boys liking boys. It's all of it, and I'm in the dark about it all. Yes, I knew where babies came from, and yes, I knew how they got there. But what about what counts? How are you supposed to *feel*? How are you supposed to *act*? How are you supposed to *be*?

Why didn't I have somebody I could ask who would give me straight answers?

Nanny? Mama? Erpy Classroom Films? Daddy? Could I have turned to him? And where *was* Daddy? Nanny wrote me he was in some sanitarium with TB. Well, goddamn him, too, goddamn them all.

Nineteen years old, and my roommate was right. I *did* act as if I'd been raised in a convent.

But why?

I cried my eyes out and reached the conclusion that the only thing that was reliable in this whole wide world was the stage, and it would be my life.

Why didn't I know things?

Maybe I did. Maybe I knew a lot more than I thought. A lot more than I was willing to admit to myself. Was I really that *simple*? Or was that the image I chose for myself? And why would I choose such an image?

Just who was I trying to kid?

Me.

I didn't want to know about things. I didn't want to know about feelings.

All those times when Mama and Nanny would be spilling their guts out to each other about anything and everything right in front of me, I'd be aware of it all for *just so long*, and then I'd find my mind someplace else, someplace . . . nice.

I used to think they excluded me from the more sordid details, that they censored themselves when I was around. But they didn't. No. They never did. Not that they ever sat me down and explained anything *to* me. It never made a damn bit of difference to them, one way or the other, whether I was in the room or not. But I heard everything.

Everything. And nothing.

They made it all sound so awfully sad.

So I ignored what I wanted to ignore. Period.

And hell, life was nicer when you pulled your shade down. Period.

* * *

Chrissy threw her arms around me.

"Sissy, I thought you were never coming back!"

It had been a full five weeks for me all right, and I had mixed feelings about Stumptown's being over and being back home. It all had gone so fast.

Nanny said she didn't like my being away for such a long time and wanted to know why I hadn't written her more. I saw the mile-high stack of letters I had mailed to her (one a day, five weeks . . . let's see, five times seven . . .) piled on top of the table next to Murphy. I apologized and said I'd do better next time.

She looked stricken. *"Next* time?" I explained I'd been asked back next summer and I wanted to go. "Why'd they ask you back?"

"Nanny, they like me."

"Well, I happen to *love* you, so why can't you stay home?"

Chrissy piped up. "Can't I go next time? Please?"

I started to open the door. "I'm going down the hall to say hi to Mama."

"She's not home." Nanny sniffed. "She's at work."

I wasn't sure I heard right.

Chris picked up the phone. "Mama knows how to work a switchboard! Let's call her."

Nanny said Mama was answering the phone at *Variety* for no money, but it was better than nothing. Bill Burgess still helped out a little, and Daddy couldn't even send us a dollar now that he was holed up in that godforsaken hospital somewhere with TB.

We called Mama. *"Variety."*

"Mama?"

"Carol? You home?"

"I got in a little bit ago. I've been up since the crack of dawn, so we could get the first bus out of San Francisco. When did you start work?"

"Yesterday. I get through in an hour. It just takes a few minutes to walk home. I'd better get off now. Glad you're back safely, honey." She hung up.

She didn't look too good when she got home, but it was the first time I'd seen her dressed in I didn't know how long. She poured herself a shot and relaxed a little.

21

I was restless. I had gained some confidence and a lot of training at Stumptown, and I couldn't wait to put it to use at school.

The new semester was under way, and I got a job for the weekends, selling purses and hose at a cut-rate shoe store on Hollywood Boulevard. It was no money, but as Nanny said, it was better than nothing. At least it took care of my carfare. And if I was clever, I could make an extra quarter for every "loser" handbag I could push on an unsuspecting customer. The women knew better, so the men were the pigeons to be on the lookout for.

They would wander in, looking helpless.

"May I help you, sir?"

"I'm looking for something for my wife . . . I don't really know . . ."

"May I suggest one of our lovely handbags?"

"Well, I think she already has one."

"A lady can't have too many Wait! I know *just* the one. You're in luck. It's the very last one we have, and it's on sale!" I'd reach down under the counter, grab one of the fake leather purses that had been on the shelves for decades, blow the dust off, wipe it with my sleeve, and jump up, presenting it as if it were the crown jewels. God, it was ugly.

But two bits was two bits.

I plunged right back in at school, trying out for every show that was holding auditions. I wasn't cast in any of the theater arts "major" productions, but I was courted royally for the one-acts and the music department's opera/musical comedy scenes for the new semester. Being a Stumptown Player had given me luster.

I was asked to be in the UCLA homecoming show to be held in Royce Hall. Like the annual varsity show, it had nothing whatsoever to do with the theater department. It was strictly a university bash done once a year for fun.

I wound up doing a sketch with the campus comedian, Lenny Weinrib, plus a Broadway show tune from *Hazel Flagg*.

The sketch was based on the Charles Addams characters in his *New Yorker* cartoons. I wore the long black gown and wig to match. My face was dead white, with a deep red slash of lipstick. Lenny was the hunchback, Igor. The premise was that I was running for UCLA homecoming queen, and Igor was my helpmate. It was the first time I had set foot on the Royce Hall stage and played to such a huge audience. Lenny and I were a perfect team. The laughs rolled in, in huge waves. I felt wonderful again.

An audience could make you forget everything.

A very nice-looking young man introduced himself to me on campus the next day and told me he thought I was going to be a star. His name was Don Saroyan, and he was a new student. He was five years older than I was and had enrolled in the TA department after getting out of the service.

We started dating.

He came over to the apartment a lot and made it a point to get to know Nanny, Mama, and Chrissy. It was the first time I didn't feel embarrassed about Nanny's messiness because he didn't seem to notice it. Mama thought he was cute, and Chrissy adored him. Nanny liked him okay, but I could tell she was worried that this might get serious. Don was as poor as we were.

He had been married when he was very young and was divorced. We talked about our dreams of Broadway. Don was an actor/singer/director. He could do it all, and he was going to do it all. He had a beautiful voice, he was a good actor, and I had no doubt in my mind he would make a wonderful director.

We teamed up with another guy in school, roping various piano players in when they could help us out, and put together a singing/musical comedy act that we performed at various charity luncheons around town.

We'd open with "Another Opening, Another Show," from *Kiss Me Kate,* then swing into a minipresentation of *Guys and Dolls.* I'd do "Adelaide's Lament." Don would follow with "Luck Be a Lady." Al and I would do "Sue Me," and we'd close singing at the tops of our lungs "The Guy's Only Doin' It For Some Doll, Some Doll, Some Doll." (Slow to half tempo and begin to raise arms high in air.) "The . . . Guy's . . . Only Doin' It . . . For . . . Some . . . Dollll!" (Deep bow, run off, come back for another bow, quick, before they could stop clapping.) After a while we worked up stuff from *Oklahoma!, New Faces of 1952,* and *Annie Get Your Gun.* We didn't always get paid, so we worked a lot.

We were big at benefits that couldn't afford "names." I remember getting my first professional check. Five dollars. My God, I thought, I would've paid *them*!

That year, I doubled and tripled so much in school productions, the extra club dates Don, Al, and I had, plus the Saturdays in the shoe store pushing plastic purses, I wound up having to drop some courses. Classes just got in my way, but I had to maintain a minimum amount of credits, or I'd get kicked out of school. I didn't want that, because I wasn't ready to go professional, and there wasn't another place I could think of where I had so many opportunities to work at my "craft." Stumptown was coming up again, and I was eager for a whole summer of plays and musicals without worrying about homework or term papers in history and philosophy, which, as far as I was concerned, were a big fat waste of time.

Cuz transferred from USC and became a UCLA theater arts major. She was more beautiful than ever, and with her acting ability, all the directors wanted her for their major productions. She won the Best Actress award her first year and became a Tri-Delt. She attended only three meetings. I pushed her into running for homecoming queen, and she made the finals. She would've won, but she cut all her hair off. Talent scouts from the studios called her, made appointments, but she never showed up. She lied to Aunt Dodo and told her the scouts didn't seem interested. Cuz didn't want any part of it.

Cuz hadn't changed, but I had.

It dawned on me—I didn't wish I was my cousin anymore. She was Janice, and I was Carol.

And it was okay.

Mama was still maintaining (barely) her switchboard post at *Variety*. She even got a kick out of it sometimes because she'd get to transfer calls coming in from movie stars to columnist Army Archerd ("He's swell . . . treats me like he does everyone else"). But I could tell it was getting to be too much for her to get up and out every day. Not that I saw that much of her. Or Nanny or Chrissy, for that matter. I'd get home just in time to conk out on the couch and be up and out before Nanny started her morning spitting routine.

I'd hightail it out of there as fast as I could. I had things to do. Even when I was home, her complaints had long since begun going in one ear and out the other. I believed Mama: "She'll bury us all." I felt guilty about Chrissy, though. She didn't have me to lean on so much anymore.

I had saved enough to spring for my bus ticket to Stumptown and have a little extra for the ten weeks I'd be gone. I was packing to go when we heard Daddy had been let out of the sanitarium and was living in Venice Beach somewhere.

Christ. It wasn't right. (Daddy, why do you have to be like that? I hate it. I hate it. I hate . . .)

Okay, okay, eyes straight ahead, keep on the track, you're on your way. Don't turn around. Haul out the blinders, pull down the shade, and you'll be all right.

The Stumptown summer of '53 was even better. Twice as good, because I was there twice as long and had twice as much to do.

I missed Don, though. He was working in L.A., trying to save some money for New York.

New York. We had talked about it all the time. Where else could I become the new Ethel/Mary and he could be the new John Raitt/George Abbott?

Broadway.

I was back and ready to tackle the new fall semester. I knew it would be my last year at UCLA. I wasn't going the whole four years. I was going to New York. I didn't know how, but I was going.

"They raised the rent, your mother quit her job, and Bill Burgess lost his."

Welcome home.

The shoe store had gone out of business, so I went back to the Iris, working weekends in the box office. At least it was quiet. I figured a sniper had done in the sidewalk sound track.

Even though I went out with other boys, I found myself wanting to be around Don more and more. Don wasn't a boy. He was a man. He made me feel protected. We had the same goal, the same dream, and he didn't want me to turn away from what I was "born to do," for anything or anybody. I didn't think it was possible, but I felt even more ambitious around him. I followed his sound advice when I was working on a song or a scene. He encouraged me and made me believe the sky was the limit.

We were as close as we could be without "going all the way." There certainly were times when I wanted to, but either I stopped it or Don did. (We had too many plans to let ourselves get waylaid by trouble.)

No.

I would wait until I got married.

If I married Don, it would be in New York.

And if we got married in New York, it would be when we were successful.

That's the way it should be. Nice.

Mama bought a parakeet for Chrissy, and it wasn't long before the bird turned into a drunk. He became notorious in the neighborhood. Mama would have her cronies in for an evening, and Tweetie would perform. He didn't disappoint anybody either. He loved to show off. Mama, Dixie, and Lucille would be at the kitchen table, having a drink or two, and Mama would haul him out of his cage and put him to work. She'd stick a shot glass filled with water under his beak; he'd take a sip and spit it out. Then she'd put a drop of whiskey in it, and he'd go to town and wind up asking for "more." They'd all howl at that. He could say, "Christine," and "Where the hell have *you* been?" Then he'd look in his little mirror and say, "Pretty bastard." Tweetie tickled the hell out of Mama. "That's the cutest damn bird in the world."

The only thing she didn't like about him was his name. Chrissy named him because he was supposed to be her parakeet.

"Mama, please, I wanna call him Tweetie. *Please.*"

"Are you nuts? Every goddamn bird in the world is named Tweetie." She made a face. "Don't you want to be original? What's the matter with you? I thought I raised smart kids. We'll call him 'Stash.'"

"No! I want Tweetie! Please, Mama!"

"Tweetie makes me wanna puke. I hate that cutesy crap. Baby, you don't want a Tweetie, for godsakes."

Chrissy was holding her own. "Yes, I do! He's mine. You said he was mine. You gave him to me! Why can't I name him? He belongs to *me!*" She started to cry.

Mama gave up. It was one of the few times Chrissy won a round with Mama.

I was happy for Chris, but secretly I liked Stash better.

Over the next few months he got a reputation as a "sex fiend," too (Nanny's description). He'd had four or five mates, and they all had dropped dead for some reason after just a few days. I'd hear them say Tweetie had "screwed them all to death," and they'd howl some more.

Tweetie loved his booze and women.

He never really was Chrissy's parakeet. He was Mama's. When she'd be asleep on top of the covers, he'd be asleep on top of her. Perched on her belly button, he'd be passed out right along with her, his little body rising and falling and rising and falling with her heavy breathing.

22

The $7.50 I was pulling in weekends at the Iris wasn't cutting it. I had to get a full-time part-time job if I wanted to stay in school. Nanny's sock couldn't cough up any more carfare and lunch money.

I got one in downtown L.A. at a place called Radio Reports, for ninety cents an hour. I worked five mornings a week monitoring and typing the "essence" of various radio shows for some sort of tabulating firm, which peddled the information to various advertisers interested in knowing where and when their products might have been mentioned on the airwaves. I had to get up every morning at 5:45, catch the 6:30 A.M. streetcar to downtown L.A., work from 7:30 A.M. until noon, catch the streetcar back to Hollywood and Beverly Hills, and transfer to the Westwood bus, making it just in time for my first afternoon class at 2:00 P.M. Classes lasted till 6:00 P.M., and then I had my extra TA department work: building scenery, doing sound for the one-acts, and grabbing a sandwich when I could. Then I'd report for the opera workshop/musical comedy rehearsals. Don and I were working on a scene from *Annie Get Your Gun*. I'd usually get sprung around 10:00 or 11:00 at night and then run to catch the bus and try to make the streetcar connection, so I could be home by midnight and, with any luck, asleep by 1:00 A.M. It didn't take a math genius to figure out that I was in the same kind of trouble I was in before. I was spending almost as much money as I was making, in transportation alone. And it didn't take a doctor to tell me I was about to keel over from exhaustion.

I needed a job on campus.

There wasn't any. "Everybody and his sister wants a job on campus. Are you crazy? Y'gotta know somebody, honey. It's all politics."

Nanny said I'd just have to quit school.

Not now. I couldn't quit now. It wasn't time.

I didn't know what I was going to do.

UCLA was getting ready to go into rehearsals for the annual varsity show. This year it was an original book musical called *Love Thy Coach*. I was asked to play the lead, Christy Addams, the female coach of a foot-

ball team comprised of eleven misfits who score touchdown after touchdown because of their love for the coach.

Some of my professors tried to talk me out of accepting the role because *Love Thy Coach* wasn't a theater arts department production and I
had already done the homecoming show the year before. The department
looked down (even frowned) on such collegiate frivolity. All serious theater majors were actively discouraged from taking any part in them. It
simply wasn't "artistic."

Well, tough.

I had my reasons for wanting to do it. First, I'd be playing the lead and
would get to sing with a whole orchestra. Second, I didn't feel I was
being disloyal to the theater arts department since I had never been given
a leading role in a major production because the professors usually chose
the more serious stuff to do in Royce Hall. Besides, the music department
(which wasn't even my major) had given me more encouragement, so I
didn't think the TA department had any right to put me down if I went
for experience someplace else. Third, if I played my cards right, it just
might pave the way for me to land an office job on campus. I had heard
through the grapevine that the varsity show people really wanted me to
do the show in the worst way.

Politics. Blackmail. But by any name, it was a gamble.

I told the producers I'd be happy to be in the show *if* they'd swing a
campus job for me ("Y'gotta know somebody, honey. It's all politics"). I
was taking a chance that they might just tell me to take a walk.

I held my breath. They came through, pulled the right strings, and I
had a job in the administration office within minutes. It didn't pay much,
but I could break even and get more sleep. Blackmail. Pure and simple.

So much for "artistic."

Love Thy Coach rehearsals were in full swing, and I was about to turn
twenty-one. I didn't feel that old. I had always thought girls who were
twenty-one were *women.* I felt eleven. But it was okay. I knew I had a lot
of lost time to make up for, and I'd take care of that before long.

I had it all worked out. I'd set a schedule for myself. Finish out this
year, get to New York some way, make my Broadway debut, marry Don,
and make enough money not to care about how much money I was
making. That way I could take care of everybody I loved and have
enough left over to give to needy people and never tell them who did it.

Don threw a surprise birthday party for me. It was in a small banquet

room in a restaurant, and a whole bunch of my UCLA buddies had
pitched in and were there from the TA and music departments. So were
Nanny and Chrissy.

They all yelled, *"Surprise!"*

And I looked at Don and said things like "Why, you . . . How? I had
no idea . . . How in the world did you ever pull this? I thought we were
just going out for a hamburger! . . . Chrissy, Nanny . . . and you
didn't make a peep! Boy, can you guys ever keep a secret! My Lord . . .
I had no . . ."

Everyone was laughing and asking me if I really was surprised, if I
really had *no* idea, and on and on. I turned and looked around some
more at all the smiling faces and stopped dead in my tracks. Over in the
corner, sitting on a chair, was Daddy.

I ran over to him, and he stood up and hugged me.

"Happy birthday, Punkin."

"Daddy, how did . . . ?" I started to cry.

"Well, that fella of yours tracked me down. He's awfully nice. I think
your Nanny helped some. I'm glad to see you, and I'm real glad to be
here. Looks like you have some pretty swell friends." He was sober, but
he didn't look too hot. He was pale. He had on an old suit I remembered,
but it looked too big on him now. "How's your mother? She coming?"

It dawned on me she wasn't there.

"She's fine. I guess she's a little under the weather tonight."

Daddy smiled. "Well, I know how that is. Give her my love, will you,
Punk?"

"Sure. How're you feeling?"

"Well, I was in Olive View for a while there, and it looks like I might
have to go back just for a little bit. Can't seem to shake this old bug, but I
will. Now, why don't you go enjoy your party? I'll be fine. Don't worry,
I'll sit right here and have a good time watching all of you."

"Can I get you something?"

"I'd love a Coke if they've got one."

Don hadn't asked Mama. He didn't ask Mama because he thought it
would be awkward for her and Daddy if they were both there. He knew I
saw Mama every day. He felt he was doing the right thing for all of us.

I got home that night, and Mama was up. She was crying. "My kid is
twenty-one, and I'm not even asked to watch her blow out the candles.
Your grandmother gets to go. Your little sister gets invited, and your

mama is left out in the cold. Even *Jody* is there, for chrissakes. I think that stinks."

She never did forgive Don.

I found out later from Don that Nanny had told him not to ask Mama.

The varsity show was over, and I was concentrating on the workshop scene from *Annie Get Your Gun,* with Don playing Wild Bill.

Finals were around the corner, and so was summer. I had to face a few hard facts. If I ever wanted to get to New York, another season at Stumptown was out, and so was another year at UCLA. I'd have to get a real full-time job and save my money. Nanny said it could take years.

Funny thing, though, I wasn't worried. It was exactly like the time I "knew" I'd get to go to UCLA. I "saw" myself in New York, and I saw it happening very soon.

Dr. and Mrs. Jan Popper were sailing for Europe that summer, and they were being given a bon voyage party by some of their friends who lived in La Jolla. Dr. Popper, the head of the music department, asked the class to join him and his wife as their guests and perform our scenes at the party as entertainment for the evening. Transportation would be provided. For the eight or ten of us in the workshop, it meant a posh Saturday evening mingling with San Diego society plus all the food we could eat. Besides, we all liked the Poppers.

It was a beautiful night with dinner and dancing under the stars. The men were in black tie, and there was chiffon everywhere, on the ladies and in the desserts. I ate so much I was afraid I wasn't going to manage even the first line of "You Can't Get a Man with a Gun," much less burp out the entire number.

After coffee there were champagne toasts to the Poppers, and then Dr. Popper graciously thanked his hosts and all the guests. He looked over at our little group huddled around a table near the dance floor and began to introduce the entertainment for the evening. My heart skipped a couple of beats, right on cue, the way it always did before it was time to get up in front of people. (The first time it happened, I caught myself feeling my pulse and thought I had inherited it from Nanny. I later learned every actor's heart cuts up at times like this, or should.) Dr. Popper was explaining to the guests that we were his students, and if we did a good job that night, he'd probably have to give us all A's. "So pay close attention. Their report cards are depending on you!" Everyone chuckled at his charm, and as he sat down, they were primed and ready to love us. The first scene was from *Brigadoon.* There were about five scenes in all. The guests were enthusiastic as all get-out. All A's so far. Don and I were the last ones. By the time it rolled around to us, I could taste the two floating islands I'd had for dessert. (All right, stop it! Just stop it. Go right back down to where you belong, and stay put for the next twelve minutes . . . *please.*) We got through it. We did our scene. The dessert behaved itself. It stayed down, and the audience stood up . . . applauding.

After the show I was starved and back at the buffet table in no time flat, loading down a plate with some fancy-looking cookies. I copped a linen napkin, put it in my purse, and was shoveling some extra cookies into it, to take home to Nanny and Chrissy, when I felt a hand on my shoulder. (Oh, God, I'm under arrest.)

I turned around and looked right into the dark eyes of a stocky, fifty-ish, black-tied party guest. There was a woman standing next to him. They both were smiling. He introduced himself and his wife and reached out to shake hands. I snapped shut my purse, with all the cookie loot, and took his hand. Don joined us, and I introduced him to Mr. and Mrs. C.

A waiter walked by with glasses of champagne on a tray. Mr. C. helped himself to one.

"We sure did enjoy you kids. A lot." We thanked them. He looked at me. "You have a pretty good loud voice there."

"Thank you."

He swallowed some champagne. "So, what do you want to do with your life?"

"Pardon?"

"This? Do you want to do this?"

"Yes. I think so. Yes, we both do. Very much."

"Well, why aren't you?"

"Pardon?"

He sounded a little annoyed that I didn't get it. "I said, why aren't you?"

Don spoke up. "All the musical theater is in New York."

"So, go to New York."

Sure thing, mister. No problem. Just hang a left at the next block, and you're there before you know it.

"Maybe someday," I politely said.

"Now! You oughta go now!" He took another swallow of the champagne. "Why don't you go *now*?"

He was beginning to get on my nerves. I looked him directly in the eye and said evenly, "Money."

"*Money*. What's money? Look at me." He pounded his chest. "Didn't have a cent when I started out! Now I'm worth a fortune! What's money?"

Don said, "I notice it's always the people who have money that ask that."

"How much would it take for you to get to New York?"

"Oh, a thousand would be nice." I was tired and ready to go home. There was a long drive ahead of us back up to L.A.

"It's yours," he said.

Mrs. C. smiled at her husband and then at us.

The drive home took about three hours. All the way back, Don and I theorized about Mr. C. Had he meant what he said, or was it the champagne he'd been drinking that had done all the talking? Did the man have all his marbles? Was he a sadist? Had we heard right? Did he actually *say* he is going to lend us each one thousand dollars? Did we actually hear him say it? Or are *we* nuts? Mrs. C. had seemed normal enough. God, it was all too much to take in.

He had given us his card and told us to come back down and see him the following week. "Hell, I'll lend you the money. Pay me back when you can." End of conversation. He had taken his wife's arm, turned away from us, and started talking to some other guests. I stuck the card in my purse, and we joined the rest of our gang. People were getting their coats and leaving. We all thanked our hosts and the Poppers for a lovely evening.

We were halfway out the door when we saw Mr. and Mrs. C. pulling away in their big car.

Nanny was asleep when I got home around 3:00 A.M. I got undressed and went into the kitchen to unload my cookie take for the night. The card he had given me had melted chocolate all over it. I wiped it with a damp rag and put it in my school bag. I crawled under the covers on the couch, exhausted. I didn't sleep.

Don and I met during our lunch break the following Monday at school. I was up to my neck in finals, and I'd been cramming all weekend. My eyes looked like stop lights. Before we knew it, I had the card out, and we were pooling our change and feeding it into a pay phone. His office was in La Jolla. Long distance. His secretary answered. "Mr. C. is at a luncheon engagement. May I take a message and have him return your call?"

We didn't have a phone, and we were out of money. "No, thank you." Just as well. He'd never remember. Forget it. Just forget it.

We borrowed some more change and called him again that afternoon. His secretary asked who was calling. We told her, and she put us right through. He didn't even say hello. "Well, when are you coming down here?" He remembered! He didn't seem as friendly, but he remembered us. He didn't say anything about lending us any money, but he remembered us.

"Friday?"

"Okay. Be here at nine A.M. sharp." Click.

Oh, God. We didn't have a car, and La Jolla was a million-mile trip. We managed to borrow an old Buick from a friend and scrape every nickel and dime we had together for enough gas . . . one way.

Thursday night was another tosser and turner, and I got up at 5:00 A.M., and tiptoed into the bathroom to get dressed. Don was picking me up at 6:00. We didn't want to be late. A Bayer's aspirin bottle crashed into the sink when I reached for my toothbrush. Nanny woke up. "What are you doing? It's the middle of the night!"

"I'm going to school early . . . to cram. Finals. Sorry."

She turned over and went back to sleep.

The sun was just coming up as I waited in the lobby looking out the door for Don and the car.

Dear God. Let it be true.

The old car heated up a couple of times, but we reached La Jolla thirty minutes early because there was no traffic that time of morning. We parked and walked around the streets, looking in the windows of the not-yet-open stores. La Jolla sure was a pretty little place, right out of a storybook. Must be nice to live there. It took us eight minutes to cover the whole town.

We found ourselves hovering outside his office building at five minutes to nine. We paced for four minutes and went in. The secretary was hanging up her coat and told us to take a seat, he wasn't in yet. The minutes crawled. I had to go to the bathroom something awful, but I didn't dare move. About fifteen minutes later she answered a buzzer. "He'll see you now."

We hadn't seen him come in. Must be a separate entrance. She opened the door for us, and we went in. He was sitting behind an enormous desk two miles across the room. We just stood there.

"Well, come on in."

Our feet dragged through the foot-high carpet, but somehow we made it to the two giant-size chairs opposite his desk.

We just stood there.

"Well, sit down."

We did. Nobody said anything. His black eyes were staring holes through us. They were positively piercing. He wasn't at all the way he'd been the night of the party. He seemed to be waiting for us to make the first move.

"Well, we made it!" I said brightly. I felt like a jerk. Don fidgeted a little in his chair.

Pause.

He finally spoke. He repeated exactly what he had said that night; only this time it sounded like a totally different sentence. "So, what do you want to do with your life?"

We told him. And we told him New York was the only place to do it. The musical comedy capital of the world.

"*Why* do you want to do this?" He looked at me.

"Because I'll never be happy doing anything else."

"What makes you think you'll succeed?"

"I don't think it. I know it." I amazed myself with the simplicity of the statement. I wasn't bragging. I just told him what I believed.

Another pause.

"Sounds like you two really mean it. You want this more than anything in the world. That true?"

"Yes."

"Well, I think you might have a good shot at it. I'm gonna lend each of you a thousand dollars. You can pay it back in five years, no interest. I want you to promise to use the money to go to New York. It's enough for a ticket, and you can stretch out the rest until you can find a job. Might take a little time. Tough business." We promised! He buzzed for his secretary. "Bring in the checks." He had already made them out.

She came in, handed them to him, and left the room. He gave one to Don and one to me. I looked down at it. I had never seen that many zeros in my life. (I must be dreaming, this isn't real.)

We thanked him over and over and started to get up.

"Wait a minute." We sat back down. "There are stipulations. Aside from this being a loan, you can't tell anyone my name, for obvious reasons." We nodded. "Also, if—I mean, *when* you do make it, you have to promise me you'll help other people out. Doesn't have to be in show business. It's up to you. Just help 'em out like I've helped you. People you think might need that one little break. Got it?"

Got it? I saw the movie.

He started going through some papers on his desk. "Good-bye."

This time we got all the way up out of our chairs and floated across the room to the door. We turned around. "Thank you, Mr. C. We're going to do it. We'll make you proud."

He looked up. "I hope so. Good luck."

We got outside and started jumping up and down, laughing and crying and screaming all at the same time. We ran to the car, hopped in, drove a block, and the car stopped dead. We had run out of gas. Between us, we had sixty-five cents and two one-thousand-dollar checks.

Unless we intended to walk back to L.A., we needed to cash one of the checks. It suddenly dawned on us . . . what if he *hadn't* given us any money! We'd have been stuck. We started laughing hysterically. We found the bank that the checks belonged to and went up to a teller. I endorsed mine and handed it to her. She looked at the check and then at me. She looked at Don, standing next to me. She took my check over to the bank manager. He looked at it, picked up the phone, and called Mr. C. I wanted to die. We hadn't been out of his office seven minutes, and we were already cashing one of the checks . . . as if we didn't trust him or something. I desperately wanted him to know we needed the money for gas, but the manager had already hung up and was on his way back to us. He eyed us up and down and okayed the transaction.

Outside I simply stared at all that green in the envelope. We found a Shell station, and while Don was getting gas to take back to the car, I finally went to the ladies' room.

"Some *man* just up and *gave* you *one thousand dollars*?"

I decided to skip school and have Don drop me off at home. He said he'd return the car and call me later. I raced into the apartment. Nanny was coming out of the bathroom, and I hugged her, opened up the envelope, and let the money drop all over the Murphy bed. She looked at the bills, and then back at me, and then back at the bills, and then back at me again. Her takes reminded me of Lou Costello. It wasn't registering with her. She looked short-circuited. I think she thought I'd brought home some new kind of Monopoly game or something. Then I told her the whole story.

This was one time I thought she really *was* going to pass out.

"No, Nanny. He didn't up and *give* it to me; he up and *lent* it to me! Don, too! Isn't it wonderful? I can go to New York! It *won't* take years! I can go now!" I got her a wet rag for her head right away and cleared the bed of all the cash so she could lie down. But she didn't want to lie down. She wanted to move. She couldn't stop moving, pacing, pulse feeling, and belching. Money excited Nanny more than Randolph Scott did. She started to gasp for breath, and I got frantic. I should have told her in steps. She asked for her phenobarbitals, and in a little while she had calmed down.

"New York? You're really going to New York . . . with all that money?" She was lying down with both hands across her chest.

"That's what he gave it to me for, Nanny."

"When?"

It was June. I had a bad tooth, and I knew I had to see a dentist. I hoped Mr. C. wouldn't mind if I used some of the money to get it fixed. I had to buy a few things plus a suitcase to put them in. "I figure late next month or early August."

She looked at me. "Well, if you're not a star by Christmas, come home."

The reaction from Mama was an odd one. There was almost no reaction.

Christine didn't want me to leave.

23

New York. It was really going to happen. And it was happening now. Someone I hadn't even known *existed* one week ago, an out-of-the-blue stranger, pops into my life, plops a thousand dollars in my lap, and bang! My whole world does a flip-flop.

It was eerie because all this happened right after I had "seen" myself in New York. Somehow, I knew it meant something was going to happen soon that would get me there. It wasn't wishful thinking. I just plain knew it, felt it. That's why I wasn't worried. I just hadn't known the "how," that's all. Now I did. Mr. C. had been the "how." I thought back again to the only other time this had happened to me, the time the fifty-dollar bill had shown up exactly when I needed the tuition for UCLA, after I had "seen" myself on campus and in the classrooms.

After finals our friends gave Don and me a "farewell-good luck-give 'em hell, New York" party. A happy and sad occasion. There was a lot of speech making, and after I had tearfully thanked everybody, somebody shouted, "Okay, Burnett, what's gonna be your first Broadway show?"

I didn't even have to think about it. A picture flashed in my mind, and I shouted back, "A musical! And George Abbott will be the director."

It took five years, but that's exactly what happened.

It turned out to be two bad teeth. Wisdom teeth. Impacted wisdom teeth. They had to be yanked. At $150 a yank. That took care of $300. There wasn't anything I could do about it. I had to be in good shape for New York.

There was $700 left.

It was early July 1954, and the countdown was beginning. I went about my business quietly, almost as if it weren't happening. I bought a suitcase and a travel outfit at Penney's. The outfit was a brown suit that cost $13.95. Perfect for those New York autumns. I put the suitcase next to the couch, and every time I bought something new, I put it in. I had two pairs of shoes half-soled and got some new underwear at Newberry's five-and-ten. I bought a red scrapbook to put my *Daily Bruin* reviews in, to show to the talent agents. That took care of all the new stuff.

I took my clothes down off the shower curtain rod, the good old shower curtain rod that had been my "closet" for fourteen years. I washed out the rest of what I was taking in the bathtub: my PJs, three pairs of stockings, a couple of sweaters, some cotton skirts, and my old high school gym blouses (I could wear them under the sweaters), two or three pairs of socks, and two cotton dresses. I left the rest for Chris. It wouldn't take her long to grow into them.

The suitcase was filled. Nobody talked about it. None of us. Even Chrissy ignored it when she came into the room.

Mama was asleep one afternoon, and Nanny was making the run to the liquor store. Chris and I were alone in the apartment. We weren't talking much. I was making out another one of my endless lists of things I had to get done before I left. I could feel her big dark brown eyes staring at me. Finally she said, "Sissy, what's a pipe dream?"

Ilomay and I used to climb the hill that led up to the Hollywood sign. The first time we made it all the way, we were amazed at how high the letters reached and how old and dirty they were up close. They always looked so pretty from far away.

We were around nine the first time we made it clear up to the top. We nosed around the back and saw that the letters were held up by a bunch of old, crisscrossed, rickety wooden planks, held together by rusty nails. It looked as if some giant had tossed his pickup sticks over his shoulder and left them just the way they'd landed.

Perfect for climbing.

We made up a game. Whoever reached the top of a letter first would own Hollywood. The first time we did it, it took over an hour. The planks moaned and moved a little under our weight, and we were scared they'd give out. We got splinters in our fingers and knees. Ilomay won, and I challenged her to a race the very next day. We went back and tackled a couple of new letters. We did it every day after that until we had climbed to the top of each and every one, and in half the time.

The *O's* were my favorite.

I found myself staring at the sign a lot as I was getting ready to go to New York. I hadn't thought of it before, but I realized a day hadn't gone by since we moved from San Antonio that I hadn't looked up at that old sign whenever I went outside. I would miss it.

It was like that with just about everything, things I never thought I gave a hoot about, things I thought I hated: Murphy, the bed that was never out of sight and never made up, the piles of newspapers (for recipes never cut out) and old strips of colored cloth (for rugs never crocheted) in all four corners of the room; Big Ben in Nanny's medicine cabinet—the whole damn mess.

"Didja ever have da feelin' dat ya wanted to *go*, yet ya wanted to *stay*, yet ya wanted to go?" Now I got what Jimmy Durante was singing about on the radio.

Don and I hadn't seen much of each other since Mr. C. gave us the checks. I'd been up to my neck in preparations to leave as soon as possible, and he was planning to go to New York later, sometime in the fall.

I'd be going alone. Suddenly I had doubts about it all. About everything.

What was the matter with me? This was what I wanted, what I dreamed about. I was given the chance of my life, and now I was almost sorry. I almost wished I had never set eyes on Mr. C. and his money. I must be nuts. There was nothing to hold me back but me.

Nanny was in a stew all the time. Mama slept all the time, and Chrissy cried all the time. She would take one look at me and burst into tears. She'd even follow me to the bathroom.

I kept looking at the calendar, trying to settle on a date, and I just couldn't make up my mind. When would be the best time to go? What difference did it make? I'd still be alone.

Oh, God, I was losing my nerve. If I put it off to wait for Don after all this, I might never go.

A guy I had dated a few times called me and asked me when I was going to New York. It turned out he and his parents were going east for a wedding, around the second week in August, and were planning to spend a few days in New York. He was a very good comedian, and we'd done some shows at army bases together with a few other UCLAites over the past year and a half. He had some introductions lined up with three or four New York agents and was hoping he might land some commercials. I liked Dave. He was talented and nice. When he told me the date he and his folks were flying, I made my reservation the same day on the same plane.

I shut my suitcase and locked it.

It was done.

24

The last time I saw Daddy was the first week in August 1954. He was back as a tuberculosis patient at Olive View Sanitarium. A friend drove me out there so I could say good-bye to him before I left for New York.

I found my way to the visitors' room in the charity ward. He came into the waiting room, wearing faded pajamas and a threadbare striped hospital robe, like all the other patients. The place reminded me of a Warner Brothers prison picture. I hadn't seen him since last April, when he came to my birthday party. He was as skinny as ever. Skinnier. He walked in a jerking, kind of goose step way, and his legs were so spindly I could see his knee bones trying to poke their way through his PJs. I remember wondering how they held him up. His old brown leather slippers made a slapping sound on the concrete floor as he walked towards me. He grinned and reached out. I ran into his arms. He hugged me hard, and as I hugged him back, I felt his shoulder blades. They were so sharp; I can still feel how they hurt my palms. He stepped back, and we held hands. His were shaking.

"Let me look at you!" He smiled broadly, and his teeth looked brown and neglected. His face was gray. I could see little tears in the corners of his eyes. I smiled back, but it was hard. "Well, Punkin, so you're on your way to New York! Your mama wrote me. When?"

"Soon, Daddy. Next week."

"Well, my goodness, how about that?"

We sat down, and he started to cough and spit into a small bottle he had with him. It lasted a few minutes. He put the top back on and put the bottle back in his robe pocket.

"It's getting a whole lot better. They analyze the sputum, and if it's still clear the next couple of months, I'll get sprung from here and get to go home." He tried to sound cheery.

I had no idea where his "home" was. He'd been in and out of Olive View so long, that I didn't think he had one. I didn't want to embarrass him by asking, so I kept quiet.

He went on, "Y'know, Punk, I haven't had a drink in almost a whole year, and I feel terrific."

"You look terrific, Daddy."

"Well, I feel terrific." He shifted in his seat. "Listen, why don't we mosey into the ward, so I can stretch these pins of mine out on the bed? These old chairs aren't so hot."

I nodded.

He pushed hard on the arms of his chair and managed to get up in sections. He looked shorter than his six feet two and a half inches. I told myself it was because I was in heels.

We walked slowly through the TB ward past the rows of beds. He greeted his roommates cheerfully and seemed proud to show off his daughter, who was paying him a visit. Some of the men were reading, some were playing cards, some were dozing, and all of them were coughing.

We reached his bed, and he looked relieved as he stretched out his narrow frame on top of the covers. He was a little out of breath. "How'd all this New York business come about, Punk? Tell me."

I told him all about the man in San Diego who lent me the thousand dollars and how I decided that now was the time to go to New York because that's where Broadway is, and that what I really wanted to be was a musical comedy actress, just like Ethel Merman and Mary Martin, and that I was going to give myself five years to "make it" (which meant to me to be able to pay the rent), and if I didn't earn a theatrical living by then, well, then I'd just come back home and try something else, like journalism . . . teaching maybe.

He said, "Well, Punkin, it sounds as if you have your life all mapped out pretty good there." He didn't say a thing about pipe dreams.

He looked at me for a little bit and then asked, "You know anybody in New York?"

"No."

"You've never been any further east than Texas."

"Yeah, I know."

"You scared?"

"No. Yeah. A little."

"That's okay." He shifted a little and covered his feet with his blanket. "You any good?"

"I don't know. I think so." I opened my purse and brought out the envelope containing the theater award I had won at UCLA and the stack of varsity and homecoming show reviews I'd clipped out of the *Daily Bruin*—enough, I felt, to impress any smart New York agent: my tickets to fame. Daddy reached for his glasses on the bedside table. I'd never seen him wear glasses before. I didn't like it. I didn't want him to have to wear them. He put them on, and I noticed there was a safety pin in one of the hinges. He read each clipping very carefully.

When he finished, he handed them back to me. "Well, you must be pretty darn good to have all those nice things written about you." I blushed a little. "You still draw your pretty little pictures?"

"Not for a long time, Daddy."

"I always loved your pretty pictures. How's Nanny? And your little sister, Christine?"

"They're fine."

"Boy, I'll bet Nanny's sure gonna miss you. You've always been her little girl, y'know. Your mama and I were doggone lucky she could take such good care of you. Doggone lucky."

During the pause that followed, a man in a dark suit and a tie marched up to the bed, shoved a small booklet under Daddy's nose, and said in a very loud voice, *"Repent now!* Let Jesus in your heart. Be sorry for your sins, and your sins will be forgiven! Satan—" He never got any farther than that. Before I knew what was happening, Daddy jumped up off his bed, grabbed the man by his tie, and, with a strength I didn't think he had, threw him against the empty bed across from us. The whole ward saw it.

"You goddamn son of a bitch, get *out* of here! I don't need you or anybody else to tell me how sorry I should be! I already *know* how sorry I am. I'm the sorriest bastard I know, and I don't want some psalm-singing sonofabitch to come in here and tell me how to patch it up with Jesus. I'm trying to do that myself, and I don't need you as my goddamn agent. This is the last time I'm gonna tell you. Now quit coming around here! *Leave me alone!"* Daddy sat down on the edge of his bed with both hands clutching the sheets, as if he were trying to keep himself from springing up again. His knuckles were blue-white. The man was half running out of the place and picking up the booklets he was dropping on the way out. The other coughers were clapping.

Daddy flopped his head down on the pillow. His face was red, and he was out of breath. I stared at him, amazed. I'd never seen him that mad in my whole life. He started to wheeze and had to sit up again. "I'm sorry, Punkin. For the language." He wiped his forehead with a corner of the sheet. "But I hate that holier-than-thou stuff. I know how I feel, and I

Rehearsal Club In Bright Revue

The **rehearsal club**, a housing project for ambitious hopefuls in the theatre (female division) put on a bright little attempt to win the attention of producers and agents last Thursday and Friday. Several discoveries were quickly catalogued.

Easily the winner in the parlay was Carol Burnett, a character-actress comedienne, who stole the honors in several skits. She can sing and pantomine with the best of them, her sense of timing is top notch.

The show originated at the Rehearsal club during a "sit around" discussion, and is expected to be an annual event.

Don Saroyan, a relative of Sir William, was called in to stage and produce the show. Both he and Carol Burnett are discoveries of Jay and Sondra Gorney who had them at their summer theatre in California some years ago. About 250 producers agents and friends were present at the Thursday opening. The show had three performances at the Carl Fischer auditorium on 57th St. Maybin Hewes did the ensemble choreography and also danced a solo number which established her as the second find of the evening. Sets and lighting by Ming Cho Lee. Original music by Peter Daniels and lyrics by Dick Allen. The big weakness was in the writing, staging and special material, altho there were two excellent skits, both featuring Carol Burnett. Joanne Perry, as her "brother" was excellent.

There were 23 girls in the all-girl cast. The critics, busy that night with the opening of "Bus Stop" did not review the show, as of this writing (Friday).

The show rehearsed about 6 weeks.

In the cast are: Patricia Kent, Pat Maloney, Jo Anna March, Carolla Soll, Susan Reiselt, Joyce Roberts, Colette Jackson, Joanne Perry, Triv-Lyn Cruse, Sally Cooper, Janina Wynn, Carleen Anderson, Cynthia Cook, Tinker Gillespie, Sally Peabody, Lovey Godwin, Peggy Kaye, Patty Maloney, Pat Diamond.

Special material by Joan Beckman, Milton Polsky, and some assists in technical, by Charles Jules, Peter Daniels, Bruce Campbell, Frank Wolff, Bill West. Publicity by Bill Landsman.

The idea is a welcome addition to institutional annual theatrical events and we expect great things for it next time. Make it soon.

... LEO SHULL

THE REHEARSAL CLUB

Presents

THE REHEARSAL CLUB REVUE

PRODUCED AND DIRECTED

BY

DON SAROYAN

ORIGINAL MUSIC	ORIGINAL LYRICS
PETER DANIELS	DICK ALLEN

ENSEMBLE CHOREOGRAPHY
MAYBIN HEWES

SETS AND LIGHTING
MING CHO LEE

March 2 and 3, 1955 - 8:30 P.M.
Carl Fischer Concert Hall

-*-

It is with great pleasure that we welcome you to our revue this evening.

This show was born of many hours of frustrating encounters with you ... but don't get us wrong, WE LOVE YOU. Therefore, we decided to ease the situation for both parties, and put on our own show.

So, we did!

It is our hope that this evening will prove profitable and entertaining for all.

-*-

PRODUCTION STAFF

Assistant to the Director - Patricia Kent

General Assistant - Carol Burnett

Dialogue - Charles Jules

Musical Director - Peter Daniels

Scenery and Lighting Assistants - Bruce Campbell, Frank Wolff, Bill West.

Publicity - Bill Landsman

-*-

THE NEWS

HOLLYWOOD HIGH SCHOOL

RNIA   TUESDAY, OCTOBER 24, 1950

Joel McCrea Likes Movie Actor Job

He doesn't look like a movie star, he doesn't ACT like a movie star (off screen), but he IS—and tops in more ways than one. That's Joel McCrea, Hollywood high alumnus, class of '24.

Literally, being an "old cowhand" at heart, he became just that not only literally BUT figuratively via motion pictures. To Joel, being in the movies was only the means to an end. The "end" being the vast ranch he now owns.

He had no ambition to be a thespian, but when director Sam Wood spotted him in a college play, Joel, without too much pressure, accepted his offer to become a part of the motion picture industry.

Gratefully shrugging his broad shoulders, he knew of no faster way to earn the money to buy that ranch he wanted. This momentous decision naturally changed his whole life.

JOEL McCREA, Hollywood alumnus, as he appears as the star of Universal-International's technicolor Saddle Tramp.

He embarked on his career playing bit parts in westerns and worked his way up to stardom. During those first lean years of acting, he
(Continued on page two)

Classes To As Red Cro

The annual project of gi will start tomorrow. Two m all first period classes a library at 8:15 a.m. Thursda

Six To Make Transcribed Broadcast

Six students will represent Hollywood high on the Young America Speaks radio program, to be transcribed in our Memorial auditorium tomorrow during third period.

Marise Cherin, Hugh Lester, Cynthia Crane, Gloria Griffith, Sau Jacobs, and Frank Fleischer wil speak on the topic, How Can Youth Best Receive Training for Living a an Adult in a Democracy?

Our school participated in thi program last year, and the discussion was so successful that KFI ha chosen to enter tomorrow's progra in a nation-wide competition, Free dom's Foundation.

BROADCAST SATURDAY

Each year, radio stations through out the United States enter som form of program dealing with free dom and democracy in this contes

Lionel Hampton To Play In Boys Gym Monday

As a special treat for the students with fully paid up student body throughout the years by living a life of exemplary conduct which is an

Joel McCrea Likes Movie Actor Job And Life as Rancher

(Continued from page one) was encouraged and helped by some of the most famous names in show business: Cecil B. DeMille, Marion Davies, and the beloved Will Rogers.

When Joel was still "green," as he puts it, he had a joke played on him that he remembers to this day.

"It happened when I was working in a picture with Marion Davies," he explains. "I was doing a scene where I was supposed to eat an apple and toss the core away.

"What I didn't know, and nobody cared to inform me, was that each time the scene was done over, all I was supposed to do was take several bites off the apple and spit them out.

"However, nineteen takes later, when the director shouted 'print it,' I was nineteen apples heavier!

"And to top it off," he grins, "the director asked me out to lunch, but don't ask what we had for dessert —you guessed it—apple pie!"

His greatest thrill occurred several years back when, instead of being dropped from the RKO acting roster as he had expected, his option was picked up, and his salary boosted from $75 to $250 a week!

Joel's favorite role to date is Stars in My Crown, in which he portrays a two-fisted, small town minister. "Though making pictures isn't as soft a job as most theater-goers believe, it's far from being dull, or routine—and any job you really like doesn't seem like work anyway."

We gather from this that Mr. McCrea had a little bit of "ham" in him all along! We like to believe that this hidden quality was nurtured in our very own HHS, when he was before the footlights for one minute flat, and had his first dramatic fling —carrying a spear across the stage!

On his fabulous ranch in Ventura, which is a paying proposition, he raises cattle and grain. Proof of the former was evident by a burn on his hand he got while branding cattle. When he's not working on a picture, he spends all of his time at the ranch with his beautiful actress-wife, Frances Dee, and their two sons, Joel and David.

His advice to young hopefuls is to get all the stage training possible before attempting the movies.

"Above everything else," he adds, "don't pattern after anyone. Be original be natural. For the most important requisite of a good actor or actress is to be yourself."

Mr. McCrea IS that- for naturalness comes natural with him!

The trip back to 102, 1985

want to pray my own way." He started to cough, and he reached for the bottle again.

After a few minutes he asked, "So what kind of singing voice do you have?"

"Loud."

"Loud? You? I used to hear you sing with your mother and Nanny in the kitchen, but you were never loud."

"I just got up the nerve a year or so ago at school. Maybe because nobody knew me . . . I don't know . . . it's just something I have to do . . . to try. The money fell in my lap out of the blue, and I just *know* I'm supposed to take it and go to New York." I looked down at the floor. "Everybody thinks I'm nuts."

He took my hand. "Well, you go ahead and do what you have to do. You'll be a success, I know it. I'm just sorry I never got to see you in any of your school shows. But Lou wrote and told me you surprised the heck out of her when she saw you . . . said you were real good. Of course, our whole family is musical, so you come by it naturally."

I squeezed his hand. It was so very bony.

He squeezed back. "Well, lookee here, no complete stranger is gonna lend you that kind of money unless you're pretty *special!*" He was starting to look awfully tired.

"Daddy, I'd better go. My ride has to get back before it gets dark."

"Sure thing, Punkin Kid." I stood up. "Now remember, when you get to Broadway, you better get me a ticket to opening night."

"I promise."

He swung his legs over the side of the bed and fished for his slippers with his big toe.

"Don't get up, Daddy. I know the way out. I'll write you as soon as I'm settled. And when I get a job, I'll send for all of you—you and Mama and Nanny and Chrissy."

"That would be great." I knew he meant it.

I bent over to him, and we hugged. He wouldn't let me kiss him.

I turned away, and he called to me. "Carol."

"Yes, Daddy?"

"I wish I could've given you the money."

"I know."

"I love you."

"I love you, too, Daddy."

I turned around again and walked past the rows of beds. I looked back, and he blew me a kiss and waved. I rounded the corner and peeked back for another look. He never saw me. He was spitting into the bottle.

25

Rain. I'm crazy about it. I always loved it. So did Mama and Daddy. They used to say it was because we all were April babies. I remember Mama saying she was absolutely "queer" for rain. Whenever she was blue, it would cheer her up. Me, too.

But there was more. I was actually superstitious about it. It had started a long time ago when I was in grammar school. I was worried about some arithmetic test (it was never my best subject), and in the middle of it the sky opened up and the rain started coming in sideways through the classroom windows. Everybody ran like crazy to shut them. The storm raged. The test continued, but the thunder and lightning were shaking everybody up. But me. I was just fine. I felt as if I were in the eye. I wasn't the least bit scared. And I wasn't nervous about the test anymore. I turned it in before anybody else was done. And I got an A.

From that time on, I usually got A's if I took an exam when it was raining.

Rain brought me good luck. I believed it.

It rained the morning my UCLA tuition showed up in the mailbox. It rained when I was asked to go to Stumptown. It rained the weekend Mr. C. gave us the money. Later on, almost every time I auditioned for a job, I got it if it rained. Almost every opening night, stage or television shows: rain. Sometimes snow and sleet (particularly the specials with Julie Andrews and Beverly Sills). Anytime there was something important to me coming up, personally or professionally, I would go into a mental rain dance. And it worked about ninety percent of the time. It would rain, I would calm down, and things would go fine.

It just makes me feel good.

Los Angeles to New York: $158.85. I had my ticket in my purse. I was wearing my J. C. Penney's travel outfit, and I picked up my suitcase. Nanny and Chrissy walked me to the lobby door. I had gone into Mama's room earlier and kissed her good-bye in her bed. "Go get 'em, kid." Tweetie didn't wake up.

I hugged and kissed Chrissy and Nanny a dozen times.

Nanny kept on waving and blowing kisses until I disappeared around the corner, just as she always did when I was little and on my way to school.

I had heard life was full of little deaths and births. This was a little death.

I had a room at the Algonquin Hotel. *The* Algonquin Hotel. I had heard and read about it. All the witty people had gathered there for years, topping one another at the famous Round Table. I was alone, standing in a room, in a strange city.

I had known the moment would come when Dave and his folks had to leave, but I wasn't prepared for the emptiness.

I was glad I had come with them. They had been very nice to me and had kept my mind off the inevitable for a few days. Now they were gone.

I decided to call home. I had already called collect the day we landed just to let Nanny know the plane hadn't crashed. We had talked fast because long distance cost a fortune. I knew I shouldn't call again this soon, but I was so lonely I had to hear their voices again, or I thought I might crack. I got the operator. Nanny answered and started talking before the operator had finished asking if she'd accept the charges.

"ARE YOU ALL RIGHT?" Long distance meant talking fast and loud.

"I'M FINE. I JUST WANTED TO SAY HI."

Mama grabbed the receiver and I told her yes, New York looks glamorous especially at night, when it's all lit up. Chrissy got on and wanted to know if I wanted to talk to Tweetie. Nanny took the phone away from her, saying we couldn't waste good money talking to some dadgum bird. Yes, Nanny, I still have a room. No, I didn't get a part yet. I haven't even got an agent. Well, yes, I'll go out and get one tomorrow. She told me about some storm around New York; they were talking about it on the radio: a hurricane. It was headed straight for my room. No, I hadn't heard about it. It was cloudy, though. . . . Yes, I'll be on the lookout for it. . . . Don't worry, I'm fine. I'll call every day and ask for myself; that way they'll know everything is okay, and we won't have to pay for the calls. Please, please don't worry. I'll be just fine.

"I MISS YOU, TOO!"

"PRAY FOR ME, CAROL. I'M NOT WELL."

"I KNOW THE TRUTH FOR YOU ALL THE TIME, NANNY! YOU KNOW THAT! I LOVE YOU ALL. BYE."

Just as I was hanging up, I could hear Chrissy yelling, "WHY DOESN'T SISSY WANT TO TALK TO TWEETIE?"

I sat down on the bed. Sissy wants to go home. That's what Sissy wants to do. Sissy would like to talk to Tweetie in person.

I got up and went to the closet—the first closet I had ever had in my life—took my clothes out of it, walked into the bathroom with them loaded in my arms, and proceeded to hang everything I had on the shower curtain rod.

It was late. I stood in my PJs and looked out the window at the skyline, what I could see of it. There were so many lights and neon signs everywhere that it looked like daytime. I pulled down the shade and got into bed. I missed my old couch. In spite of the shade being down, I could still see everything in the room, clear as anything. A huge neon sign was winking, right at me. It might as well have been in the room. I shut my eyes tight and tried to go to sleep. It sounded as if all the car horns in New York were stuck.

After a few minutes I heard a new sound—like pebbles being hurled against the windowpane. It got louder and louder.

Rain. I started to cry. It was the first time rain couldn't cheer me up. It got louder, and I got louder. When it let up a little, I let up a little. We went on like that all night. A wet duet. I fell asleep around daylight and woke up feeling better. The cry had helped. The rain had helped me cry. I got dressed and went to a coffee shop to get a doughnut. It was still coming down, and a radio was talking about Hurricane Carol hitting New York full force. Well, I'll be damned. I had *two* doughnuts.

I hurried back to my room to take stock. I got out my pencil and paper and started figuring. Unless George Abbott called me right away, I knew, before I even started adding it all up, that I had to find another place to live, but quick. I was spending $9 a day at the Algonquin, for just a room. (Lord, and 102 was $36 for a whole month.)

Okay, let's see. The wisdom teeth had cost me, with the anesthetic, $300. I'd already spent $45 for my hotel room, and it was going to be $9 more when the clock struck noon. Clothes, suitcase, scrapbook, airplane ticket, ground transportation, food . . .

I had been as careful as I could, and I had a little more than $350 left out of the $1,000.

And I'd been in New York five days.

I picked up my imitation red leather scrapbook and began to leaf through it. There they were, all the rave reviews from the *Daily Bruin,* the clippings from the Stumptown Players summers, plus photographs of all the characters I'd played from the different shows and sketches I'd done, all carefully and neatly pasted in, with red pencil underlining the pertinent paragraphs. I had even included my special award (on parchment) for "Outstanding Newcomer," presented to me my first semester from the UCLA theater arts department. Surely, if some big Broadway agent would just look through this book and read these nice things in print . . . well, that's all it would take.

DeNeut had given me one New York telephone number. I fished for it in my purse and finally came up with it. It belonged to Eleanor Eby, the girl who was so great as Nellie Forbush in the scene from *South Pacific,* where I'd lasted a hot ten minutes in the chorus. I didn't know her very well, but she had seemed friendly enough. She'd been ahead of me in school and was pretty much of a star on campus when I enrolled as a freshman. She had graduated and come to New York for the same reason I had. She was also kind of engaged to one of my best friends from school, Larry Swindell, who was now in the armed forces off somewhere serving our country.

Larry was one of the most brilliant people I had ever met. He was always brutally honest with me, and I didn't dare ask him what he thought of one of my performances on campus unless I really wanted to know.

I hoped Ellie's number was still good. I hoped she'd remember me. I picked up the phone and gave the number to the hotel operator.

After about twelve rings a voice answered, "Rehearsal Club."

"Excuse me?"

"Rehearsal Club, who do you want?"

"Eleanor Eby . . . is she—does she—"

"ELLIE! PHONE!"

Whoever answered dropped the receiver, and I could hear it banging against the wall. I could also hear a lot of female voices. I waited. Somebody yelled, "Will *someone* pick up the goddamn phone? I'm expecting a call! It might be a *job* for godsakes!" Footsteps. Someone picked up the receiver, and I heard a breathy "Hello?"

"Ellie?"

"Yes? Who's this?"

"Carol . . . Burnett. I just got to New York. Larry and Dick DeNeut said I should give you a call and say hi."

"Carol Burnett?" (She'd forgotten me, I knew it.) "Oh, God, how great! I heard you might be coming here. Where are you? Can we get together?" (She was as wonderful as I thought she'd be.)

"I'm at the Algonquin."

"The *Algonquin!* Good grief! It must be costing a fortune!"

I looked at my watch. Five minutes past noon. It sure was. She told me to get out of there fast, that she could swing a bed for me where she was living. It wasn't the Algonquin, but it had a roof, food, and was a *lot* cheaper. She gave me the address. I was packed and checked out in ten minutes. If I'd only called her at eleven forty-five, I'd have been nine dollars richer. I lugged my suitcase the nine blocks up to Fifty-third Street. It was pouring. I checked the address. Here it was, an old brownstone between the Avenue of the Americas and Fifth Avenue. I climbed the steps and rang the doorbell. Nobody answered. I rang again. "It's open!" I turned the knob and pushed against the door with my back, trying not to drop my purse and my suitcase. I felt like a drowned rat. My new travel outfit was clinging to me like wet Kleenex. "Carol! Heavens, let me take your suitcase. You're drenched! Hurry up . . . get inside! Do you *believe* this storm?"

I turned around, and there was Eleanor Eby. She looked like an angel. I swear, I thought I could make out a halo. She was blond and tall and graceful and positively beamed, and there was a lilt when she spoke. I remembered her lovely, clear soprano when we'd rehearsed the workshop scene in school. Yet, with all this ladylike demeanor, she somehow reminded me of a St. Bernard puppy. (Years later, when I first met and worked with Julie Andrews, I thought, "She reminds me of an English Ellie Eby.")

My feet made squishing sounds in my shoes as I followed her and my suitcase through the hall, past the staircase, and into a back parlor, where a pretty white-haired woman was sitting at a desk. "Miss Carlton, this is my friend from California I told you about." Miss Carlton explained that she didn't have much in the way of a room for me. In fact, there was only one available bed, and it was located in the transient room, on the first floor right next to the hall where the pay phone was. The room faced a small courtyard, though, and I would have a cot, a dresser, a bathroom, a closet—and four roommates. I nodded, and she proceeded with the rules of the club.

1. The residents are young women who must be actively pursuing a career in the theater. They are allowed to take other jobs, as a means to pay the

rent, but no resident can expect to hold down a full-time job outside the theater and remain at the club permanently.

2. No drinking. No unruly behavior. No loud noise.

3. No men allowed to visit anywhere other than the common parlor, and all men must be off the premises by 10:00 P.M. weeknights, midnight on Saturdays.

I would receive room and board for eighteen dollars a *week,* payable in advance. I dropped my purse, grabbing for my wallet. "Wouldn't you like to see your quarters first?"

"No, thank you. It's just . . . fine." I handed her the money before she had a chance to change her mind.

Miss Carlton smiled and shook my hand. "Welcome to the Rehearsal Club."

My rain had come through, again.

We walked down the hall past the pay phone on the wall, and she opened the door to the transient room. At the moment, it was empty. There were five cots and a dresser next to each one. It reminded me of a barracks. The bathroom was small and packed with the belongings of the four girls who had already staked their claim: magazines on the floor by the toilet, shampoos, curlers, toothbrushes, toothpaste, soaps, and razors all around the tub and sink area. Stockings and underwear were soaking in the sink and hanging from the towel racks and the shower curtain rod. The medicine cabinet was chock-full of makeup, sanitary supplies, aspirin, Q-tips, razor blades, and deodorant. It didn't look as if another hanger with anything on it could possibly squeeze into the already bulging closet.

I was back home.

I was given two sheets, one blanket, and a pillow. I unpacked, and by some miracle I was able to squeeze a few of my clothes into the one small closet that already looked as if it were about to explode. I left my sweaters in my suitcase and pushed it under the cot. I put the rest of my stuff in and on my dresser, made up my bed, and fell on top of it.

The next thing I knew, the overhead light was shining in my eyes and there was activity in the room. I got up and headed for the bathroom. A girl with huge breasts was coming my way, naked with a towel around her head. She glanced at me, went to her dresser, and bent over to get something out of the bottom drawer. She wasn't the least bit self-conscious. "Hi," I said, looking at a spot on the wall a good two feet above her head. "I just moved in. My name's Carol . . . Burnett."

She didn't even turn around. "So?"

When it finally dawned on me that that was it, I headed for the bathroom again. I turned the knob. The door was locked. A bright, cheery voice from the other side called out, "Busy!" I would have to pass Miss Congeniality if I went back to my station, so I decided to wait outside the bathroom door until Miss Busy was finished. After a while I began to think Christmas would be here before I'd ever see the inside of that bathroom again. Finally the door burst open (just as I was about to), and out she popped. "Next!" I flew past her so fast and slammed the door I didn't even see what she looked like. So far I had almost met two of my four roommates.

The Rehearsal Club had been established years before and was endowed by a bunch of rich New York society women who wanted to help "young ladies who were seriously interested in pursuing a theatrical career." That's why the rent was so cheap. "Our Ladies of the Fund," as the girls called them, contributed the rest.

It was a four-story brownstone, and most of the rooms were doubles. The average occupancy was around fifty girls. The cafeteria was in the basement. Everybody complained about the food but me. I thought it was terrific. The others had never had Nanny's fried salmon balls.

The club was famous. The play and the movie *Stage Door* had been written about it.

And the room I shared with four others could have come right out of the play. It was as if we'd been typecast for the roles. There was the Tough One who had been around the block a time or two (the one I'd nicknamed Miss Congeniality); the Ballerina, who did her barre every morning on the sink at the same time she washed out her underwear; the Serious Actress, who slept with Stanislavsky books under her pillow and hardly ever bathed or changed her clothes; Miss Busy (from the bathroom), who had a thick English accent, was relentlessly cheerful, kept an appointment book, always had things to do and places to go, and was into Spanish dancing at the moment. And me. I guess I was the hick . . . from Hollywood.

The hick slept late that first morning and woke up suddenly, not quite remembering where she was.

I jumped out of bed the wrong way and banged my forehead against the corner of the dresser. The Tough One was on her way out the door (fully dressed, thank God), caught what I had done to myself, and tossed a "nice going" my way before she disappeared. The other beds were empty. I headed for the bathroom and turned the knob.

"Busy!"

I rubbed the knot that was blossoming on the side of my head and went back and made my bed. There was a lot of commotion outside our door in the hall. The pay phone was on the wall directly on the other side of my bed, and I could hear six or seven girls yelling, all at the same time, wanting whoever was on the phone to make it fast, so somebody else could have a crack at it. I stuck my head out the door. Everyone I saw was dressed and seemed to have a mission in life. I smelled coffee. It was coming from the basement. I was hungry and asked one of the girls if breakfast was still being served. She said, "Yes, and good luck." I went back into our room and waited for the bathroom to be sprung. Tinker (that was Miss Busy's name) finally burst through the door, fully made up and beaming. She chirped in her British accent, "All yours!"

I tried chirping back, "Thank you!" Mine wasn't as good as hers.

She and her dark brown curls bounced over to her dresser. She collected her purse, her castanets, and her appointment book, checked herself out in the mirror, smiled at what she saw, turned and clicked her castanets and said to me, "Bye-bye, and toodle-oo. I'm off! I hope we all have smashing luck today!" She bounded out of the room as if she were on a pogo stick. I could hear her greeting everybody in the hall and her high heels making a clickety sound clear out the front door. Bye-bye and toodle-oo to *you*, Tinker, and I, too, hope we all have smashing luck today. The bathroom was all mine.

By the time I was dressed and got downstairs for breakfast, all the tables had chairs on them upside down, and there was only some watery coffee left. Lunch wasn't until noon.

I walked back up the stairs. The house was silent. I climbed up to the fourth floor and stuck my head into Ellie's room. It was empty, and the two beds were made. I envied her having only one roommate. There was a picture of Larry on her dresser. I went back downstairs and wandered into the parlor. I sat down and leafed through some old magazines. There was an old upright against the wall. I wished I could play the piano.

I sat there for a very long time, and it finally occurred to me that I had absolutely no idea what I was supposed to do now.

* * *

So I asked questions and copied everybody else.

After that first morning I didn't miss one meal. The next day at breakfast all I could see was coffee cups and everybody's nose buried in a newspaper I'd never heard of before, called *Show Business*. I scanned the room, looking for someone whose hands or feet I might recognize, and spotted Tinker's curls sticking up over her paper. I sat down across from her and asked her what it was that everybody seemed so interested in. She lowered the page for an instant and explained. "Darling. This is our bible! It's the only way we can find out what's going on in this town!" She circled something in red, jumped up, grabbed her stuff, and said, "I'm off! Toodle-oo."

So I bought a *Show Business* at the corner newsstand. It was a kind of tip sheet on who, where, when, and what was auditioning. I got a red pencil and did some circling of my own. Then I began "making the rounds."

Making the rounds turned out to be trying (and failing) to get past the receptionist who worked for the agent, producer, or director you were desperately trying to see. (All he had to do was look at my scrapbook, for godsakes.) Making the rounds meant having to give *her* your photograph (which you paid cold, hard cash for) and knowing damn good and well that the minute you got back in the elevator and pushed the down button, she was busy filing your eight-by-ten glossy in her wastebasket. Making the rounds meant having her say, "Don't call us, we'll call you," or "Let us know when you're in something, and we'll try to come see you." When I asked how does anybody get in anything without an agent, she'd give me a vacant smile as an answer. Once she asked, "Are you Equity?"

"What's Equity?"

"The actors' union."

"No."

"Then we can't help you get a job."

"How do I get in the union?"

"Get a job."

They all had the same receptionist.

I was going broke, fast. I thought back to Mr. Freud's advice when I was a freshman at UCLA: "Don't walk into an audition looking hungry; it makes producers nervous." I had to get a real-life job if I was going to be able to make the eighteen-dollar-a-week nut I had for rent alone. And for the first time in my life I was becoming aware of a thing called winter. I needed a *coat*.

I bought a real newspaper and began circling the want ads for part-time work. It was impossible. Every actor in town wanted a part-time job. I missed out on everything I applied for. You had to know somebody for that, too! God, you'd need an agent in this town to get a job as a street cleaner! And if I got a full-time job, the club would kick me out because it wasn't in the "theatah." And where else in New York could I get room *and* board for eighteen dollars a week? I didn't know what I was going to do.

I was mulling over my fate, trying to choke down some pea soup at dinner one night, when the Tough One, Joyce, set her tray next to mine and pulled up a chair.

She had landed a job as a hatcheck girl at a restaurant on Forty-ninth Street, Susan Palmer's (a ladies' tearoom), across the street from Rockefeller Center in the Time/Life Building. She had a proposition for me. How about being partners? The job was six days a week. We'd each work three, alternating the days so that one week I'd work Mondays, Wednesdays, and Fridays while she'd take Tuesdays, Thursdays, and Saturdays. The following week we'd switch, giving both of us some weekdays off to "make the rounds." Susan Palmer's offered no salary, just tips. We'd be on our honor and split the take, bringing home our tips every night to divide. A real-life part-time job.

"Why'd you ask me, Joyce?"

" 'Cause you look honest." She smiled at me. We shook hands.

I'd have to think up a new nickname for Joyce.

There was only one thing neither of us had thought about. Ladies don't check their hats.

There would be a letter from Nanny every day. Sometimes two. I didn't turn off my light at night until I had finished a letter right back to her, to mail first thing in the morning. It still didn't help.

My Darling Carol,

Are you up for anything good? Has anybody important seen you yet? Why don't you go out and get an agent? Your mother says you're wasting your time back there. She says you spent all that money to go to New York, and for what? Just to check hats. Winter coats cost money. I'm so worried about you that my heart has been acting up and skipping beats ever since I watched you disappear around the corner August 9th. She's in bed all the time now. I can't get her to eat. She just wants to drink. Sometimes I think I'm going to go out of my mind. Nobody should have all these worries. Christine is growing so fast. She misses you. You probably won't recognize her if you ever see her again. I'm worried about her. She's getting titties. Are you warm enough? Don't let those roommates open the window when it snows; you could freeze to death in your sleep. Your blood is thinner than theirs. I had bronchitis all last week. I spit up all the time now. I can hardly lift my head up off the pillow to open a can of soup, but I have to, because nobody here is going to give me a hand. I never know where Christine is anymore. She doesn't come home from school, just stays out as long as she pleases. Your mother says everyone in the world thinks they can make it in show business, and she says if *she* couldn't "what makes Carol think she can?" She says she has more talent in her little finger than the whole family. I reminded her how talented and versatile all us Joneses were. Brother Edgar had a beautiful voice, and so does Eudora. I never had a chance to express myself because your mother and Eudora were my life, until you came along. I just pray you're doing the right thing. You can't trust everybody. There's more crime in New York than anyplace in the country. I'd better close. My breath is getting short again, and I really should try to lie down, but I know I won't get any sleep, because I get dizzy if I don't keep my head up. I pray every night to God that I will get a letter from you in the morning. Sometimes I wonder if you're getting mine. New York is a huge city. I love you more than anything or any *one* in the world. Don't forget to know the truth for me. I love you more than my own life.

All my love, always,
Your Nanny

P.S. I didn't care too much for that publicity picture you sent. It just doesn't look like you. I hope you didn't get gypped. I'm going to buy a frame tomorrow, if I can make it to Kress'. This heat makes me faint. Pray for me. I love you.

Your Nanny

Please let there be a letter from you tomorrow.

Lord, it could get cold. I'd never been this cold in my whole life. Nanny had opened up her sock and sent me twenty dollars for coat money. I thanked her in every letter for fourteen days running. I bought the Coat in Klein's bargain basement for thirty-five dollars. It was a black-and-white tweed with nubby little balls of wool all over it. It did the trick. I was warmer, and I thought I looked swell in it until one of the girls remarked that it looked like "unborn linoleum."

I'd walk real fast through the cold to my job at Palmer's, with my chin buried in my chest, hoping my nose wouldn't freeze off until I could make it to Radio City Music Hall, where I could cut through an underground passage and avoid two and a half blocks of freezing wind.

And this was only fall.

Joyce and I averaged thirty dollars apiece each week. After I coughed up the rent to Miss Carlton, I was left with twelve dollars to go crazy with. Even though ladies didn't check their hats, they did check their packages and, sometimes, their coats. The average tip was twenty to twenty-five cents.

There was an oyster bar downstairs for the men. The men were a hundred times cheaper than the women. They avoided me entirely—not even a "No, thank you," after my polite "Check your coat, sir?"

The enemy below was a row of hooks on the wall that didn't require a tip. The men would actually leap down the stairs to avoid eye contact. I took to standing directly in their way as they came in the door. They had their choice: Give me their coats or knock me down the stairs. They started giving in to the Poor Little Match Girl.

And the Poor Little Match Girl figured out a way to get a little more out of them.

While some unsuspecting gent was enjoying a martini and a cup of lobster bisque below with his buddies, I'd take the coat he'd left in my care and pull the threads out of the tiny strap inside the collar that looped over the coat hook. Then I'd sew it right back on, using a different color thread, usually red or white.

When he presented his claim check, I'd say to him, "Oh, sir, you know that little strap in your collar? Well, it was torn, but I sewed it back on for you . . . see?" I'd get an extra dime for that one. I just had to be careful not to pull it on the same guy twice.

There really was a little bit of Nanny in me.

26

"Nobody gives you anything in this world, baby. You make your own breaks." Mama used to say that.

It was Saturday night, and I was sitting on my bed, staring out the large window at the courtyard next door. Joyce was working the weekend shift, and everybody else had a date. The club was quiet.

I was thinking about Mr. C. and how he had given me something. *He* had given me a break, a big one, a thousand-dollar break. Now it was gone, and here I was, letting us both down. I was lonesome and feeling sorry for myself.

Don was supposed to be coming to New York soon, along with some other UCLAites, but it seemed as if it were never going to happen. It was his fault I was so lonesome. It had been so long since we'd seen each other I wasn't even sure I loved him anymore. I would remain alone forever. I'd wind up staying at the club my whole life and become Miss Carlton: counting everybody else's money and watching everybody else move.

Tinker had left a newspaper on her bed, and I picked it up and turned to the theater section. Broadway. A five-minute walk. A million miles away.

The ads for the shows were so beautiful. There it was again, his name: George Abbott. "THE PAJAMA GAME . . . GEORGE ABBOTT'S 'THE PAJAMA GAME.' " Another Abbott smash in a steady string of Abbott smashes. I remembered bragging to my friends that I'd work for him someday. I had "known" it then. I wasn't so sure about anything now.

I heard a sound against the big windowpane. Rain. I cheered up a little. I took the paper, walked back to my bed, and flopped down on top of the covers again. *The Pajama Game,* starring Janis Page, John Raitt, Carol Haney, Eddie Foy . . . wait a minute. Wait a minute!

I grabbed my tweed coat out of the community closet and threw my clear plastic raincoat over it. I plowed through the shelves, looking for my galoshes, and came up with one. I put it on and searched for the other one. No luck. I found one that belonged to Yvonne, the Ballerina. I figured she wouldn't mind if I borrowed it for just a few minutes. I slipped it on, tied a scarf around my head, grabbed my purse, and ran out into the downpour.

The St. James Theater was about ten or eleven blocks away. *The Pajama Game* was playing to packed houses every single night. There were taxis and limos waiting out front for the show to break. When I got to the stage door, I waited in the rain until the show was almost over. Around ten forty-five I opened the door and slipped inside. It was my first time backstage in a Broadway theater. It smelled great. I was soaked. I reminded myself of Anne Baxter in *All About Eve.* The old man who was leaning back against the wall in his chair next to the door looked up from his paper. He was exactly like all those characters they called Pops in the Betty Grable backstage movies I had loved so much; he would have played the kind old geezer who stood in the wings and gave the thumbs-up sign to the understudy going on for the first time. I smiled at him.

"Whaddya want?"

"I'm here to see Eddie," I said, "Foy."

Eddie Foy, Jr., had a scene-stealing, starring role in Mr. Abbott's smash, and he was my new hope.

A year or so before I left to come to New York, a neighbor of ours in Hollywood was a "star" of sorts—to me anyway. His name was Jack, and he did a lot of small bits in movies. He was always working, usually playing Irish cops. He had played one in a movie that had featured the well-known stage comic Eddie Foy, Jr. I remembered Jack telling Nanny, Mama, and me stories about his adventures on the set. I was wide-eyed at the mere thought of it all. Jack had said that Eddie Foy, Jr., was one hell of a guy. "Not only funny, but nice to everybody, not just the big shots."

I was staring into space. Pops had said something.

I came to. "Pardon me?"

"I *said,* 'Are you a friend of Eddie's?' "

"I'm . . . from California, just got in."

"Bring this rain with you?" He chuckled.

I chuckled back. I looked down at my feet. Oh, my God. My galoshes weren't the same color. One was black, and the other one was light brown. There was a sudden thunderclap. I jumped. Then I realized it was the sound of applause when the curtain falls on a hit. The audience was cheering and clapping and up on their feet, bravo-ing all over the place. And I was right there, backstage, hearing it! Smelling it . . . I couldn't get over the smell—what was it?

Curtain calls. Seemed like dozens. After a while the backstage area was a sea of bodies—dancers and singers running upstairs to scrub off their greasepaint as fast as they could, so they could hit the town on a Saturday night. People everywhere shouting, "Have a nice weekend! *Oh, no!* Christ, it's *raining*! Goddammit! See you Monday! Let's take in a movie tomorrow. . . ." I caught a glimpse of Janis Paige and John Raitt and Carol Haney heading for their dressing rooms, all stars and all within touching distance. I was in heaven. But where was Eddie? I was searching the crowd for him. What if I missed him? I spotted him the same time Pops did. The old man called to him, "Hey, Eddie!"

The wiry figure turned our way. He had on a baggy pair of pajamas, his costume for the curtain call. He looked pretty funny. "Yeah?" He walked towards us. He was soaked with sweat and was wiping his face and head with a towel.

"Friend here to see ya. Says she knows you from California."

Eddie Foy, Jr., looked at me and said, "Yeah, kid? Whaddya want? Do I know you?" He wiped his head again.

This was it. "Well, in a way you do, Mr. Foy. You see, a very close friend of my family's, Mr. Jack Shea, worked very closely with you in a motion picture in Hollywood. He played the Irish cop? You had lots of scenes together, and anyway, he said you were the very nicest person he had ever worked with in his many years in the business and suggested that I should be sure to look you up when I got to New York!" (Whew.)

"What for?"

Okay. "Well, you see, Mr. Foy, I'm in the business, *too,* but I've been mainly stationed out in Hollywood, and Mr. Shea thought—*said* you'd be just the person to ask for advice about New York, you being so nice and all."

Most of the cast was leaving or gone. The last few people were saying good night. I could tell Mr. Foy wanted to say good night, too. He was still blotting his face. He was wetter than I was.

"Advice?"

"Yes, sir. *Please.*" Before he could make a getaway, I spilled out as much as I could, as fast as I could: about how impossible it is even to *see* an agent, much less to *get* one, and how do you get in a show if you don't *have* one? No producer or director will even look at you, and how do you *get* one unless you're in a show? I didn't give him a chance to open his mouth. I was scared that if I stopped to take a breath, he'd vanish. I told him about the "complete stranger" who had enough faith in me to lend me practically a fortune and how just trying to live in New York had swallowed it all up. I told him about my rave reviews in college, about working in summer stock, about my dream to work in an Abbott show . . . and on and on.

He was shifting his weight from one foot to the other. I was just about to launch into how musical all the Joneses were when he stopped me. "Okay, okay! Whaddya . . . sing? Dance? Maybe I can get you an audition for a replacement in the chorus." He *was* nice.

"Well, Mr. Foy, I have a pretty good singing voice. It's very loud, and I've been told it's perfect for Broadway, but it's not a trained voice, and I can't read music. And I'm afraid I'm not a very good dancer. I had a lesson once, in the samba, but I'm not a trained dancer by any means. . . . I'm sorry . . . I haven't had any training in anything. I'm afraid I'm not good enough for the chorus." I was proud of my honesty.

He looked frustrated. "Well, then, what kind of job *do* you want?"

"I'd have to have a featured role."

I remember a pause.

He finally said, "Where you living?"

I told him about the club and wrote the pay phone number and my name on the back of an envelope from one of Nanny's letters. I gave it to him.

"Okay, I'll call you." He made a beeline for his dressing room.

I shouted, "Thank you, Mr. Foy!" I looked at the stage door man and said, "Night, Pops," and floated out of the St. James, and into the rain humming "This Is My Once a Year Day."

He called me the following Monday. He had made an appointment for me to *meet his agent!* Before I could get into thanking him properly, he interrupted me with "Yeah, that's okay, you're welcome. Good luck, kid," and hung up.

I met with his agent, who politely flipped through my scrapbook and glanced at the publicity picture Nanny didn't like. He said he'd keep me in mind "if anything came up." I asked him what I should do in the meantime. He jokingly said, "Well, why don't you put on your own show?" I thanked him and said good-bye.

What a good idea.

Four years later, in 1958, Eddie Foy, Jr., and I happened to be the guests on the Dinah Shore summer replacement series one week. He and I were featured together in a sketch and a song. He still perspired a lot and had a towel with him all the time. Somebody remarked about it in rehearsal, and he said, "That's flop sweat, kid, y'never get over it." I hesitated to mention our first encounter since he showed no sign of remembering it, but when he told me he thought I had a good loud voice for Broadway, I took the plunge and told him all about that rainy night, the promise he'd made and kept, and my visit with his agent, which was the very first time I'd gotten past a receptionist. I told him about the agent's off-the-cuff remark about putting on my own show, which I did, about four months after I saw him.

He looked a little uncomfortable at first. He didn't remember any of it. He started to walk away, and then he stopped and turned around and said, "I did all that?"

"Yes, you sure did, Mr. Foy."

He smiled and said, "Well, that was very nice of me."

It sure was, Mr. Foy.

I heard it ring even before it woke me up. I was always the first one to hear it anyway, since the phone was on the other side of the wall opposite my pillow. It was late. I usually ignored it most of the time. I'd put the pillow over my head, turn over, and go right back to sleep.

I picked it up after the third ring. It was for me. I knew it was for me.

I was barefoot. And I'd left my robe on the bed. It was cold in the hallway. "Hello?" There was a crackling sound. The connection was awful.

"Carol?"

"Mama?" I could barely make out her voice.

"Carol. It's Mama."

"EXCUSE ME, THIS IS A PERSON-TO-PERSON CALL FOR CAROL BUR-NETT." I tried telling her that's who they got when I heard Mama crying.

"Carol . . . oh, God."

"Is it Nanny?"

"EXCUSE ME, THIS IS A PERSON-TO-PERSON CALL FOR—"

"YES!" I screamed.

"IS THIS SHE?"

I was beginning to hate her. "Yes! This is *she!*"

"GO AHEAD, PLEASE."

"Carol . . ."

"Mama . . . is it Nanny?"

"Jody's dead."

Daddy.

Daddy. It hadn't even occurred to me. I felt stupid. He had been released from the charity ward a few weeks after I'd visited him three months ago. I just saw him. He was alive three months ago. He had written me a couple of cheery letters, saying he was staying with some good friends in Venice Beach.

"He woke me up," Mama was saying, "out of a sound sleep. I could hear him calling to me. 'Lou, Lou!' " Mama used to brag about her "visions." And this had been one of them. He was dying and calling to her. She tracked him down and got there in time. "I took Christine with me. It was the middle of the night, but I found him, baby, I found him." She was crying hard now.

Nanny got on. She started telling me how she had always "liked Jody; he was always so sweet to me. In spite of everything, I liked him. Always did."

They kept trading the phone back and forth. My feet were freezing. I don't remember hanging up. I walked back into the transient room and sat on the bed. I could make out the four sleeping figures of my roommates. Tinker, Joyce, Yvonne, Barbara. I wondered about their fathers . . . bet *they're* all alive tonight.

I'm in New York, and he's dead. In Venice Beach, somewhere . . . with a bunch of wino buddies. And I don't have any money to get to him.

Too late.

He never saw me in a school show. But I was going to bring him to New York someday . . . a ticket for opening night . . . I had promised him. He had promised me. My throat hurt. It was on fire.

It was just beginning to get light when I finally cried. I reached back and got my pillow and pushed it up hard against my face so I wouldn't wake anybody up. I screamed into it as loud as I dared. God*dam*mit! Why'd you have to go and do that to yourself? What's the matter with you anyway? Don't you care? Don't you know how much it hurts, how much *I* hurt? You were doing okay; you *told* me you were doing okay. Ohhhh. Why couldn't you have been okay . . . Daddy . . . for *me*?

27

Don finally arrived. I was never so glad to see anybody in my whole life. I took one look at him and fell in love again. Two other Bruins, Frank and Bruce, were in town, so the boys pooled their resources and moved in together. They shared a one-roomer across the street from the club.

By this time I had graduated out of the transient room to one of the tiny double rooms upstairs, with only one roommate, Sally. I was closer to heaven in more ways than one. It was a four-flight walk-up.

It felt so good not to be lonesome anymore. UCLA had invaded West Fifty-third.

We all were broke. I'd sneak what food I could to the boys from the club and Palmer's restaurant. We found ways to entertain ourselves, spending endless hours, hysterical with laughter, telling "rejection stories" that came out of our daily round making. They became our "Receptionist Routines." We saw all the second acts of closing Broadway shows, or flops, by mingling with the ticket buyers at intermission and innocently drifting into the theater with them when the buzzer sounded.

Don and I resumed our steady relationship, but we were never alone long enough to suit me. There was no place to go to *be* alone. He lived with two other guys, and I lived in the "convent across the street."

I didn't want to be a nun anymore. But I was following Nanny's orders, in spite of myself, to "get the ring" first.

Nanny had said to me, "If you're not a star by Christmas, come home."

But by Christmas I wouldn't even have the fare home. At the end of November I was checking Christmas packages while the Palmer's patrons pranced in and out for eggnog, blasting me with the icy wind every time they came through the restaurant doors. I got an offer from the USO to go to Australia to entertain our troops at Christmastime. Work! Not checking coats in a tearoom but a chance to work at my craft. If I couldn't be home, I could be artistically productive. I was thrilled at the prospect of the trip. (Australia! And it was *summer* down there!) I arranged to have Barbara take over my partnership with Joyce while I was gone. By the first week in December I had filled out all the forms the

USO sent, and once I had followed up on the rest of their instructions, they would send me my airplane tickets. I went to a doctor, got the required shots—and promptly came down with whatever it was I got the shots to *prevent.* I had never, *ever* been that sick in my whole life. The plane took off without me.

When I got a little better and could lift my head up off the pillow, I'd crawl down the four flights of stairs to the dining room for some soup, and the joint would empty in seconds. Everybody steered clear of me, and during the entire holiday season I was dubbed The Typhoid Mary. Not that there were that many girls left to infect. Ellie had moved out of the club and show business. She and Larry got married. And just about all the rest were home for Christmas with their families, including Sally. I had my little room upstairs all to myself, but there was no way I could enjoy this newly discovered luxury: privacy. I was miserable. Miserable, ill, and homesick. It was my first Christmas away from Nanny, Mama, and Chrissy. I was sick, and there was nobody to really and truly take care of me. Don was across the street but was helpless because of the "no men allowed in the rooms" rule. I felt like an abandoned two-year-old. I was, as Nanny would've put it, "Pure-dee-pitiful." And I'd soon be broke again. Barbara had my job until after New Year's, and even if I hadn't given it to her, I wouldn't have been able to lift a hat to hang on a hook if my life had depended on it.

The week between Christmas and New Year's I was finally able to sit up in the parlor, and Don and some of the other UCLA homeless came to call. Our spirits were low. We tried to cheer each other up by singing carols and thinking up clever gifts that didn't cost anything. None of us felt like singing, and none of us was very clever.

It was snowing, but it didn't feel like Christmas.

28

It was 1955. A new year. The club came back to life, and so did I. As a bonus, I was elected club president. It didn't bother me that nobody else wanted that particular honor. It would look good on my résumé.

I was off the critical list and back working at Palmer's. One good thing about winter: Everyone wore a coat. In fact, I was averaging four to five extra bucks a week.

Fine. But it was time. Time to "make your own breaks."

I'd been stewing for three months about something Eddie Foy's agent had said to me: "Why don't you put on your own show?" Well, why not? *Why* not? He had been kidding, but I wasn't.

The new president called a meeting. I got a few surprised looks. Nobody had ever called a meeting before. Nobody could remember one anyway. There was a suggestion box, that's all, and the suggestions were usually homemade dirty limericks about the quality of the food we were served (those were the polite ones). I announced the meeting at dinner. I stood up and rapped my fork on my milk glass. "There will be a meeting of all the residents in the parlor after dinner. I have a very important matter to discuss with you *all,* so please come upstairs as soon as you've finished dessert. It won't take more than ten minutes." I paused. "And it could very well change each and every one of our lives." I exited up the stairs. That ought to get 'em.

I was waiting in the parlor. Tinker was the first one to arrive. "What is it? What *is* it?" I kindly told her to be patient, she'd know soon enough. The rest of the girls arrived and settled down pretty quickly. A few of the older members straggled in and hung out in the doorway, lighting up cigarettes.

I called the meeting to order, and Tinker was the last one to stop talking.

"Girls, a while back I actually got into an agent's office and met one face-to-face. Contrary to popular myth, they do exist." Laughter.

"Get a job out of it?" one of the smokers asked.

"No."

"Next time don't put out." She exhaled. Loud laughter.

She was good. I waited. "No . . . I didn't get a job, but I got an idea" —pause—"a great idea."

I let the moment breathe. Silence. I was good, too.

Then I continued. "He told me to let him know when I was in something and he'd be more than happy to come and see my work. Naturally, I asked him how does one get in something in the first place without an agent, and he said to me, *'Put on your own show.'* "

There. It was out. I had said what I wanted to say . . . what this meeting was all about. Grinning from ear to ear, I looked around the room at all the faces, expecting applause.

Or *some*thing.

I lost one right away. "Oh, f'chrissake . . . an' I got a *date* tonight." She stubbed her butt out in an ashtray and left the room in a huff. We all watched her go. A couple of others started to get up.

"Hey, wait a minute!!! Come *on!* Why *not?* Let's do it; let's call him on it. Let's *put on our own show!*"

Quite a few more left the room.

I felt my throat squeeze. "Hey, you guys!" (Forget them, concentrate on who's left. Who *is* left? About twenty. Okay, that's okay.) "What's the matter with us anyway? Look at us, what are we doing? We keep pounding the pavements day after day"—I pounded the coffee table with my fist—"leaving our glossies that cost us a fortune, *that we probably got gypped on* with some dumb receptionist who uses them for wallpaper! Every day we go out *begging* for a break, just a little one, every single day, and—and—and just *who* do we think we are? Is somebody gonna up and *hand* it to us?" I saw a few heads shake. "No, I don't think so either! It's *not* gonna be dished out to us on a silver platter. *We* gotta do it. It's up to *us!*"

I had 'em. "Like my mama done tol' me, *'You have to make your own breaks!'* " I was out of breath, and my vocal cords were shot. (Thank you, James Stewart, Frank Capra, Mickey and Judy.)

I got my applause. Tinker started it. "Great! I'll do my Spanish dance!"

Maybin, who danced, volunteered her services (as choreographer) and her boyfriend, Peter. Peter was a very talented songwriter/pianist. I volunteered Don. He would direct and produce. Ming Cho Lee, one of the UCLAites, would do the scenery and lighting.

We brought the guys in for another meeting the next night, and we wound up meeting every night for the next two weeks (before and after my hours at Palmer's).

Planning. Lots of planning. We had the cast (twenty of us), the director/producer, the writers, and the scenic designer. We'd each be responsible for our own costuming. It was all falling into place. We had just about everything. Except the show, the theater, and the money.

The other tenants complained that we were completely taking over the parlor and told us please to go some place else to play Let's Pretend. Sourpusses.

We paid for a rehearsal hall by chipping in a quarter apiece every night. Anybody could be in *The First Annual Rehearsal Club Revue,* come one, come all, for two bits.

Now we needed something to rehearse.

We kicked around lots of ideas and finally settled on basing the whole show on "truth." A show about a show. Why not let the audience in on How Our Revue Was Born? Brilliant. We came up with a rough rundown:

ACT I. OPENING

1. Parlor. Girls are sitting around, despondent, lethargic, depressed. They complain about the tough times they're all having trying to get discovered in this cruel town. Receptionist bits, etc. Song: "LAZY AFTERNOON." Solos and chorus.

2. Carol bursts in. Bubbling over with energy, she sings about how exciting it all is. Song: "I LIKE NEW YORK IN JUNE (HOW ABOUT YOU?)" Added special material verse by Peter Daniels. Song ends. Girls throw pillows at Carol; maybe some shoes, too. Carol tries to cheer them up. They'll have none of it. Song: "WHY, OH, WHY, OH, WHY, OH, WHY DID I EVER LEAVE OHIO?" Solos and chorus.

3. Discussion follows about how to solve their dilemma. The Idea is born. "Let's put on our own show! We'll make the agents, producers, and directors come to *us*!" Songs: "PICK YOURSELF UP, DUST YOURSELF OFF, AND START ALL OVER AGAIN" and "NEW YORK, NEW YORK, IT'S A HELLUVA TOWN." Entire cast.

INTERMISSION

ACT II. THE REVUE

Every one of us would get a solo shot at showing our stuff in the second act. Perfect.

We zeroed in on our dates.

The Carl Fischer Concert Hall on West Fifty-seventh was the cheapest theater we could rent. It was available for two nights the first week in March—for $100 a night. We passed the hat and came up with a $50 down payment. The invitations would go out as soon as we drummed up the rest of the dough, $150.

Make your own breaks.

We got in touch with "Our Ladies of the Fund," the wealthy women who sponsored the club, and invited them to a rough run-through of the first act. We told them that we wanted their creative input, that we wanted to draw on their "expertise." It was a total con. What we really wanted to draw on was their pocketbooks, but we had to win them over first.

We cleaned the dirty rehearsal hall as best we could and set up the folding chairs for the ladies, wiping each seat thoroughly so they wouldn't soil their Chanel bottoms. They arrived pretty much on time, looking very pulled together. None of them wore the same outfit, but it looked like it. There were about ten of them.

Don got up and made the Welcome to Our Rough Rehearsal Speech: "We're so happy you could take time out to be with us tonight. As we explained over the phone, this is a rough run-through, which means no scenery, costumes, or props"—not that we had any—"just the raw talent of the young women of the Rehearsal Club. We know you all have imaginations, but tonight I'm afraid they'll have to be working overtime." They smiled. "As for our show, we hope to invite every producer, director, and agent in town, and we intend to make them sit up and take notice! They haven't put us in a show yet because they just haven't seen what we can do, so we decided to take the bull by the horns and put *ourselves* in one! As my father used to say, 'There's more'n one way to skin a cat!'" The ladies laughed and applauded (charming, isn't he charming). Don continued. "But before we did that, we wanted you to come here as our guests tonight and be the very first ones to see the effort we've been putting in, these past few weeks, to make *The Rehearsal Club Revue* an annual event; we wanted to let you know that your devotion and generous contributions to the Rehearsal Club, and all it stands for, have not been misplaced. It's our way of thanking you personally, the best way we know how—with our talent."

The women were positively beaming.

For the next hour and a half we strutted our stuff.

When we finished, we hit them up for the $150.

"Our Ladies of the Fund" came through. Not only with enough to rent the hall but an extra hundred to boot, for any added expenses (like postage and programs . . . and scenery). *Two hundred and fifty smack-eroos.* They also got Katharine Cornell to sign the invitation. Miss Cornell was a famous Broadway actress and a member of the board.

Dear ——,

We are happy to invite you to the first annual Rehearsal Club Revue to be presented at the Carl Fischer Concert Hall, March 3 and 4 at 8:00 P.M. These young women have been told you'd be happy to "see their work" when they are "in something." Well, they've written and produced their very own showcase, JUST FOR YOU! So please, keep your promise, and come see their work. There is no charge. Simply produce this postcard at the door. It will serve as your ticket. Those of us on the Board of Trustees are very proud of these talented performers. We're looking forward to seeing you there, so you can "discover" them for yourselves!

Sincerely,
Katharine Cornell

She signed them just the way we wrote them. The penny postcards were mailed to everybody we could think of.

We rehearsed around the clock: in the rehearsal hall, in our rooms, in the dining room, in the hallways, and on the stairs. I recited lyrics to myself over and over while I was checking stuff at Palmer's.

March was around the corner.

We were as ready as we'd ever be.

"Five minutes, everybody, five minutes! Break a leg!"

(Oh, God, oh, God, oh, God, please don't let me forget anything. Oh, God, I've never been so scared in my life . . . please. . . .)

It was here. March 3, 1955, our opening night. We could hear them coming into the hall. We were getting an audience! It had worked. They got our postcards and came! Actual agents. I peeked through the curtain. They looked like agents or the way I thought they were supposed to look. They were sitting there—just like real people. And then I spotted . . .

"Ohmygod!" I screamed.

"What *is* it?" Tinker rushed up. Her mantilla was crooked.

The club had friends in high places. I let her peek. *"Ohmygod!! Marlene Dietrich . . . Celeste Holm!"*

The houselights dimmed, and the piano overture began.

And I thought I was going to die.

The place was packed. I stood in the wings, waiting to go on for my big comedy number in the second act, shaking with fear. Then out of nowhere I hit a calm.

I remember thinking, "This is it. If they don't like me, I'll quit, so *please,* God, please make them like me."

I heard my cue and started trembling again. I was going to sing "Monotonous," the Eartha Kitt number from *New Faces.* It was a sexy, funny number, and Kitt had been very sexy and funny in it when she introduced it on Broadway in 1952. It was about a hot-looking dame bored with being adored. She had sung it in skintight toreador pants and slithered her way over and around six poufy chaise longues (I saw the movie a dozen times back home). The New York audience was familiar with the song and began to laugh at the piano intro. I walked out onto the stage. I was in a frumpy old print housedress I'd found at a thrift shop and scruffy loafers, had curlers in my hair, and entered lugging three broken-down kitchen chairs, which I plopped down on the floor and proceeded to trip over and get all tangled up in while doing my best (worst) to slither sexily, like Kitt. It was a complete takeoff on her original version.

I got three bows and lots of bravos. I wouldn't have to quit. Thank you, God.

It seemed as if the entire audience was milling around backstage after the show. You couldn't move. It looked like a bucket of worms. Everyone was jumping up and down, screaming, giggling, crying and hugging and kissing each other, including "Our Ladies of the Fund."

Marlene Dietrich, looking just like Marlene Dietrich, complimented us all, and Celeste Holm, elegant and friendly, got me aside and said if she could help me in any way, she'd be delighted. I was delirious with joy. And to top it all off, the *agents* were introducing themselves, passing out business cards, and asking me for my phone number!

That night I fell into bed exhausted and unable to close my eyes. I was afraid if I closed them, I might wake up. If this was a dream, I wanted it to go on forever. And then I heard it against the window: rain. It was raining . . . just for me. I drifted off, dreaming of footlights every color of the rainbow.

The following Monday there was a terrific review for me in good ol' *Show Business* (refer to photo insert), but it wasn't so hot for the show itself, although it encouraged our efforts. No matter, the pay phone on the wall was ringing off the hook. The agents were calling *us*.

"Carol! It's for you! Now it's somebody from William Morris!"

Ring. "Maybin! It's for you, hurry . . . MCA!"

I'd been keeping in touch with my old buddy from UCLA, Dick DeNeut. He was in the service. I wrote him about the show and sent the review from *Show Business*.

Sunday - March 13, '55

Dearest DeHootie -

Now a report on the
East - Coast happenings.

The show was a huge
success. We closed to an SRO
audience of top agents, producers, directors, Marlene
Detrich and Celeste Holm!

The next day, Dick,
I received TWENTY calls from
just about the best agencies
in town. Needless to say, I
was thrilled — but confused.
I didn't know who to sign
with — I called Celeste Holm
as she came backstage, & said
that she was very impressed
with me, & any time I wanted advice I could ask her.

So, I went up to her place
last Saturday afternoon,
and she spent two hours (!)
explaining the pros & cons
of agencies to me. I finally
decided to sign with
the Wm. Morris office for
a year — She was so nice.

I already have my
first job as a result of
the show — MCA hired
me for an industrial
show in Chicago, to take
place the last week in
April. At last I feel
as if I'm progressing.
I did good, Dick. I
didn't go overboard on
anything. I did a straight

song in the first act called,
"I Love New York, but I'm
Scared" — a good tune,
but not much of a vehicle.
In the second act, I
repeated my role of "Stan"
(a boy) in Whats in a Name?
Shades of a UCLA one-act!!
Then, I did "Monotonous" —
BUT not like before.
It was a complete take-off
on Kitt. Instead of sexy
toreador pants & six satin
couches — I had: a
baggy print dress, loafers,
and three broken-down
kitchen chairs to work with.
It was the best I've ever
done it. I got three

curtain calls each
performance - I was
thrilled, as this was
probably the toughest
audience I'll ever
have to play for. I
wish you could've been
here, Richard - I think
you'd have been proud.
I thought of you before
each performance.
I think we started
a tradition, as the Board
of directors is already
talking of a show for
next year. This makes
me very happy, as the
whole mess was my
idea.

Please write soon
Dick — just how soon
are you heading for L.A.?
When you get there, give
everyone my love & I'll
keep you well-posted on the
doings here.   Love ya —
                    Carol

29

The week after the show I met with representatives from MCA, William Morris, and just about every other agency I'd heard of and not heard of. Don got calls about his directing, and he was running around on interviews, too. It was working out just the way we had planned it. I loved walking up to the receptionist, giving her my name, and having her smile and say, "Oh, yes, he's expecting you!" A sensational feeling. I almost asked a couple of them if they remembered giving me the brush-off, but I didn't. I was in too good a mood. How beautiful to be wanted!

The man I liked the best wasn't with a big agency at all. In fact, he wasn't even with an agency but worked for a management company. It had a very small client list, all "names." His name was Arthur Willi, and he wasn't like any of the others. He really seemed to care what I was going to do with my life. I sat in his office across from his desk, and he laughed and confessed that he had wanted to go home right after our first act, but it was his wife, Laura, who had persuaded him to stay for the rest of the show. He didn't try to push me into anything, and he said that no matter whom I signed with, he would always make himself available to me if I needed any advice.

I chose the William Morris Agency, because it was the most famous, and I signed on for a year.

But I kept going back to talk to Mr. Willi every other week or so. His door was always open, and his advice was always better than anybody else's.

Monday, May 9, 1955
New York City, USA

HELLOOOO OUT THERE!

Saints preserve us, I thought
they'd frozen you & packaged
you in aluminum foil for future
generations. I'm glad to know
you're still living - er - alive -
er - existing. In other
words, I almost gave you
up, De Nootie.

your letter was wonderful.
I'm keeping them all on file,
in case you want to write
a book some day — that is,
if your fingers aren't frozen.

How much longer will this
outrage continue? And when

are you coming to me?

As for East Coast news, I'll attempt to relate all in detail; although, I may not finish until Thursday. However, I'm sure you'll have the time — that's the only thing I <u>am</u> sure of.

#1. After the revue, I signed with the Wm. Morris Agency (as you already knew). They, in turn, got me a fine job with a summer company at Green Mansions — a summer resort, 200 miles upstate N.Y. I will play "Jenny" in Three-<u>penny</u> Opera (a (ugh!) SERIOUS

role)... also parts in My Three
Angels, I Am a Camera, &
Oh Men! Oh Women! As yet,
I don't know what parts,
plus, skits and songs in
several variety shows.
One of the writers will be
Sheldon Harnick of -AHEM!-
"Boston Beguine" fame. The
director is an ex-B'Way
stage-manager; his last
chore being The Girl in
Pink Tights — name's Perry
Bruskin — looks very much
like Dennis Saunders, inciden-
tally. Anyhoo, that's the
summer agenda.
     #2. Did an industrial
show for aluminum foil
through MCA, in Chicago

April 18th Much fun, also much money — it enabled me to fly to L.A. for a 10-day visit. In fact, I just returned to New York a week ago today! Saw everybody. I'm so sorry that you & I missed connections. It was good to be home. Nanny is fine, & Chris is 5'2" tall & wears a size 7 shoe!! (no more playing "Don't step on the green;" her feet are too big!!)

Saw the Swindells — They're on their way here now, driving back.

It rained most of the

time I was home. Wayne
Hubbard & Phil Abramson
tossed me a 22nd birth-
day party at Phil's place
in Beverly Glen. Everybody,
but everybody was there.
Joanie Beckman with Bob
Fremont (remember him?),
E. g. André with Mrs. André,
Eddie Hearn, Earle Jones
with Gail Kobe, Nanny
with Christine, and many,
many others.

     #3. If you can get hold
of a copy of Theater Arts
(May Issue) yers trooley
is on page 12 doing "Monotonous" from the Rehearsal

Club Revue. I'm a horrible mess, but it is a good picture. I've already received several offers of stock as a result of it. Don got a promotion at work as a result of the show, also. He's now assistant to the director of MCA Industrial Shows!!

I'll be going up to Green Mansions June 18th. I'm really looking forward to it. Danny Kaye & Imogine Coca played there in their youth. I should profit a great deal.

In the meantime, I'm working on the revue material, some of which is extremely funny. I'll elaborate on it in my next epic to you.

In the meantime, be good, & don't take any wooden igloos.

Write again soon, Richard.

Love,

Carol

30

The dress was bright orange—so orange you could probably see it in the dark. High neck. Long sleeves. Tight at the waist. Full skirt. On sale, for twenty dollars.

The four of us, Sally, Barbara, Mary, and I, chipped in five dollars apiece, and it was ours. It would be our community audition dress. The color would stand out at any cattle-call audition ("Excuse me, would the girl in the orange dress step forward, please?"), and the style fit each one of us. We hung it in my closet, signed it out when we needed it (first come, first serve), and whoever used it last was responsible for having it cleaned and put back in the closet (one-day service, naturally).

Mr. Willi had told me always to wear a bright color if I wanted to be noticed in a large audition. So when I spotted this dress at Bloomingdale's, I ran back to the club and talked the other three into the investment. It was a wonderful dress. I didn't always get the job, but I always got a call-back.

The Morris office was sending me out for all the summer stock auditions, and I landed a job that would start in June at a resort called Green Mansions in upstate New York. Every summer the hotel hired actors, producers, writers, and directors and did standard and original pieces as entertainment for their guests. I was signed on as the comedienne.

Don was working, assisting an industrial show director, and I auditioned for an industrial show for aluminum foil that would be done in Chicago in the spring.

("Excuse me . . . you . . . yes, you . . . young lady, the one in the orange—")

I was hired for seven hundred dollars. When the show was over, I splurged and bought a plane ticket home. It had been eight whole months since I'd seen my family, and I was homesick. My twenty-second birthday was around the corner, and I wanted to go home for a visit before I had to report to Green Mansions. I wasn't the star that Nanny wanted, but I was a *working* actress.

I couldn't get over how much Chrissy had grown. God, I had missed her. I had missed them all so much. And it was great getting together with some of my old UCLA buddies, who tossed me a birthday party, but after a few days, I started to miss New York . . . a lot. Nanny and Mama hadn't changed at all. They still fought all the time. Nanny got her spells, and Mama drank and got her hangovers. Chris was the only thing that had blossomed. Nanny didn't want me to go back to New York because she wanted me with her. And I could tell Mama didn't want me to go back because she was jealous. I found myself getting depressed. New York was life. This was decay. One morning I walked into Mama's apartment, and she was asleep on top of the covers as always, with Tweetie settled down on top of her stomach. Mama was snoring softly. I had the sinking sensation that I had *never left at all,* that it had all been a dream, a cruel joke, that I might *never* get out.

"WHERE THE HELL HAVE YOU BEEN?"

I almost jumped out of my skin. It was the parakeet.

"New York, Tweetie, and I'm going back as soon as I can."

Friday, June 10, 1955

Hiya!
    Got your "gem" this A.yem.
You sound fine Richard,
just fine. I sure do wish
we could've seen eachother
in L.A. Fate is against us,
De Nootie — but as long as
there's a mail service, we
won't lose touch. I leave
for G.M. a week from
tomorrow. My new address
will be: Green Mansions
                    Warrensburg, N.Y.
    Did a show up there
Memorial Day week-end; a
truly beautiful resort. .
methinks 'twill be an enjoy-

able summer.

Guess what? <u>I was an</u> <u>extra</u> <u>on</u> <u>the</u> <u>Martha</u> <u>Raye show</u>! (Sounds like a "title, doesn't it?) I called Nanny long distance to tell her to watch, & Chris answered — when I told her, she screamed, "Oh Sissy! Is Martha Raye sick?" Anyhoo, 'twas much fun. She's nuttier than I am - and Erroll (sp) Flynn is fat, but pleasant. What did I do? I sat in a "Tunnel of Love" boat, and necked with some idiot whose name I never <u>did</u>

learn! However, the dough will keep the wolves from the door, until my departure. What one won't do for $.

Glad to hear you have your tootsies in a theater venture. Have you considered Time Out for Ginger? That was a 50's hit, y'know. Keep me informed on the progress.

I'm working on a night club act for G. M. Variety night shows, that I can put to use in the fall, when I return to the City. The

Morris office made a
deal with two writers and
a director — I'll have
all summer to test it
out before an audience —
if it's good, it'll be
booked into one of the
clubs here. The director is
Mickey Ross, who directed
the Sid Caesar show for
quite awhile, before he
quit to go into producing
& directing on his own —
He's very well respected
around town, and he seems
to have a great deal of
faith in me. The writers
are Lee Adams & Chas.

Strouse — young fellows,
who wrote some stuff for
the _Shoe string Revue_. I
don't want to be a night
club comedienne for the rest
of my life, but as the
Morris Office says, it'll:
1. Keep me before an
   audience. 2. Provide a
good show case. 3. Give
me T.V. material — I'll
keep you posted.

    Well sweetie, that's 'bout
all — Larry & Ellie _are_
here now!! (almost
forgot to tell you!) Today's
Larry's birthday, so we're

all getting together tonight -
I'll give him your address,
and he can keep you
informed on their progress.

When next you write,
send it to G. M? My
letters will try to be
prompt, but I don't imagine
they'll be as long.

Be good - what else can
you do? - and write when
you can. Again, good luck
on your theater venture -
I love ya - "and someday
I'll find you."

your Lorac

I was never so glad to get back to a place in my life. From now on New York was *it*. I would *have* to be a star, so I could set up Mama, Nanny, and Chrissy in a Park Avenue penthouse, where everybody would be well and happy.

In the meantime, I was treading water until it was time to go to Green Mansions. Palmer's restaurant was a lost cause in May, but the manager said Joyce and I were welcome to come back in the fall, when the weather changed. I was hoping I wouldn't have to, but it was comforting to know the job would be there.

The Morris office got me a couple of television jobs as an extra. One of them was *The Colgate Comedy Hour*. It was a thrill to watch Martha Raye do her stuff. She was inspired, and they should've sold tickets to the rehearsals. I wasn't impressed with television, though. The cameras got in the way. You couldn't see the audience. No matter, those bit parts paid my rent that month, and come June, I'd be on a real stage—all summer, as the main comedienne—for five hundred dollars and room and board.

Sunday- Aug. 14, 1955

Well- here I am- and I bet
you don't believe it for a
minute!

    This is honestly, absolutely,
positively the very first chance
I've had to set myself down,
and answer yours of July
5th. I'm ashamed De'Nootie,
please forgive me.

    It has been so long, I
don't exactly know where
to begin, but here goes.

    At Green Mansions, I am

a success — I can say this
to you, as I know you'll
understand — I'm honestly
not doing my best, Richard.
Perhaps, its because I'm
tired — or maybe I haven't
had a role I feel I can
really do — nonetheless, the
management is pleased, even
tho' I'm privately mad at
myself. There _is_ one thing
I do that I have fun in —
Dorothy Parker's one-act
about newlyweds, <u>Here We Are</u>.

I also enjoy doing "Jenny" in <u>Three</u> <u>Penny</u> <u>Opera</u> — other than that, nothing much excites me up here. But I <u>am</u> learning to do things I don't like — which is a big lesson to me — so I don't feel the summer has been wasted.

Now for some big news — I'll preface it by saying that there is nothing definite, but the events leading up to it are very exciting.

Three weeks ago, the Morris
Office called me — and said
to report to the Cort Theater
on July 28 — 10:30 AM to sing
for Rogers & Hammerstein's
Pipe Dream — I flew down
And blasted out "Monotonous"
for both Mr. R & Mr. H —
plick; it was the most
thrilling moment of my
life!! — they smiled
& laughed all the way
through the number, &
when I'd finished, Mr. R.
asked if I could come
back in two weeks to sing

And read for Harold
Clurman (Bus Stop) who's
directing the show for them.
So I went back last Thurs.
and sang and read — They
seemed very pleased —
So I had the Morris office
Call Barbara Wolferman,
(R&H's gal Friday) — she
said that they were very
impressed, & that she's
pretty sure that if there's
a good small part for
me, I'll be in the show!
And even if there is

nothing, she said that
they know & like me, &
that ~~there wont~~ they will
use me when there is a
part I could do in a future
show. Anyhoo, that's just
about the most exciting
thing that has happened
to me since I've been in
New York. I'm sitting on
pins & needles, praying
for a little part — I'll
probably know within
the next couple of weeks
or so — . And I'll let you
know immediately.

Now, how about you?
I sure do miss ya, De
Nootie — there have been
so many times when
I've wanted to talk over
personal-type matters
with you — I'm just sorry
I haven't had the time
to write oftener — but
now that things have
eased up somewhat, I
promise to be a better
correspondent. How's
your theater venture?
Details, please.

I saw Damn Yankees when I was in town — loved it. Verdon is the end.

Larry is working on a local newspaper in Tudor City — and — as was expected, has taken over the sports section, and is still spreading. He's due for big things. A wonderful boy — Oh when will we all get together again? They are moving soon, and when they get settled again, I'll send you their address.

WEll honey — nuthin'
more to report — I'm all
writ out — Please
write soon — & Remember,
I loves ya —
    Carol

31

I didn't get the job in Rodgers and Hammerstein's *Pipe Dream.* I came close, but I missed out because I was looped to the gills—on cough medicine. I had been called back a *third* time. I was right in the middle of my stint at Green Mansions (a six-hour bus ride from New York), I had a rotten cold, and my final call-back was a Monday afternoon. The producers at Mansions gave me the day off to go into the city. I could hardly talk, much less sing, and I was frantic. After the show Sunday night, I took the late bus to New York and collapsed in my bed at the club around 4:00 A.M. praying for a miracle before I was due to sing for Mr. Rodgers and Mr. Hammerstein at 2:00 P.M. I coughed my way through the night and the next morning. I hadn't closed my eyes, and when I saw myself in the mirror, it showed. I felt my head. Yep, a fever all right. Oh, Lord, why? Why now? Downstairs I hacked my way through a breakfast of tea and toast. I started to cry. All the girls in the club were recommending home remedies. I remembered the times Nanny had put mustard plaster on my chest and covered it with a flannel cloth to break up congestion, and it had still taken days before I recovered. I didn't have days. I had about an hour and a half.

Then Barbara said she had a whiz of a cough medicine and gave me a slug of it in a tablespoon. I stopped coughing almost immediately. That stuff was good. I got dressed. As I was going out the door, she gave me another swig for good measure, and I was on my way.

I don't remember much of the audition, but I do remember trying to get home. I staggered all the way back from the theater, turned the corner, saw the club in the middle of the block, and fell to my knees. A man was walking towards me as I collapsed on the sidewalk, and I remember asking him to help me up. He crossed the street. I was dying, no question about it. And I wanted to. I knew I had lost the job. They had been very polite, but they only said, "Thank you very much." Broadway talk for "get lost." Somehow I got up the steps to the club and leaned my body against the doorbell. I looked up at the skyline. The buildings were swirling above my head. Maybe I'd wake up in Oz.

I woke up the next morning in time to catch the bus back up to Green

Mansions. I had slept fifteen hours. The cough was gone—but so was my chance for *Pipe Dream,* the new Rodgers and Hammerstein musical, opening that fall.

Ironic, that title.

Green Mansions was over, and I was back at the club. The Morris office sent me around to auditions every once in a while, but I was usually the wrong type: not a star and not a chorus girl. Most of the producers I sang for were complimentary, but compliments didn't pay the rent.

I found myself back checking coats at Palmer's, just as I had the year before. Was that it? One tiny splash, and it's all over?

I went to see Mr. Willi. He asked me all about the summer, and I told him how hard we had worked and how much I felt I had learned, but that things seemed to be at a standstill once again. The Morris Agency wasn't courting me anymore, the people there acted as if they didn't even know I was signed with them; I felt like an old girlfriend who had been tossed aside. He gave me a pep talk and said now was no time to think other people would do my work for me. I had to keep plugging. He suggested I work up some new material for auditions—material I could use in a club act if I had to. "You'll make it, Carol, if you don't give up on yourself. I believe in you." I left his office feeling better. Thank you, Mr. Willi.

I remembered a young man who had followed me into the hall after one of the dozens of auditions I'd had last spring for stock, he had been accompanying the singers on the piano. I had been on my way out of the building when I heard him call my name. He introduced himself, said he really liked the way I worked, and felt sure I was a shoo-in for a stock company that summer and much bigger things in the future. He was a coach and special-material writer. He gave me a piece of paper with his name and number and said he hoped we could work together someday.

I had asked a few people up at Green Mansions if they'd heard of a coach named Ken Welch. They had, and they all said he was terrific. I'd filed the information away in the back of my mind.

After Mr. Willi's advice, I dug around in my wallet for the piece of paper Ken had given me six months before. I found it, called him, and we made an appointment. We began to work together on audition material. He charged ten dollars a session, and I paid him in the quarters and dimes I got from my job at Palmer's.

It was the start of a professional and personal friendship that's still going on.

The day I did my first show on the Paul Winchell kiddie TV show on NBC was the day I first pulled my ear as a signal to Nanny back home. December 17, 1955.

I had called her from the Rehearsal Club, thrilled with the news that I had been signed for a few weeks as a regular member of the cast. I'd been hired by Paul Winchell himself! He couldn't be nicer, and I was going to get to sing "Over the Rainbow" to Jerry Mahoney (Mr. Winchell's alter-ego dummy) on my very first outing. She could catch me every Saturday morning!

She was excited, too. "How much are you making?"

I told her it wasn't a lot, but it was a major stepping-stone in my career. She then said, "Well, say hello to me when you get on television."

I explained that I couldn't do that. It was a scripted show, and the producers wouldn't let me break out of the story to say hello to her on national television.

"Well, tell 'em it's for your grandmother who raised you."

"Nanny, please, I can't do that! It's my first regular job. And besides, it's not my show."

"I don't see how one little 'hello' could hurt NBC."

I had a brainstorm. I had worked the aluminum foil industrial show that fall with Bud and Cece Robinson, a dance team, who had a four-year-old son, Danny. We all had become good friends. Whenever Bud and Cece did their act and Danny was watching, they'd pull their ear-lobes for him as a special secret signal, which meant "We love you, Danny."

"Nanny, I'll pull my ear for you."

"Your what?"

"My *ear*. It'll be our special secret signal. From me to you. Telling you, 'I love you, Nanny.'"

She liked that a lot.

What she didn't like was that I told her Don and I would be getting married after the show that same day.

We settled down in a one-room apartment directly above the kitchen of the old La Scala Italian restaurant on West Fifty-fourth between Sixth and Seventh, for $110 a month—a fortune.

My job on the Winchell show lasted thirteen weeks. Neither one of us was working full-time, and we had to watch our pennies. Directing jobs for Don weren't any easier to find than acting jobs for me. He worked at anything he could get. He even drove a cab part-time.

Thank God I was eligible to collect unemployment: $36 a week, more than I ever averaged at Palmer's. I reported to the unemployment office every week and stood in line for hours.

I got the same awful woman just about every time. "An actress, huh?" Then she'd look at me and make a face. She made me feel like a crook. "Did you seek work this past week?"

"Yes." (No, I love being here with you every Tuesday. I want to spend my life here.) I explained that I had auditioned three times the past week for Broadway shows that were casting, *plus* worked up a new routine on "Different Types of Singers" with Ken Welch, so I'd have some funny new audition material. I started to do one of them for her.

I could tell she hated me. Actors made the unemployment office people furious because they couldn't send you out on regular jobs. If they could figure out a way to get me an audition for George Abbott, I'd be more than happy to forgo my $36 that week. My pleasure. But in the meantime, I'd like the money I'm due.

She would practically throw it at me.

Don and I hadn't been able to save much out of the $115 a week I had made on the Winchell show, but with my unemployment and his working at odd jobs, we were paying our bills. We bought a pull-out couch that doubled as a bed, a dresser, two kitchen chairs, and a coffee table. The table was a plain door that you could buy at one of those do-it-yourself furniture stores. It came with four attachable legs.

If we watched our budget very carefully, we could have friends over for dinner every once in a while. Spaghetti. We got a reputation for being the best Italian cooks in our circle. Our sauce couldn't be beat. Our secret was plain tomato sauce and an open window. The aroma from the La Scala kitchen below would waft up and into our tiny apartment, and everybody's nose did the rest.

Nanny was not happy that I had married Don. She let me know it in no uncertain terms in her letters: "Your mother says you were a fool to marry him. He has no money, and you'll wind up freezing to death with a bunch of babies. Besides, he's not even one of us. He's Armenian! You'd better watch out you don't get pregnant!"

I would tear it up, but there would be another one just like it the next day in the mailbox, beginning with "Your mother says . . ." The letters made me so mad I'd wind up crying.

I wasn't sorry I had married Don. He was gentle and sweet, and we had fun together. It wasn't the rotten picture Mama and Nanny had always painted, and it infuriated me that every time I opened another letter, I'd read another dig. Okay! So we don't have any money! So what? We're young. We're healthy. We're talented. And we're in love! What's so bad about that? Please . . . Dear God, make them lay off! Please, we're going to be just fine!

It's all just fine, exactly the way I pictured it. Every show business couple is supposed to struggle at first. It's part of it, it makes it all the more wonderful when our big break comes.

And then I started to get luckier than Don.

Mickey Ross, who had been the director up at Green Mansions, called me to audition for Max Liebman (the producer of the wonderful *Your Show of Shows* with Sid Caesar and Imogene Coca). Mickey was assisting Mr. Liebman, and they were putting a television show together for Buddy Hackett—a half-hour live situation comedy called *Stanley*. I went over that same day, read with Buddy, and got the job.

Don and I were ecstatic. That night we ate downstairs in the restaurant.

My one-year contract with the William Morris Agency was up during my thirteen weeks on the *Stanley* show, and I didn't re-sign. They hardly ever called me anyway, so I was just as glad they didn't notice (or care) when the year was up. I went over to Mr. Willi, and he took me into the fold.

I spent the summer of 1956 doing stock at another summer resort, Tamiment (catering to young singles), in the Poconos in Pennsylvania. Ken Welch was along as a writer-composer, and so was his talented (singer-writer) future wife, Mitzie Cottle.

Tamiment had been the beginning for Danny Kaye and Imogene Coca. I was hired as the lead comedienne. We did an original musical revue every week as part of the resort entertainment (just like Green Mansions). Since the audience didn't pay to see us (we were part of the whole resort package for the week), we *had* to be good, or they could just get up and leave and go neck in a rowboat and we could find ourselves playing to empty seats. They never did.

That fall I auditioned for a CBS talent search project (doing the material Ken and I had worked up, with him at the piano), and we were sent up the ladder to Garry Moore.

Garry Moore was the star of his own CBS-TV morning show five days a week. On Fridays he introduced new young talent to his audience. He was the kind of man who held the auditions himself. He wouldn't let anybody else do it for him. I remember how friendly he was when he introduced himself to us and how he made us feel right at home. I was the least nervous I had ever been at an audition. When we finished, he came up to us and said he would put me on his show the following Friday and *anytime* we had any new material. All we had to do was call him, and he'd book us—no need to audition for him again! Ken and I went to town coming up with new stuff as fast as we could.

I still collected unemployment when I didn't work the previous week, but I did a lot of guest shots for Garry's morning show that year, and as a result, Don and I were able to move to a small one-bedroom apartment over on Eighth Avenue (this time above a tiny grocery store), where we celebrated our first anniversary. I called Nanny and Mama and Chris over the holidays, and all Nanny talked about was wanting me to make sure I didn't get pregnant now that Don and I had to pay more rent. She whined during the whole conversation, and Mama sounded sick. When I hung up, I felt guilty as hell about Chrissy. God, would I *ever* be able to do anything about that mess?

Then I got a Merry Christmas call from Mr. Willi. His office had shown a kinescope of one of my appearances on Garry's show to *The Ed Sullivan Show* producers, and they booked me for a guest shot the first week in January 1957. Ed Sullivan! Things were definitely looking up.

Two weeks after the Sullivan show, I was back in the unemployment line. I stepped up to the Wicked Witch's window—two whole weeks since I'd laid eyes on that fabulous face. My form was all filled out and waiting for her approval. I was tickled silly and found it hard to keep a straight face.

She looked at the form. "You've made a mistake."

"I did? Where?"

"You put the numbers in the wrong columns." She shoved the paper back at me.

I tried to look concerned. "I did? Where?" I was having a wonderful time.

She lost what little patience she had. I had gotten her goat but good. *"Here!* Where you wrote you earned *seven hundred and fifty dollars for one day's work!* You'll have to fill out another form and wait in line again." She tried to wave me off with her pencil. "You'll want to put down *seventy-five dollars* or, more likely, *seven dollars and fifty cents,* but not *seven hundred and fifty!*"

"No, I won't."

"What?"

"I wrote it in the correct columns. I made seven hundred and fifty dollars two weeks ago. May I have my unemployment check now?"

"In one day?" she screamed.

"Yes, if you'll read further down, you'll see where I was a guest on *The Ed Sullivan Show* a week ago Sunday."

Her face paled, and she gave me my check. She looked dazed.

I smiled sweetly. "Sorry you missed it. I'll let you know before the next time! Bye!"

I had written Mr. C. when we did *The Rehearsal Club Revue* and told him all about the terrific response we got. I wanted him to know we were working hard and keeping our promise to him.

I let him know when Don and I got married and when I was on the Winchell show.

I wrote him when I did my first *Ed Sullivan Show.*

He never wrote back.

32

The summer I was at Tamiment, Mama went on the wagon.

Chrissy and Cuz had been invited to visit some of our relatives in Texas for a few weeks, and Nanny called me to see if I could scrape up enough money for part of Chrissy's plane fare. Don and I had a little saved up, and we were able to pop for a one-way. Cousin Irene helped with the other half. I was glad she was going to get to go. If anybody needed a change of scenery, it was Christine.

I called Chrissy the day before she was leaving. I'd never heard her so excited. She was eleven, and this would be the first time she had ever been outside Los Angeles.

"Oh, Sissy! I'll bet we get to ride some horses!"

"Sure you will. Just make sure you hang on!"

"Do you think we'll see some cowboys?"

"Hey, what do *you* think? You're gonna be in *Texas*! I just called to tell you to have a terrific time."

"Oh, I *will!* Thank you! Thanks for the ticket!"

Nanny grabbed the phone. "Did you get my letter?"

"Hi, Nanny. Which one?"

"The one I sent two days ago."

"I'll probably get it today. The mail gets here in the afternoon—"

"Christine will be gone forever."

"No, she won't, Nanny."

"I hope I feel up to going to the airport tomorrow, so I can see Christine off, but Parker's driving them, and he drives so fast he about gives me a heart attack every time he gets behind that wheel. I wish Eudora would drive. She knows *how* to drive. But he won't let her when *he's* in the car—"

"How's Mama?"

"She says she's going to quit drinking."

"*When?*"

"I'll believe it when I see it."

"Is she there? Can I talk to her?"

"Christine! Run down the hall and get your mama. Tell her Carol's on the phone . . . wake her up. Tell her it's *long distance!*"

"Nanny, never mind, don't wake her up—"

"She *says* she's going to get herself sober while Christine's in Dallas and surprise her when she comes home. I told her I just hope I live to see the day. You know how she shakes in the mornings when she hasn't had a drink yet. I'm not looking forward to it, I can tell you that. I wish *I* was going to Texas."

"Well, maybe next time, Nanny . . ."

Her voice went away from the phone a little. "Louise! Hurry up! It's Carol! She's calling from that summer stock place in Pennsylvania!"

Mama said, "Hi, kid."

"Hi, Mama. I didn't mean to wake you up."

"You didn't. I've been up for days."

"How are you?"

"I'm o*kay.* I've got some news for you. I'm goin' on the wagon. When the baby leaves tomorrow, I'm tossing out my booze. It's tap water for me from now on." She laughed. "And for Tweetie-bird, too."

"Mama, that's wonderful."

"I'm gonna surprise Chris when she comes home. I'm gonna be pretty again, goddammit. And she's gonna love *me!*"

"Mama, she loves you."

"The old lady's not buying it, but I'll show her. Christine will be mine again. I'll show 'em all."

She did, too. For a while.

I got pieces of the story later, from Cuz, Christine, Dodo, and Uncle Parker.

Chris and Cuz were on their way home, and Mama and Nanny were waiting at the airport with Dodo and Uncle Parker for the plane to land from Dallas. She had made it. She hadn't had a drop in weeks—not since Chris left home. And she looked terrific. She had fixed her hair and put on some makeup. She had on her best dress, high heels, and stockings. She started shaking a little when the plane began to unload and held on to Uncle Parker for support.

Cuz and Chris came through the door. Chrissy spotted Nanny waving.

"There they are! There's Nanny!" They got closer, and she stopped and looked at the woman standing next to Nanny.

"Mama?"

"Hi, baby."

Chrissy couldn't stop hugging her. "You look so beautiful! You look so beautiful!" She hadn't seen Mama dressed in over a year.

On the way home in Uncle Parker's car, Chrissy wanted to sit next to her.

The next few days she spent more and more time with Mama in their apartment.

It didn't last.

I heard different versions of the story.

One was that Mama simply fell off the wagon, and that was that. Another one was that she got the shakes so bad one night, Nanny offered her a drink just to calm her down.

33

It was August 1957, and Mr. Willi had booked me into the Blue Angel three months before. The Angel was *the* "in" cabaret, over on the East Side of Manhattan. The management specialized in featuring new young talent. It was an important showcase. We did two shows a night, seven nights a week, and I was getting two hundred dollars a week. There was a headliner and three other acts. I was one of the other three. Ken Welch had written a solid twenty-minute act for me, mainly original comedy songs, and I had been well received. Don and I were just keeping ahead of the bill collectors. The Angel managers wanted to renew my contract if I could put a new piece of material into the act. I hurried over to Ken's, and we went to work to come up with something fresh.

Ken got a brilliant idea. It was the height of the Elvis craze, and he wrote a song about a young girl going ape not over a rock star but over our secretary of state, John Foster Dulles. Mr. Dulles, as far as his public image was concerned, was aptly named. He wore glasses and a hat, and he never smiled. He was uptight and ultraconservative. Some people in the media went so far as to call him a pickle puss. He was the least likely candidate for *anyone* to swoon over, and that's what made the number so funny. We decided to open the act with it.

I sang the first line, "I made a fool of myself over John Foster Dulles," and the audience fell down laughing. It was an instant hit. Word got around, and soon audiences were coming into the Angel to see "that girl who sings the song about John Foster Dulles."

Then Jack Paar booked me on his NBC late-night show on Tuesday, August 6. The Parr show was one of the most popular shows in the country, and like the Sullivan show, it was live.

"So won't you join me in welcoming a bright new comedienne, now appearing at the Blue Angel?" He said my name, and the band played an intro. I walked out, stood on the mark, looked into the camera, and trembled. There was polite applause.

When I finished, the place went wild.

I went back to the Angel to do the second show, and the phones were ringing off the hook, people wanting to know how long I'd be appearing there and making reservations. By the time the sun had set the next day, my whole life had turned around. I was the talk of New York, of the whole country for that matter. Newspapers. And not just the show business section. Front-page stuff. NBC had received hundreds of calls and reported that 152 of them had been protest calls from people thinking the number was in poor taste. The other callers had thought it was a riot. Reviewers raved, and there were even editorials. Some said the song was political. James Reston, of the New York *Times,* wrote a tongue-in-cheek editorial about the political ramifications of the song. Was it pro-Republican or anti-Republican? I was famous.

Mr. Dulles had missed it, so the State Department (through Mr. Dulles's TV adviser, John Waters) requested a repeat performance (the Paar show again) on Thursday. Mr. Waters was quoted as saying, "The secretary would very much like to see Carol do the song." Then Ed Sullivan had me sing it on his show on Sunday night. Three network appearances in *one* week.

Interviews. Newspaper columnists. TV talk shows.

"Miss Burnett, tell us, did Mr. Dulles finally get to see the number?"

"Yes, I believe so."

"And?"

"And I was told he liked it, a lot."

"Have you heard from him?"

"No, but I watched *Meet the Press* the other morning, when he was on, and the very last question was: 'What's going on between you and the young lady who sings that love song about you?' "

"What did he say?"

"Well, he kind of smiled . . . an actual *smile* . . . and I swear, I could see a twinkle in his eye . . . and he said, 'I make it a policy never to discuss matters of the heart in public.' "

"What do you think of that?"

"I think he *does* have a sense of humor."

"Are you still appearing at the Blue Angel?"

"Oh, yes. Seven nights a week, two shows a night."

"So anyone who missed the song on TV can catch you doing it at the Blue Angel?"

"You bet. . . . You don't think I'd leave it out, do you?"

The Angel hadn't seen that kind of activity in a long time, and I *never* had. I was lapping it up, basking in my newfound limelight. (Boy, am I good. I am *really* good.)

As far as I was concerned, nobody in the world *was* ever or *would* ever be that good. Period. I had it all figured out. I had found the key, the answer, the secret. I knew how to wrap that audience around my little finger and make them love me forever and ever. I knew it all.

What I didn't know was that the whole thing had gone to my head.

It was a Monday night. And we were packed. Again. Mondays were notoriously slow for nightclubs. But not *us,* boy, not since me. Me and "Dulles." They were lined up around the block.

I was cool as a cucumber, and as I was putting on my lipstick and fixing my hair in the dressing room, I thought back to all those silly times I had been nervous about performing, how my heart would race when I heard the crowd coming in and settling down before the lights dimmed. The butterflies in my stomach just before the music began. The anticipation, backstage and out front. The stage fright. A silly waste of time. I winked at myself in the mirror. (That's all in the past, kiddo. That's all in the past. Relax, you've got it made.)

I remember whistling in my dressing room before the first show that night. I had two dresses: one for the early show and one for the midnight show. (Lemme see, should I wear the red or the black?)

I was introduced and sauntered onstage in my red. The audience was eager to see me. They greeted me with the huge round of applause I had come to expect. I pointed to the piano player, shot a look at the audience, and, oozing cocky confidence, patiently waited for him to finish the intro.

"I made a fool of myself over John Foster Dulles . . .
I made an ass of myself over John Foster Dulles . . .
The first time I saw him 'twas at the UN.
I never had been one to swoon over men,
But I swooooned and the drums started pounding and then . . .
I MADE A FOOL OF MYSELF, OVER JOHHHHNNNN FOSTER DULLES. . . .

Something was wrong. They weren't laughing. They usually laughed after the first line. Not "usually." Every time. Something was definitely wrong. I couldn't figure it out. I was halfway through the song, and they were still just sitting there, staring at me. It wasn't that they were unruly or not interested. That wasn't it. It would've been better if that *had* been it. I *wished* that had been it—there would have been a reason for all this —but *they were paying attention.* They were listening. And they weren't laughing.

And that was only the opening number. I had twenty minutes to go.

Not one laugh. Not one real laugh. A polite titter or two, and that was it. (Ohmygod, I've *lost* it!)

I thought I would never get out of that nightmare. I raced through the routines and prayed no one I knew was in the audience. I prayed to die (wasted, because I already *had*). I prayed my armpits would dry up. The twenty minutes dragged on and on, even though I was pushing like crazy. It was just like trying to run in a dream. After what seemed like days, I finally finished and made a hasty exit—hardly enough applause to get me off the small stage and over to the back stairway. Usually I'd get all the way up the stairs and have to come back down for another bow because they were all shouting, "More! More!" Not tonight.

I had bombed. Royally.

And in my gut I knew why. I had been too cocky, too sure of myself. I wasn't human anymore. And it showed. It affected (*in*fected) my whole attitude. I wasn't funny. I was abrasive.

I headed for my dressing room down the narrow hallway, and a customer was weaving toward me on his way to the men's room. Drunk. We had to pass each other. I knew he had just seen what I had done downstairs on that stage. I looked at the floor and tried to inch past him (goddamn hallway—ought to be a fire law or something). I hoped he wouldn't notice me. I was too humiliated and embarrassed for anyone to notice me, even a drunk, and the specter of the midnight show coming up was already starting to haunt me. I was crying like crazy, and the tears were spotting my red satin jumper. (*Why* hadn't I worn the black?)

"Hey, there," he said to me. "Hey, aren't you—"

Oh, God. I wiped my eyes with my fingers and looked at him. He had kind eyes. Blurry but kind.

"Hey there, little lady . . ." His voice matched his eyes.

"Yes, sir?" Please, God, don't let me blubber. Let me get to my room with some dignity.

"Well, my goodness." He reeled back against the wall. He was really out of it. "Aren't you the little lady . . . I just saw this very minute? Downstairs . . . just now, on the stage?" He cocked his head and smiled at me. He had a sweet smile. I felt a little better.

I smiled back. "Yes, sir . . . I am."

There was a pause.

"Boy. You stink." And he disappeared into the men's room.

* * *

My heart was racing, and I had butterflies in my stomach before I went on for the midnight show.

It went a lot better.

Chrissy knew I was coming out for a few days before the holidays. Nanny had told her. I didn't know why, but I felt it was very important for me to go.

We really didn't have the money, but I had saved a little from the Blue Angel job, and I'd been collecting unemployment since September. The Dulles number had made me hot in the business for about ten minutes. It didn't take long before I had cooled down and was thought of (when I *was* thought of) as "that girl who sang that song about John Foster Dulles." The past year I'd done a couple of shots on Sullivan, eight weeks at the Blue Angel, and Garry Moore's morning show, whenever I had some new material to break in. The weeks I didn't work, there was always the old unemployment check. Don was able to land a few one-shot directorial jobs here and there and still drive a cab part-time. We were managing. But New York was expensive.

I called Nanny. "I'm coming home!" I explained it was just for a few days. Don would stay in New York, and I had to be back before our second anniversary, December 17. She snorted something about her not surviving another Christmas. I told her I'd be there before she knew it, and we all should be happy I could afford to come home for even a little while.

I arrived in the early afternoon the first week in December 1957. Nanny cried when she saw me. I hugged and kissed her a lot and then went down the hall to see Mama. The shades were down, and she was asleep.

"Sleeps all the time these days," Nanny said.

I decided to head straight for Le Conte, where Chrissy was a seventh grader. I figured it would be fun to surprise her on her way home from school.

We spotted each other at the same time.

"Sissy!" she screamed. "You're here!"

I think I was more surprised at what I saw than she was.

She had shaved off her eyebrows. Her perfectly arched, thick black eyebrows looked like five o'clock shadow. She had replaced them with black pencil. She was wearing apple red lipstick and a matching red sweater that emphasized her 34C chest. She was sauntering up Bronson Avenue from Le Conte with about three or four guys, horsing around on the street outside the bowling alley. She was twelve.

She ran up to me and kissed me. She said to the guys, "This is my big sister! Here she is . . . this is *her* . . . I told you . . . she lives in *New York,* and she's in *show business*!! Tell 'em, Sissy, tell 'em . . . I'm not a liar! *Tell* 'em."

I wanted to cry. I had to do something.

It had been a couple of years, or close to it, since I'd been home for a visit. It had been bad enough the last time, but now it was even worse. Everything had changed, gotten older, more worn-out: the building, Nanny, Mama. Especially Mama. She looked awful. She was bloated all over. Her puffy cheeks were covered in broken blood vessels, and the once beautiful, big blue eyes looked milky. Her long eyelashes had all but vanished, and her hair was thinning and stringy. Even though she couldn't eat much of anything, her stomach looked as if she had swallowed a basketball. She lived in one old nightgown and never left her apartment. The room reeked of Gallo, smoke, and—I didn't know what the other smell was. She was forty-six.

I'd been lying awake on the old couch for two nights in a row when I finally made up my mind. It had been driving me crazy, and I wasn't sure I knew how to handle it, but I had to do it. For Christine's sake. I would have a talk with Mama. Alone. I didn't want Nanny in on this, because I knew she would queer the deal.

There was no way in the world they could handle Christine. Mama was too sick, and Nanny was too old and nervous. It was up to me. But the deal had to be struck with Mama. I had to let her in on it, make her a part of it. I couldn't leave her out. She was so sick. It would be too mean. My plan *had* to have her blessing.

Christine was at school, and Nanny was at the store. It was midmorning, a good time to get through to Mama. Her hangover would be somewhat in check, and even though she'd be on her way to getting drunk all over again, she wouldn't be there yet. I went into her apartment and locked the door.

"Where the hell have *you* been?" Tweetie was still at it. The shades were down, and the old faded flowered curtains blocked out any cracks the bright Hollywood sunshine might be able to peep through. She was on top of the covers, bathed in sweat. God, the room stank.

She was awake. "Hi, kid, what's cooking?"

"Can I turn on a light, Mama?"

"Sure, what the hell."

"How about a little air?"

"Why not? It's hot in here, isn't it? Let's go for broke."

I pulled up the window a good six inches. It helped a little—not enough, but a little. Mama got up out of bed and threw on her old robe. We sat on the couch. It was the first time we'd had a chance to be alone together since I got home. She fussed a bit with her hair. "Gotta do something with this mess, don't you think?" I looked at the red birthmark on her right temple. I remembered how she used to conceal it deftly with a curl or a wave. I remembered how beautiful she'd once been. She lit a cigarette. "You were pretty good on the last Sullivan show you did. Must've been a kick meeting Elvis—God, I'm nuts about him—and if you ever meet Marlon Brando, give him my number, will you?"

We talked about New York. She brightened up a little. "I always wanted to go there. Yeah, New York's my kinda town. I'd have made it there. That's where all the smart ones are. . . . Did I tell you your father appeared to me in a vision in the middle of the night—the night he died?"

She had, but I said, "Tell me about it."

"It was the damnedest thing. I was right there in that bed, and out of the blue I could hear *Jody,* calling to me, 'Lou, Lou,' and next thing I knew, I could actually *see* him. He was lying on a cot somewhere, and he was trying to get through to me. That was three years ago, and I remember it as if it was yesterday."

I felt the lump in my throat.

Mama inhaled the smoke. "Well, I got right up out of that bed and started phoning all over town to track him down. I knew he was trying to reach me. My intuition never fails me, you know that, and this was a goddamn *vision.* Something was definitely wrong. I got hold of a few of his old cronies and finally found out he was in some dump in Venice Beach. I woke up Christine, and we got dressed and took the streetcar and the bus clear out there. It was damn near dawn when we found him. It wasn't easy, believe you me, but I *found* him. He still had TB . . . plus pneumonia . . . Christ." She ground out her cigarette in the old Stork Club ashtray she'd had for years. She sighed and went on. "There he was, lying there in this filthy shack, surrounded by a bunch of passed-out winos. I'd heard he'd gone off the wagon and was on the streets in

Venice—" Her voice broke. "He was dying, Carol." She got up and poured herself a shot. She was shaking, and she turned and pointed a finger at me. "I always loved Jody. I want you to know that, baby. He was weak as hell, but there never *was* one any sweeter. *Never.*" She put the shot glass to her mouth, held her wrist with her other hand to steady it, threw her head back, and gulped down the whiskey. She closed her eyes and held her breath. I could tell the booze was burning her throat. "He was so thin, so awfully thin. I mean, he was never fat . . . but he looked like a skeleton lying there on that bed. . . . I stood at the foot of the bed, and he stared at me for a minute . . . and I said, 'Jody, do you know who this is?' . . . and he said, 'You were once my wife.' Well, that did it, Carol, I started crying and couldn't stop." She reached for another cigarette and lit it.

She sat down again, and I braced myself for the next line.

"He said to me, 'Carol was here. . . . It's a shame, you just missed her. She came to see me.' Yeah, he thought you'd been there. . . . I didn't have the heart to tell him you were still in New York."

We both were crying now. She wiped her eyes with her fingers. "Christ . . . life."

"Mama, let me have Christine. Let me take her to New York."

"For how long?"

"For keeps."

She looked at me, scared. "How 'bout just for Christmas? She'd get a big kick out of *that.*"

"Mama, she's growing wild out here. Let me have her; you know I'll take good care of her. I love her, too."

Just then Nanny tried to open the door. "Louise, don't lock this door . . . I can't get in! Why'd you lock the door? Louise!" She started turning the knob back and forth. Mama put her finger up to her mouth to shush me. She didn't want Nanny in on this any more than I did. Nanny started banging on the door. "Louise! Carol? Are *you* in there? Open up!"

Mama screamed at the locked door. "Get lost! Carol and I are having a private conversation!"

I could feel Nanny stiffen on the other side. It was quiet for a few seconds, and then we heard her walk down the hall and slam her door.

We didn't say anything for a while, and then she looked at me. "For keeps?"

I nodded.

After a very long time she finally spoke. "Okay. I won't say anything. We'll tell Christine and the Old Lady it's just for the holidays."

We were thinking exactly alike. We knew Christine wouldn't leave with me if she thought she wouldn't be coming back. And we knew if Nanny got wind of it, she'd tell her. I'd secretly check Chrissy out of Le Conte, and we'd leave for New York the end of the week. Mama would tell Nanny once we were gone, and I'd tell Chrissy after I got her to New York. It would all be okay. It was for the best. In the meantime, mum's the word. I hugged Mama, and she smiled and cocked her head. She looked almost pretty.

"Take care of the baby for me, will you, kiddo?"

"You know I will, Mama."

It was the best talk we had ever had. And it was the closest I'd ever felt to her in my whole life.

One month later she was dead.

Chrissy was ecstatic when I told her I was taking her back to New York with me for the holidays. She and Nanny had no idea I had already been to Le Conte and told the principal she wouldn't be returning after New Year's, that she'd be moving east. Mama had backed me up in the lie.

"New York! Oh, Sissy, will it snow?"

"I don't know, but I bet we see some from the train."

"The *train?*"

I had always wanted to go across the country by train, and I figured it would be a terrific trip for the two of us. It would be something we'd always remember. The last time I'd been in a train was when Nanny and I sat up all the way from San Antonio. A hundred years ago.

Chris was thrilled.

Nanny wasn't. "Now I won't have either one of you here this Christmas."

Chrissy said, "I'll be back, Nanny. It's only for three weeks."

"Long enough," Nanny replied, downing a couple of Bayers. "January's a long time off." She looked old and lost.

I couldn't look at them. Dear Lord, let this be the right thing. Please.

After my talk with Mama, the next hurdle was Don. I knew it would be okay with him for me to bring Chris to New York for Christmas, but having her as a *permanent* responsibility was another matter.

I called him collect from a pay phone to insure my privacy. It was okay with him. I was grateful that he was willing to take it on.

I hung up and leaned my head against the phone booth.

Oh, God. Another mouth to feed. And school—what about school? I didn't want her winding up going to school in the city. It would be riskier than Hollywood. No, it would have to be a private school somewhere. But where? How?

I didn't dare think about it anymore. First, I had to get her out of Los Angeles.

We kissed Nanny and Mama good-bye the morning of December 11, 1957, one day before Chrissy's thirteenth birthday. I was scared to death Mama would back down and change her mind, but she didn't. We went into her apartment, and she was trying to get up. Nanny said, "Don't bother, Louise. I'll go into the lobby with them. Why don't you just stay in bed?" Nanny always had to be the last one to say good-bye and the last one to get a kiss. It was a thing with her. Mama accused her of having a "star complex."

"Why don't you stay put, Louise? I'll see them off."

Mama shot her a look. "I am perfectly able to walk them to the lobby, thank you very much." She put on her house shoes and reached for her robe.

The four of us walked into the lobby, and I turned to Mama. I kissed her and whispered, "Thank you, Mama. It'll be okay." She squeezed my arm. Then I kissed Nanny.

Chrissy started to kiss Mama, and Mama said, "Kiss Nanny good-bye first." Nanny started to say something, and Mama stopped her with "I wanna be last, this time."

Christine got her snow.

The second day on the train was her thirteenth birthday. She blew out her candles in the dining car, and the other passengers sang "Happy Birthday," along with the waiters and me. She wished for Mama to feel better and for snow.

It was the perfect time of year for a train trip from L.A. to New York. Especially for a kid whose native tree was a palm. We rolled along on the tracks that cut through the Rocky Mountains, and we gazed out the windows at Christmas card pictures come to life. At night I listened to the wheels clicking on the tracks and found myself saying over and over, *"How'm* I gonna tell her? *How'm* I gonna tellher?*How'm*Igonnatellher . . . *how'm*Igonnatellher . . . ?"

* * *

She loved being in New York with Don and me. She slept in the small living room on the foam rubber couch with the screw-in legs. It was the first time she'd ever slept in a room alone. We window-shopped along Fifth Avenue and toured Bloomingdale's, top to basement. We bought chestnuts on a street corner and wondered how anything that smelled so good could taste so rotten. She learned how to flow with the pedestrians: dodge the traffic and cross against the lights. We decorated a small tree, and the three of us celebrated our first eastern Christmas together.

And her eyebrows had grown back.

Christmas Day we called Nanny and Mama. I was a little nervous about it. Nanny asked Chris when she was coming home, so I knew Mama hadn't spilled the beans yet. Chris told her she'd be back before school would start again, right after New Year's.

"Let me talk to Carol."

Chris handed me the phone. "Hi, Nanny, I love you. Merry Christmas. How do you feel?" She told me.

"It's the worst Christmas I've ever had. Your mother hasn't put a foot out of her bed since the two of you left. I wanted to go to Eudora's today, but I can't leave Louise, and she won't go with me. I don't feel like going anywhere anyway." I heard Mama yell something at her in the background.

I asked, "Is she there? Can I talk to Mama?"

"All right, but don't hang up before I can say good-bye."

She gave Mama the receiver. "Carol?"

"Hi, Mama. Merry Christmas."

"Same to you, kid. Is my baby there?" She sounded more tired than drunk.

I gave the phone to Chris. "Merry Christmas, Mama. I miss you, too. I'm having a wonderful time! I'll be home soon! I'll see you next week! I love you. Lemme say good-bye to Nanny! . . . Hi, Nanny! I hope you feel better soon. Merry Christmas. Good-bye! . . . Here's Sissy! I love you!"

I was right there. "Hi, Nanny. I hope you feel better soon. Here's Don. He wants to wish you both a Merry Christmas." Don got on and off as fast as he could, and then it was my turn again. "Nanny, I'd better say good-bye now; this is costing a fortune."

"Have either one of you two got a job coming up?"

"Something'll happen soon, Nanny. It's always slow around the holidays."

"Well, I hope I live to see it."

"You will. I'll know the truth for you. I love you. I'd better hang up
now. Merry Christmas! I love you!"

"I love you, too! Pray for me."

"I will . . . good-bye."

Just before New Year's, Chris and I were getting ready to cross the street
at Fifty-fourth and Eighth. We'd been grocery shopping, and we were
loaded down with bags. She said, "Sissy, school's starting next week.
What day do you think I should leave to go back home?"

Here it was.

"You're not, honey. You're going to stay here and live with us." I
blurted it out before I had a chance to think about it. She dropped the
bag she was holding. She simply let it fall from her arms. Groceries were
all over the sidewalk. I remember a large grapefruit rolling into the middle of the street and being crushed under the front wheel of an Eighth
Avenue bus—juice and seeds spurting everywhere.

She started to scream. "You can't *do* that! I belong in California! I *live*
there. I don't *live* here, and you can't *make* me! Mama and Nanny won't
let you!" I tried to explain. She screamed louder. *"You kidnapped me!"*
Even the most insulated New Yorker turned his head on that one.

I got her across the street and into the apartment before any cops
could nab me. I was trying to calm her down when Don came home. He
tried, but she was hysterical.

I explained it was the best thing for her. "One door closes, another
door opens . . ." and that Mama knew all about it and thought so, too.

She wouldn't believe me. "You're lying! Mama would never give me
up!" Then *I* started crying.

We called Mama. Now Chris would believe me. But Mama had
changed her mind. As soon as I heard her voice, I knew she was drunk.
She told Chris she wanted her to come home. Now they both were hysterical, and Nanny was busy having an attack because she hadn't been let
in on it. Dear God.

I found the right words. I convinced them at least to give it a chance. I
would get the money somehow, even if I had to borrow it, and find a nice
school out in the country somewhere for Chris. I would see to it she got
the braces she needed for her teeth. Easter was right around the corner,

and I swore I'd find a way for her to go home and visit everybody during vacation, so she could tell them all about life in New York. And then, before anyone would know it, summer would be here, and she could spend it in California (I kept going, hardly taking a breath), why, she wouldn't be giving up California, at all . . . this just meant she'd have *two* homes, and after all, Mama always felt New York was the place to be, and wasn't she happy the baby had a shot at this big opportunity?

"Mama, please give me the chance to give Chris a chance."

It worked. They calmed down and agreed to a tryout. Nanny wasn't for it at all, but when I told her this situation might take me to California more often, she piped down.

I hung up the phone, exhausted.

Christine looked at me through her red eyes. "Sissy, will the braces give me pretty teeth?"

We were almost a week into the new year, 1958.

I woke up late one night and saw the living room lights were on. Don was sleeping, and I slipped out of bed to check on Chrissy. It was around 3:00 A.M. She was sitting up on the couch, writing a letter.

She looked disturbed. "Sissy, I had a dream about Mama, and it woke me up. I just wrote this letter to her and I have to mail it now." I asked her if it could wait until tomorrow.

"No . . ."

She read it to me. In it, she told Mama how much she loved her and apologized if she had ever hurt her in any way.

Chris insisted on mailing it immediately.

Mama got it a few days later, in time. Just in time. It was almost as if she had waited for it to reach her . . . and when it did, she let go.

We got the call from Nanny on January 10.

"Carol? Carol? Is that you?" She was crying.

"Nanny! What is it? What's wrong?"

"She's gone. Louise . . . my baby."

Oh, God. Oh, Dear God. Mama. I knew it was coming. Down deep I knew it. That's why I took Chris. Mama knew it. That's why she let me take Chris. And Chris—she knew it, too.

"I just knew it," Nanny was saying. "Eudora and Parker came over last night, and we tried to get her to eat a half a chicken sandwich, but she wouldn't touch a thing. I couldn't even get her to swallow a raw egg with her whiskey, like she does sometimes. She kept reading that letter she got from Christine to us. I didn't sleep at all last night, and I got up early to go down the hall and check on her. Something was different. I felt it even before I went into her room. She was on top of the covers like always, but she wasn't breathing. She looked so bad. Oh, Lord . . . she's gone, Carol." I had never heard Nanny sob like that. "What am I going to do without her? She was my baby. I don't know how I'm going to stand it. Nothing is worse than losing your own child."

Chrissy and I couldn't be there. We didn't have the money, so we couldn't be there. We were three thousand miles away when Mama was cremated. I remembered her saying, "No hole in the ground for *this* kid. I'll come back and get you if you ever let 'em throw dirt in my face."

It had been such a beautiful face.

35

We picked a school for Chris in a small town in New Jersey—all girls, uniforms, and Episcopal nuns. I couldn't believe she'd go for that, but she did. She got her braces. She said that's why she wanted an all girls' school, so there wouldn't be any boys around to tease her about the railroad tracks on her teeth. As for the nuns, I think down deep she was starved for some structure and discipline. The school was out in the country in a beautiful setting, about an hour from New York. She could come home on weekends. We borrowed money from the bank, with Mr. Willi cosigning the loan. Now all we had to do was keep working.

I was booked on *The Dinah Shore Show* in March. It was shot in California. Home . . .

I got a room for two weeks at the motel just up the street from Nanny and 102.

Nanny wanted me to move her from Yucca and Wilcox. She didn't want to live there anymore. The memories were too painful. And she didn't even have Tweetie to keep her company. Mama had given him to one of her old buddies after Chrissy had moved in with me. She didn't want him around because he reminded her of Chris. (He lived to be eighteen.)

There was a one-bedroom apartment available in a building a couple of blocks away, on Cherokee.

When I looked at the mess Nanny had accumulated in 102 over the years, I felt like making a run for it. She even had the clothes, washrags, strips of cloth, chipped dishes, cups, old magazines, newspapers, letters, and drawings she'd brought from the San Antonio house, eighteen years ago. It boggled the mind, but I didn't bolt. I held my breath, rolled up my sleeves, and plunged in.

I moved her between rehearsals for the Shore show, lugging all her stuff by hand in shopping bags—*all* her stuff. She wouldn't let me throw out one single old newspaper or magazine. "My recipes!" (Lord save us, she'll never change.) It took a hundred trips and all weekend to carry all of it over to the Cherokee apartment. My hands were raw, and my back was breaking, but I kept thinking, "Well, at least she's got that extra room. There'll be more space for all this junk." I finally got her moved in, and there wasn't any more room in the new place than there had been before. The stuff had multiplied during the move. Downright spooky. It had a life of its own. I hung up her clothes in the closet and stacked everything as neatly as I could in the cupboards. But Nanny cut through all that, settled in pretty fast, and had it looking like 102 in no time flat.

One night I walked back to the old building and went in. I went down the hall to Mama's room. There was a light under the door, and I heard a radio blasting away. Somebody else was in there now, somebody else.

"I miss you, Mama . . . I wish I'd gotten to know you."

I walked back up the hill to the motel where I was staying. I threw my key on the dresser and sat on the bed for a few minutes. This was the first time ever that I had not been with Nanny when I was in Hollywood. I was sleeping in a bed, not on my couch. I was a grown-up who would be a quarter of a century old next month, and now I was responsible for Nanny. I felt so funny . . . as if I were in a whole other life now . . . a new one. I wasn't the same person anymore, and I never would be again.

Later, as I was falling asleep, I remember smiling to myself. The motel I was in was sitting smack-dab on top of the vacant lot where we all had played when we were kids.

The year flew by, and Don and I were apart almost as much as we were together.

That summer I worked for Ed Sullivan at the Desert Inn in Las Vegas for four weeks. I was one of the ten acts he took with him. I sang the Dulles number and did a couple of comedy routines. Chris was with me. Don was back in New York.

Vegas. Mama and I never *had* made it to a show that time—the time we got stranded and wound up sitting on the lawn in front of the depot, waiting for Nanny to bail us out. And we didn't catch one when we were on the "honeymoon" with poor Bill Burgess. She blew any money they had on roulette *that* trip, too. And now here I was, appearing in one of the shows in one of the fancy hotels on the Strip.

She would've had a ball.

After I closed with Sullivan, Chris and I went to California. I'd been booked for a couple of Dinah Shore summer replacement television shows, hosted by John Raitt, Janet Blair, and Edie Adams.

I was doing okay. I wasn't a star by any means, but Nanny was. She told everybody in the neighborhood (and out of it) who she was. If they hadn't heard of me, *I'd* catch it. She was turning into a stage mother. "Why aren't *you* hosting Dinah's show? You could do that. What's the matter with those agents of yours, anyway? Why do you put up with that?"

"Nanny, I haven't had the experience . . . I wouldn't *want* to. I'm not ready! Give me time!"

She'd sniff. "Well, you're not getting any younger."

It was February 1959. A drizzly Sunday.

Don and I were home, and the phone rang. I picked it up.

He looked at me after I had hung up. "What's wrong? What is it?"

"The Garry Moore Show."

Garry still had his daytime show every morning, and now he had a terrific variety hour on CBS, once a week, Tuesdays at 10:00 P.M. I never missed it.

"What do they want?"

"Me. Martha Raye's the guest this week. . . . She's got a bad cold; she can't make it. . . . They want me to fill in for her."

"My God, that's great."

"How'm I gonna *do* it? They've been rehearsing all week—and they want me to learn it by *Tuesday!*"

I ran all the way to the rehearsal hall. But I kept thinking, "This is nuts . . . I'm crazy . . . I'll never get it all down . . . I'll blow it . . . I'll bomb, and Wednesday morning I won't be able to get *arrested.* . . . Nanny'll never show her face in the neighborhood again . . . she'll kill me! I'll let Garry down, and he'll never call me again. . . ."

I got to the rehearsal hall in about fifteen minutes, and Garry greeted me with a great big hug. "Am I glad you were home! Martha's flat on her back with the flu. Carol, you're a lifesaver. I can't thank you enough!" He was the nicest man in the world.

I mustn't let him down.

It was right out of *42nd Street.*

Tuesday night at 11:02, the security guard at the backstage desk hollered to me, "Carol! Someone's on the phone for you!"

I was still in the finale costume. We all had just taken our bows, and the show was off the air. CBS was into the 11:00 news. This show was history. But not to me. Everybody was gathered around me and cheering. Garry was hugging me and thanking me. I was hugging him and thanking him and all the cast, crew, orchestra members, ushers, janitors, and anybody else I could find.

Garry, in his inimitable, personable way, had explained to the audience, both at home and in the studio, that I had been a last-minute replacement for Martha. He made them want me to do all right. He made them root for me. It couldn't have gone better. I was crying with relief when I took the receiver from the guard.

"Hello?"

"Carol?" The voice was raspy.

"Yes?"

"Martha."

"Excuse me?"

"Martha . . . Raye."

"Oh, my! Oh . . . *Hi!* Oh . . . how do you *feel?*"

"Rotten. But this is the last time I'm ever gonna get sick and let you fill in for me. . . . You were too good."

I started to cry all over again.

After we hung up, the guard said, "Oh, by the way, these came for you during the show." Two dozen beautiful red roses. From Martha.

About a week later I got a call to audition for a revival of Rodgers and Hart's *Babes in Arms.* The producers were going to open it in Florida, work out the kinks, and bring it to . . . Broadway . . . in the fall of '59. I was called back to sing half a dozen times over the next two weeks. The producers liked me a lot, but they were leaning towards a "name." The television appearances I'd made didn't count for much on Broadway, but I had the director in my pocket. He wanted me, and if *he* wanted me, he could convince them to take a chance on me . . . couldn't he? The director always had the last word . . . didn't he?

My God. Broadway. At last. The part was mine. It *had* to be. That's why I'd come to New York in the first place. And this was the closest I'd come . . . and I was so *very* close. Okay, so my first show *won't* be with George Abbott, as I'd always thought. That's okay.

The phone rang. The director said they wanted me to come for (yet) another audition that morning. Could I be there in thirty minutes? The producers were having a tough time making up their minds. (I was going out of mine.) This time they wanted me to read for them, not sing.

I got dressed in two minutes. Don was out, and Chrissy was home on spring vacation. I told her I wouldn't be gone more than an hour . . . and to pray for me. This could be *it*.

I waited backstage for them to call me on. I was uneasy. Nervous is good. *Too* nervous isn't. (Calm down. Why can't I calm down?)

I stood on the stage of the theater, next to the pole with the naked light bulb on top. I held the script, and my hands were shaking. (Please, God, don't let me lose this.)

I lost it.

I knew I'd lost it the minute I opened my mouth to read. I was awful. The words came out in a shaky whisper. It was as if I had never, ever been on any stage anywhere. I was better in the Le Conte ninth-grade senior play, f'godsakes . . . and I'd probably been better when I was zonked on the cough medicine that time when I screwed up so royally with *Pipe Dream*.

I opened the door to the apartment, and Chrissy looked up expectantly.

"Forget it. I blew it." I burst into tears.

She put her arms around me, and I let myself be cuddled by my fourteen-year-old sister. "Sissy, it's okay . . . it's okay. . . . Remember what you always say: 'One door closes; another one opens'?"

I wanted to punch her in the nose. Then I had to laugh.

We hugged each other, and I went into the kitchen to throw together our "poverty special" (macaroni and hamburger) for dinner that night.

The phone rang.

"Sissy, it's for you."

"Hello."

"Is this Carol Burnett?"

"Yes."

"Are you free to audition for a show this afternoon? We're starting rehearsals in two weeks, and we open in May, at the Phoenix Theater."

"Uh . . ."

"It's a musical, based on 'The Princess and the Pea,' the Hans Christian Andersen fairy tale—"

I knew the story.

"Would you be interested in trying out for the lead? George Abbott's directing."

36

One door closes.

It happened. It happened the way I "saw" it back at UCLA.

George Abbott. My first . . . and only Broadway director.

Once Upon a Mattress opened in May 1959 and was a hit.

Mr. Abbott. At last.

Mattress was to run for only six weeks off-Broadway, as part of the Phoenix Theater's summer season. Mr. Abbott was directing it because he enjoyed discovering and working with new young talent. I wouldn't have cared if it were supposed to run six minutes: I was being directed by George Abbott!

But under his magical guidance our modest little musical was one of the surprise hits of the season, and after the six weeks, we moved uptown and played on Broadway for more than a year.

He was everything I had dreamed he would be. He had directed some of the biggest hits in Broadway history, but he treated us as if this were his very first one.

I remember the day he staged me in the bed pantomime sequence. As the character Princess Winnifred, the Woebegone, I was on top of twenty mattresses and couldn't sleep because of the tiny pea that had been placed under the bottom one, by the Wicked Queen. I was supposed to flail about, roll myself up into a ball, jump up and down, sock the pillow, almost fall off the bed, and wind up exhausted, counting sheep. By the time we had finished choreographing the six-minute pantomime (which took all afternoon), I *felt* like Winnifred. I was wiped out. But Mr. Abbott, who had been matching me move for move, looked as if he'd just had a good night's sleep. He was seventy-two and I was twenty-five.

As I write this, he's ninety-nine and in the middle of preparing his next show, number 125.

That June, five years to the day, I sent a certified check for one thousand dollars to Mr. C. He didn't write back then, either.

I finally saw him again years later.

Mrs. C. had called me at my office at CBS, where we taped my show, to say hello . . . out of the blue . . . "hello" . . . after about seventeen years. My God. Mr. and Mrs. C.! I was dying to see them. We arranged to have lunch in La Jolla at the beach club they belonged to.

I was nervous and very excited. I spotted them at their table right away, and we hugged each other and cried a little. It was . . . a moment. I don't know how else to describe it.

He looked good. Gray hair now, a little heavier. Mrs. C. hadn't changed much at all, and she kept the conversation going throughout the lunch. He was very quiet, almost shy. I asked him if he had received my check in 1959, and he smiled. "Yes, and you were right on time."

After lunch, on the way back to our cars, Mrs. C. got me aside and said, "He's so proud of you, Carol. He's just too embarrassed to tell you, and he never answered your letters because he never wanted to look as if he were trying to take credit for your success. You know, in all these years he has never said a word to anyone about helping you that time— even when you would tell the story about the mysterious benefactor to the newspapers and on television. And if your name ever popped up in conversations for any reason, he would just look over at me and smile."

I kissed them good-bye and whispered in his ear, "Thank you, Mr. C., for giving me my start."

"You're welcome."

Not long after that I got the news that he had died.

In October 1959 Garry Moore asked me to be on his Tuesday night variety show every week. So for a year I doubled—in *Once Upon a Mattress* and as a regular cast member on Garry's show—and I loved every hardworking minute of it. After *Mattress* closed, I was with Garry two more years.

That was the beginning of the most durable positive professional relationship I've ever had.

Garry Moore.

There was a uniqueness, a special quality about Garry that encouraged all of us around him—myself, Durward Kirby, Marion Lorne—to do our very best, take chances, have fun, and not be temperamental—all that, without his ever having to spell it out for us. He simply set the tone.

And Lord, he was generous to us. I remember sitting around the table in the rehearsal hall on Mondays, and if he thought another one of us should be given a funny line the writers had put in for him, he'd say, "Give this one to Durward, or Marion, or Carol. It's better if *they* have this." When he'd be complimented on being generous, he'd laugh and say, "No, I'm smart." He was both.

And he is loved by everyone who worked with him.

Because he cares.

It was March 1960. I remember looking at Don one evening and saying simply, "It's over, isn't it?" I was hurting, and I saw the hurt in his eyes. He nodded. We knew it had been coming on for a long time. I felt sad.

It would have been easier if we had been mad at each other, but there was no one to be mad *at*—no yelling, no fighting.

There just wasn't anything to talk about anymore, and there hadn't been for quite a while. How could there be? We hardly saw each other. For the past five months I had been doing eight shows a week in *Mattress,* plus Garry's show—a major network television show, seen by millions every Tuesday night. People even stopped me on the street and asked for my autograph! It was all so exciting and wonderful. My dream had come true.

I had a whole other life—apart from Don.

Parallel lines.

We had changed. It all had changed.

But I felt guilty, as if I had done something wrong.

Was that it? Was it because *I* got the breaks? Because I was "cooking"? Because it looked as if I might be off unemployment for good?

Was it because I was doing what I came to New York to do, and it hadn't happened exactly the way we dreamed it would, *together*?

And Don—was he *pressured* into being supportive and cheerful when (sometimes) he just damn well didn't *feel* like it? Did he feel left out, not wanted, resentful, helpless? And if he did, did *he* feel guilty about having those feelings?

I wondered what would have happened if I hadn't kept pushing to get married.—(*"Get the ring!"*)—if we had given ourselves a chance to go after our dreams separately. Would we have made it? Would we have even married?

I didn't know then, and I don't know now.

But it was over.

And we parted as friends . . . which was what we had always been.

New York City, February 1985

Oh, my God. I can*not* believe what I heard, not ten minutes ago, from Cuz.

We've been kicking around our childhood over the telephone ever since I started writing all this, and I was asking her about the family history, especially about Nanny's lesser-known husbands.

I told her about the day Mama blasted out the news to me about Nanny's shady secret, right after they'd had a doozy of a fight over Tony —the day Mama caught Nanny about to rip up the only snapshot Mama had left of her and Tony.

I had never talked to Nanny about it, and Mama never brought it up again.

So I asked Cuz because Aunt Dodo would be the one who'd know the most, even though she has been pretty sick lately and her memory hasn't been too good. I knew the "six husbands" information had always been hush-hush, a major skeleton, but maybe Dodo might have dropped a tidbit or two about some of her other daddies around Cuz, at one time or another.

"It's a shame you didn't get more out of Aunt Doo." Cuz had always called Mama Aunt Doo. We don't know why.

"Well, let me think now, Cuz." We still call each other Cuz.

"The last one was Papa John (White)." Yes, we both remembered him. We were real little when he died, but he was the only grandpa Cuz and I had known. Number six.

Cuz was having trouble.

So I suggested we start from the beginning.

"Okay, Bill Creighton was number one." (Right. My grandfather, the one Mama named me after. Dodo and Mama's daddy.) "Then there was Herman Melton—"

I interrupted. "Right, Nanny married him, and he later kind of adopted Mama, I guess, because I have some old love letters of hers from James Trail addressed to Louise *Melton.* She had been Louise *Creighton* before that—"

"Oh, no," Cuz said. "Mr. *Melton* was Aunt Doo's father."

"What?"

"I said Mr. *Melton* was your mother's daddy—"

Janice had to be mistaken. "Cuz, Mama was Louise *Creighton* when she was little. I've seen books of hers where she signed her name that way on the inside covers. She took Melton's name *after* he and Nanny got married, but Bill Creighton was her father."

"No, she and Mother weren't whole sisters."

"What?"

"You never knew?"

Knew? *Knew?* No! I was dumbfounded. "Cuz, are you sure?"

"Oh, yes. I've known that ever since I can remember. The whole family knew it. I can't get over the fact *you* didn't."

(Neither can I, Cuz; neither can I.) "Who told you? How do you know this?"

"Lord, it was so long ago. I think Mother must've told me. It was such a secret . . . I just figured *you* knew it all these years, too."

No. Sure didn't. I looked at the calendar on my hotel room desk. It's 1985, and I'm just now finding out that the grandfather I thought had been mine, that Nanny had told me had been mine . . . wasn't. I wasn't a Creighton after all.

It sure did explain the difference between Mama and Aunt Dodo. Dodo, a brown-eyed blonde, who turned to the Bible, and Mama, a blue-eyed brunette, who turned to the bottle. Personalities, attitudes, humor, everything—different, different, different. Snow White and Rose Red.

Cuz went on. "Don't you remember how Mother always talked about how Papa Bill loved her so much and hated Louise?" (Yes, yes, and I remembered the fights they had about it and how Mama had said it wasn't true: that Eudora was just jealous, that's all.)

Oh, my God. *Mama didn't know either!*

"Janice!" I was yelling over the phone to Cuz. "Janice! *Mama* didn't know it either! Nanny never told *her* either. . . . *Nobody* ever told her! I *know* Mama never knew it! She *died* never knowing it!" I was beside myself.

"Cuz, Aunt Doo *had* to have known."

"No, no. Why would she and Dodo have fought over which one of them he loved the most, if she didn't think he was her *father?* And she would *never* have given me 'Creighton' for a middle name. I mean, why name me after a man who not only *wasn't* her father, but who *hated* her to boot? You got a picture of Mama doing *that?*"

"Maybe you're right," Cuz said. "But I don't see how they could've kept it quiet so long when everybody else knew—even me."

"The wife is the last one to find out. Only in this case, it's the *daughter!*"

But *why* the secret? Unless . . . Nanny was pregnant with Mama (Mr. Melton's baby) *before* she divorced Mr. Creighton!

That's it. Of course, that's it.

Janice and I continued trying to piece it all together. "And I'm right, Cuz. Mama didn't know it because if she had, don't you *know* it would've come out all those times when she was drinking—when she and Nanny were at each other's throats! Nanny never could have gotten away with all the rotten things she said about Mama and Tony if Mama had had the *slightest* inkling that Nanny had *done the exact same thing!*"

Good God.

I asked Cuz to talk to Aunt Dodo and try to jog her memory. We're also going to get in touch with the vital statistics and records departments in Belleville, Arkansas.

Nanny, the Belle of Belleville. Yes, indeed.

More later.

I can't get over it. It's like a soap.

Two Days Later

Cuz just called. She talked to Dodo, who said she and "Sister had different daddies . . . that's a fact." Cuz then got hold of someone in the records department in Little Rock, where all the Belleville information is now. They turned up Mama's birth certificate:

INA LOUISE CREIGHTON
MOTHER: MABEL EUDORA CREIGHTON
FATHER: WILLIAM HAROLD CREIGHTON

So . . . Nanny had put Creighton's name on the birth certificate, which means . . . she was *still married to him when she had Melton's baby.*

But she made damn sure Mama was legitimate.

* * *

I've been thinking about this for hours.

Somehow, some *way*, Nanny must have "persuaded" Bill Creighton to claim Mama as his own. Maybe he did it for Aunt Dodo's sake, so the scandal wouldn't touch the one daughter who was his. . . .

Maybe he loved Nanny enough to do it for her.

Dodo used to tell the story about how Nanny broke his heart when she divorced him. "My daddy was a gentleman through and through. I was just a little bitty thing, but Mother dragged me into the courthouse with her, and she said such awful things about him. I hated it. I would cry and cry. She kept wagging her finger at him, and he never answered back. Not a word. And he could've put her in her place, believe you me, but he didn't. He didn't open his mouth, but I could see the tears in his eyes. He was such a gentleman."

That's the only thing I remember Dodo talking about. She never said anything around me about her and Mama not being "whole sisters." ("He could've put her in her place.")

I called some relatives in Texas, some cousins of Mama's. *They* all knew Mr. Melton was Mama's daddy. I'll be damned. The whole world knew it—except Mama and me. Even Mr. Melton hadn't told her. Nanny probably would've killed him if he had.

If there's an afterlife, Mama's fit to be tied. I can hear her now lacing into Nanny: "What the hell's going on here? All this time you were telling me how *awful* I was for screwing around with Tony, and now it comes out *you* did the very same thing with Herman Melton, and I was the result? Oh, my God! Are you ever *something*! And you had the *gall* to preach to *me*? At least Christine *knows* who her father was, but you let me live my whole life . . . and *die* . . . wondering what it was I did that was so bad—bad enough to make my own daddy hate me so much?"

Three Days Later

Cuz and I haven't been off the phone with each other. She has been calling all over Arkansas to find more records. Nothing has turned up with Nanny's and Melton's names on it.

I'm thinking about going to San Antonio and talking to some of our relatives who were around back then. Some of them are pretty old now, but they might be able to shed some light on this.

* * *

Next Day

Just got a marriage license in the mail . . . result of Janice's calls to Arkansas and Texas. It's Nanny, all right, but it's not Melton.

THE STATE OF TEXAS
COUNTY OF BEXAR
HOLY UNION OF MATRIMONY (March 4, 1922)
JOHN REESE AND MABEL CREIGHTON

He's a new one. Must've been number three. But Nanny put down "Mabel *Creighton*" as her name. Does this mean she was never Mabel *Melton*?

Appears that way. They probably never were married.

Nanny, you were something all right.

I called Chrissy with the news. She is as astounded by the Herman Melton saga as I am. Just like me, she had always thought Creighton was our grandfather.

I can't believe Chrissy's forty now . . . and a mother.

When she was growing up, she would ask about Tony over and over again. Mama would tell her all about him, and Nanny would come down with a spell whenever she caught them with their heads together.

Since I had met him when he was going with Mama, I described him to my baby sister many times: his dark good looks; the black eyes. Chris had seen only a picture or two, before Nanny's raid. Mama said she wanted to choke Nanny every time she thought of how Nanny destroyed all the photographs she found of him. Mama said she'd never forgive Nanny for tearing up Tony's face.

Christine had talked all her life about wanting to track down her father.

I wanted to help her find him. So, in August 1984, I went all out and hired a detective, but I didn't tell her, in case nothing turned up.

The detective did his job. He found Tony. Too late. He had died a year and a half before, on Christmas Eve. I was sent all the information that had been dug up. I learned that the name Tony had used as an actor had been "Hollywooded" up. I had his birth date, birthplace, the names of his parents, his brothers and sisters, and his widow—the same woman he was married to when he was in love with Mama. They never had children.

I remembered a story that had gone around the family right after Chrissy was born. It seems that Tony had called Mama and said that he and his wife would be willing to take the baby if Mama would promise never, ever to try to get in touch with them or Christine. She told them what they could do with that idea and hung up.

I felt so bad when I turned all the information over to Chris. If only I had tried a couple of years earlier, she might've been able to meet him. She never wanted anything from him, just to see him and ask a couple of questions, so she could tell Jenny and Max about her dad's side of the family. And she wanted to look in his eyes, the eyes she inherited. She wanted to touch him . . . that's all.

When I told her about Mr. Melton, all she could say was: "Poor Mama."

I love my sister so much, and I'm so glad Mama had the guts to have her. I never realized at the time how brave she was. . . .

Now, when I think back to that early December morning in 1944, I want to cry. I picture Mama walking down Wilcox in the dark and waiting on the corner for the streetcar to take her to the hospital clear downtown . . . young, scared, and desperate for someone to love . . . someone who would be all hers. She came home with the best present she ever gave me: Antonia Christine, six pounds six ounces.

Guts. That's what Mama had all right. Not too many women in those days would've gone through what she did, especially knowing up front she'd never see Tony again; knowing she'd have to put up with the "scandal of it all"; smug looks from the neighbors and Nanny's constant "I told you so's." She wanted that baby, and she *had* that baby.

Then somewhere along the way it all became too hard and too ugly to put up with, and she lost Christine, too.

Oh, Mama, dear Mama. I wish you were here now, so I could hold you and tell you and show you that your two girls are fine, that between us, we have five beautiful children of our own. Creightons, Meltons, or whatever the hell, who cares? We all love each other, and we're glad you were born.

38

San Antonio, Texas, 1985

I'm here visiting relatives who were around when Nanny was.

None of them was familiar with John Reese or with whoever might have lived with her after *he* bit the dust and before she finally got around to Papa John White. Mama said there had been six in all. So we're missing the two between her marriage to Reese in 1922 and her marriage to Papa John, sometime in the early thirties. She sure was busy.

The folks here remember only Creighton and Melton.

They wrote some of their recollections about Nanny down for me. I'm reading them now.

Mr. Creighton was such a nice man. He showered Mae (Nanny) with diamonds . . . a bracelet, locket covered with diamonds. Three rings with huge diamonds . . . Herman Melton and three other young men had beautiful voices. Mae told them to come to her house two or three times a week, and she would play for them, and teach them to read music. Mae and Herman became interested in each other, and finally married, she was twelve years older than he . . . his mother and father were very much opposed to their marrying, and wouldn't speak to them. They moved to San Antonio. Mae went to town and a movie every day. He left her and went back to Belleville.

Another cousin wrote:

When she had a big party, she did not want to use "homemade" bread, so she ordered "store-bought" bread and would go down to the depot and pick it up. She never kept house. She would wrap a white bandanna around her head, and tie it real tight, so as to keep her head from splitting open, her headaches could get that bad. She'd sit on the porch and fan herself with the ice sign. She would say it was the worst spell she's had. But when friends or neighbors passed by and asked her to go to town or a show, she'd get well real fast.

Here's one from a niece:

Edgar F. Jones was the eldest one. Aunt Mae was next . . . Grandpa Jones,
as they grew up, gave them a choice as to what they wanted . . . Aunt Mae
wanted piano, furniture . . . Daddy chose travel . . . Chicago World's
Fair, etc. Aunt Mae controlled two rooms . . . the living room and her
bedroom. I never knew her to go into the kitchen, her head began to ache
before the meal was cooked but cured up by mealtime or if there was somewhere to go. Theirs was a very well-to-do family until Grandpa went broke.
The bottom fell out of the cotton market . . . Aunt Mae was good at gossip
. . . harmful kind and lies . . . my family was not fond of her, and she had
no use for us. Their going to California was (in) the hope of movies and
welfare the state gave. Mother and Daddy went to see them and were horri-
fied at the way they were living. Aunt Mae was said to have more diamonds
than anyone in the county . . . my father (her brother) gave her diamond
earlobes . . . .

She must've hocked 'em.

Nanny hated one psalm. The twenty-third. She hated the "death" part.
"Yea, though I walk through the valley of the shadow of death. . . ."

"I don't know why they have to keep harping on 'death.' There *is* no
death; that's what Mrs. Eddy says." Then she'd pop a couple of pills.

She was visiting Chrissy and me in New York in 1960, when I was
working on *The Garry Moore Show*. The show was in the top twenty, and
I was doing really well. Chrissy was home for Thanksgiving, from board-
ing school. She was settled and happy. Life was beautiful. I was twenty-
seven and Chrissy was sixteen.

Nanny was seventy-five and having the time of her life. I had flown her
all the way from Hollywood. This was her first time in New York, and
she was living it up, going to the tapings and telling everyone she was my
grandmother. Garry would introduce her in the audience, and she'd
stand up (with her blue hair and apple red lipstick), throw her arms up in
the air, clasp her hands together, and make like Joe Louis. I wanted to
die. She even signed autographs.

One night the three of us were having dinner in my Central Park South
apartment, when she suddenly looked up at Christine and me and asked
us where we wanted to be buried.

"What?"

"Where do you want to be buried?"

"Who, me?" Chris asked.

"Either one of you, both of you. Where—"

I said, "Nanny, I really haven't given it much thought, but if I had to make a choice right now, I'd pick New York, because I've . . . found my happiness here."

"Me, too," Chrissy said.

"Bull. If the two of you think I'm going to fly six thousand miles a year to put flowers on your graves, you're crazy."

She died in 1967.

The year you were born, Jody.

She had met you, Carrie, even baby-sat you a couple of times, when we came out to California to visit, but you were too little to remember.

Before she got too sick to stay in her apartment on Cherokee, your dad and I visited her there. I was pregnant with Jody.

I remember trying to show her some baby pictures of Carrie and complaining about the green Japanese lanterns she had all through her apartment.

"Nanny, why don't you get some light in here? You can't see a darn thing."

"That's my love light." She had a forty-year-old boyfriend. He was a jazz musician in Redondo Beach.

She was eighty-one.

Six months later she wouldn't eat, and she was hallucinating.

She was in a nursing home and giving everybody holy hell. She would calm down at night and gaze at the ceiling. Your dad and I were there one evening, and she was lying there, staring straight up, not blinking. I was trying not to cry; she looked so pale, and thin, and awful. She burst out laughing.

"What?"

She was tickled pink. "There he goes. There he goes, again . . ."

"There 'who' goes again?" I asked her, looking up at the ceiling and not seeing a thing.

"Why, that daddy longlegs."

"Who?"

"*I said, 'That daddy longlegs!' Up there!*" She pointed a bony finger. "Plain as day. Right up there in that corner! Whatsa matter . . . you *blind*?" She'd get real mad if you weren't getting it . . . and madder if you said so.

"Oh, yeah."

She was pleased as punch. "Here every night 'round this time."

Oh, God. Spiders on the ceiling. She thinks she sees spiders on the ceiling.

She chuckled. "Yep, they come one at a time to him . . . one at a time . . . he's a smart bugger . . . gets 'em in that corner, where they can't get away"—then she turned her head toward us and grinned—"an' he humps 'em *all* to death."

Cuz and I were sitting next to each other, staring at the closed coffin. Christine was on my left. We were in the special section reserved for the family, stage left of the preacher's podium, and closed in by a curtain.

The service was a combination of Christian Science, Unity, and Church of Religious Science. Aunt Dodo had made the arrangements as Nanny's remaining daughter. The minister hadn't known Nanny, but Dodo had filled him in.

I couldn't believe it. "It" had happened to Nanny. She had talked about it ever since I knew her, and it had finally happened to her. My God. She was dead.

Christine and I had gone to the "Slumber Room" the day before, to see her.

The lid was open, and she was lying there in the dim light. We walked up to her slowly, and when we reached her, we touched her folded hands.

She looked terrific. Except I knew she would have said the lipstick was too pale.

(Oh, old girl, I love you. I always have, and I always will. I never thought you'd leave me. Oh, boy . . . Oh, Nanny, this feels so weird. I don't believe it's you in there. How am I ever gonna really let you go? I never could, you know.)

We sat there for a long time. We cried, and then we talked about her and Mama, and then we cried some more.

When it was time to leave, we kissed her good-bye so she wouldn't come back and haunt us.

The service was about to start.

I could spot friends through the curtain, walking down the aisle to their seats: DeNeut, Larry and Ellie Swindell. Flowers covered the casket. The organist plowed into "Red Roses for a Blue Lady." Dodo and Cuz had told me that was her and the boyfriend's "song."

Well, good for her. Good for her. She was a character all right. I thought of the story Cuz told me about the time, a few years before, when Nanny was at Hollywood Presbyterian Hospital for tests (I was in New York doing Garry's show), and Cuz and Dodo went to visit her. As they approached her room, they noticed a lot of people in the hall, lined up and waiting, some in *costumes,* to see Nanny. Cuz pushed open the door to Nanny's room and saw a little girl in a tutu, tap-dancing at the foot of Nanny's bed, twirling a baton. Her father was in the room with her, whistling "Dixie." When it was over, Nanny said, "Well, that's awfully good. I'll be sure and tell Carol about you. On your way out would you send in the next one, please?"

When Cuz and Dodo had asked her what that was all about, she said, "Well, I was bored."

The minister came on.

I looked at Christine. (We're all that's left. We're the only ones who can remember what it was really like . . . because they're *both* gone now.) She looked at me. Her face was tear-streaked, and she tried to give me a little smile. (I don't want to cry. I'm tired. I don't want to cry anymore.)

I left my body. I hadn't done that in years. I was floating over my right shoulder, watching me watch the whole thing.

The minister began. (Who is he talking about? He didn't know Nanny. He's talking about somebody else. He's at the wrong funeral because he's certainly not talking about Nanny. He doesn't know a thing about her, that's for sure.) I tuned out. He droned on and on, and I kept floating . . . and then . . . something he was saying jolted me back to where I was.

"Yea, though I walk through the valley of the shadow of death. . . ." Oh, my God, that fool. I expected her fist to shoot right up through that closed lid and deck him flat.

Cuz and I started to giggle, just as we used to in church almost thirty years ago: a small, choking sound at first. We tried our best to stifle the noise; then Dodo's long arm reached out, and she pinched the hell out of Cuz. Cuz yelled, *"Ouch!"* and I lost it. I doubled over laughing.

And that's when I couldn't stop crying.

She was buried two doors away from Nelson Eddy, just up the hill from Tyrone Power, and there's no birthdate on her tombstone.

She's *got* to love that.

39

Well, dear Carrie, Jody, and Erin,

This wraps it up. I certainly had no idea it would take a couple of years to get around, at last, to "Love, Mom."

Memory is a tricky thing. It all has to do with our own point of view, which always puts us center stage. I talked a lot with Aunt Chrissy this past year, picking her brains about certain episodes that involved us both, and most of the time, even though we weren't too far apart, she had another viewpoint . . . hers. Same with Cuz . . . and dear Ilomay . . . but I don't think it matters that much one way or the other, because what I really wanted to do was let you know my take on it all—to share my feelings with the three of you. And if I succeeded, even a little, it was worth it.

I was never able to share that much. I closed myself in real early because it made me feel safe. I put a wall up . . . (what Mama called "Carol's shade"), remember?

And then I was able to let things out only by being somebody else. It worked. It's what kept me going, I know it. I felt more secure. More accepted. More loved. (I thought.)

Funny, even after I was grown-up, there were times when I was more at home in front of millions of people than I was at *home.* If I have one regret, it's that I didn't know then why that was. The good news is I know it now. And the best news of all would be if I could do something about it. Because if I can, I'll be a hell of a lot better off as a person . . . and it would show you that it's never too late to make up for lost whatevers.

But I was lucky. I've had a lot of happiness, and I'm not afraid to expect more . . . and that's a big step.

I kept wishing, as I was writing this, that Nanny and Mama and Daddy had left a diary or two around for me to puzzle over. They didn't, but thank God Nanny was a pack rat. I found lots of old photographs and letters in her trunk after she died, and it's wonderful to have them. Now you know why *I'm* starting to save everything. However, as you also know, I'm a lot neater than Nanny. But then so was Oscar Madison (*The Odd Couple* slob).

I discovered a lot of things for *myself,* in writing this for you. I wound up understanding Mama a whole lot better than I had when I was a kid. When Nanny and I got off the train from Texas, Mama must've known she had lost me the minute she saw her seven-year-old baby clinging to Nanny for all she was worth. I remember the times she tried to get close but was too tentative, and I didn't pick up on it. It had to hurt her. But I know she never stopped loving me. It's just something I know.

If only she'd had a grab at the brass ring before she gave up and drowned her hope.

I'll always remember what she had to go through to have Aunt Chrissy. To hell with everybody and what they thought was "right" or "wrong." She kept that baby. Today it's no big deal. But believe me, it was then.

I still think of her, in labor, waiting for the streetcar to take her to the hospital in the middle of the night . . . and it just kills me.

And I never knew what a special person Daddy was until I started writing about him. They'd said he was so "worthless." No. He wasn't. The picture of him telling me always to love my little half sister, that he loved her, too, and that he was glad she was here for me will be in my mind until I die. I don't believe he had a hateful bone in his body. Some people might say that's why he didn't survive. I'd like not to think that. He had a disease, and it killed him.

Nanny. Well. Nanny. She's the toughest one to figure out. I can't, and there's no sense trying. She tried to act like the weakest, but she was the strongest. She hung on. And like any of us, she hung on the only way *she* knew how. If she had to cheat to meet the rent to keep a roof over our heads, she cheated. If she had to lie to the relief lady to get enough food money for us, she lied. But she pulled us through.

There were times this past year, as I was writing about her, when I found myself wanting to kill her—even though she was already dead. But I've come full circle. I know that I'll never know the whole story about Nanny and her past, what made her do some of the things she did. And so what? What I *do* know is she was *there* for Christine and me. She was our rock. And she never faltered when it came to that. She gave us what little stability our childhood had. She loved us, and she showed it. And we knew it.

They *all* were okay.

They all loved me the best way they knew how.
And maybe . . . one day . . . I'll be able to let them go.
And that's a good thing, too.

Last August 18 I went back, for the first time in years, to Yucca and Wilcox and 102. The people who live there now let me go in alone and sit for a while. I took my tape recorder. I walked in, and just stood there for a few moments.

I pressed the On button:

"Well, I'm here. I'm in, ah, I'm in one-oh-two. It's August of 1985, and the last time I lived here, in this neighborhood, was 1954 when I left to go to New York. It's . . . as small as I remember it. The people here . . . they're neater. Then I guess you could say that about anybody . . . being neater than Nanny, I mean. Murphy bed is gone, they've put a shower curtain up over the hole in the wall. Closet is still in there. Almost looks like the same carpet. Oh, Nanny. Oh, God. I'm lookin' out the window . . . [at] the Mayfair, the window I crawled out of, back into . . . the time I kept fooling Asher, and I'm lookin' out at the victory garden area . . . just below the window. Ilomay and I used to run up and down that strip of dirt. It's the same kinda white tile in the kitchen, hasn't changed, and I'm walkin' now into the little dressing room and, uh, closing the door. There's a mirror, full-length mirror—not cracked anymore, somebody fixed it—where I used to pose and pretend I was Betty Grable. And, uh, I'm in the bathroom. I'm lookin' at the shaft. 'Hello. Helllooo' up [there] to the roof . . . and the tub where I used to play Little Mermaid. They haven't changed the sink, same old sink. There's no medicine cabinet [!]. Holes in the wall where it was taken down . . . same drawers in the dressing table."

I pushed the Off button for a couple of minutes and walked back into the main room. I was crying like crazy. It was a peculiar feeling. Here I was, *weeping* and recording it. I wanted to put my feelings on tape, but I had the weirdest sensation that I was intruding upon myself . . . spying.

I was getting in my own way.

Time out.

I let myself go. It felt good. A couple of minutes went by.

I pushed the On button: "You think when you're gonna go back that it's going to look different . . . maybe smaller, because you're taller, I don't know, but this is *just* the way I remembered it: the same walls, the same size, the same *colors*. Ohhhh . . . I remember lying over there with the chicken pox . . . and Daddy sitting just about where I am now . . . and Nanny was out . . . Mama makin' the chocolate pie. . . . Oh, God, oh, God. Ohhhh, it's something. It's *really* something . . . oh . . ."

Off.

On.

"I asked, uh, if I could spend an hour here. He was kind enough to say yes. I've been here about . . . maybe . . . fifteen minutes. I think that it's enough. This'll be the last time I'll ever see it, I know that. . . . All the years I've been having those dreams about this room . . . how I kept re*doing* it. Remodeling it, opening it up, *breaking down walls!* Ohhh, God . . . those dreams. I was trying to re*do* the past, wasn't I? And it hasn't changed. I think it's time to go."

Off.

I'm fifty-two now. I'm one whole year older than that dark, secret age Nanny was, way back when Nanny wouldn't tell anyone how old she was and I wormed it out of Goggy that hot summer day on the porch in San Antonio. That was the day I wanted to know how long it would be before I'd have to put *my* teeth in a glass by the bed, the way Nanny did. When Goggy whispered the forbidden number in my ear, I was shocked and relieved at the same time. Shocked that Nanny was so very old and relieved that I had such a long way to go before *I'd* need store-bought teeth.

I still have my teeth.

And I'm not so old.

I love you so much.

Mom

About the Author

Carol Burnett makes her home in California and likes to divide her time among California, Hawaii and New York, and plans never to retire.